THE LOST SEASONS
Cricket in Wartime, 1939–45

Eric Midwinter

THE LOST SEASONS

Cricket in Wartime, 1939–45

Methuen

First published in Great Britain 1987
by Methuen London Ltd
11 New Fetter Lane, London EC4P 4EE
Copyright © 1987 Eric Midwinter

Printed in Great Britain
by Redwood Burn Ltd, Trowbridge, Wilts

British Library Cataloguing in Publication Data

Midwinter, Eric
    The lost seasons: cricket in wartime, 1939–1945.
    1 Cricket—Great Britain—History
    —20th century   2. World War, 1939–1945
    —Great Britain
    I. Title
    796.35'8'0941   GV928.G7

ISBN 0 413 14230 2

Contents

Introduction

Although I have nebulous childhood recollections of white-garbed figures flitting about a green field, my first distinct memories of cricket date from World War II. A hundred and more conversations persuade me that this is true for many of the generation now in its fifties. Certainly, there are very many cricket-lovers who talk nostalgically of the Victory Tests of 1945, when, out of the shadows, a series of pre-war style three-day matches emerged and seized a rapt public's attention.

My father was a scorer of much repute in and around the environs of Manchester and, had it not been for his anxiety about employment during the eight non-playing months, would have accepted a scoring job with Lancashire. No less an authority than Lord Winstanley of Cheadle, a highly proficient and all-round club cricketer of that epoch, has reminded me that my father was one of the first scorers to use a glorious spread of coloured pens to map batsmen's strokes around the wicket and deploy other statistical and presentational devices.

Thus it was that, provided he could be freed from his wartime fire brigade duties, he was frequently invited to score for the various entertaining charity matches which were arranged. There was always the need for a small boy or two to operate the score-board rollers and crash the number plates about, and so, free of charge, I was initiated into the wondrous culture of cricket.

It was chiefly Lady Kemsley's 'Daily Dispatch' War Fund

XI versus a side captained by some notable. I lived some five or ten minutes travel from Old Trafford so it was, of course, Lancashire stars who provided the attraction. Names that I had heard talked of round the kitchen table, faces I had collected on cigarette cards were suddenly in action on local cricket grounds. Eddie Paynter would crack straight drives into the tennis courts; Charlie Hallows, dark and sleek of hair, would play a lordly innings; George Duckworth would amuse with his traditional appeal, that stentorian accusation, with right arm extended judicially skywards, which led Neville Cardus to christen him 'the Chanticleer of wicket-keepers'; a young Cyril Washbrook would give his ferocious square cut and towering hook an airing.

There were some famous West Indians: Learie Constantine, deliciously agile in every phase of the game; Achong, foxily deliberating over his slow 'chinamen' and himself of oriental extraction; and E. A. Martindale, extremely quick bowler and dispenser of glass-splintering sixes among the nursery greenhouses adjacent to the ground. They would be joined by a handful of local players, keen to show their excellent club form was no delusion and tremendously cheered on by a partisan crowd. They would be given early runs by kindly county bowlers, and the assembly was mightily pleased. Apart from the gate money and the raffles, local worthies would offer half a crown to war charities for every six hit, and so this splendid procession would delight the wide-eyed scoreboard attendant.

On one occasion, Martindale was bowling at an alarming pace, excited, it was rumoured, by an unfriendly lbw decision against him when batting. Three or four dismissed batsmen were strolling around the ground including, I think, the two Lancashire batsmen Bunny Oldfield and A. E. Nutter, both of whom afterwards migrated to Northants. One or two of them wore RAF tunics in lieu of the conventional blazer. They stopped at the score-box and explained to my scorer-father that, as 'Manny' Martindale was exerting himself so angrily on not the best of pitches, they had 'not stayed around'. The notion of giving up one's wicket was an alien one to my young ears, for, in our backyard and park games, I practically had to be prised away from the bat even if the stumps were shattered. Curiously, I recall that piece of professional self-reliance as clearly as Eddie Paynter lofting the ball over the tennis netting.

Then, in 1944, and with some of the war damage repaired, there was cricket at Old Trafford, and the silent ground, which I passed so often on the train, was open for business. Herbert Sutcliffe captained a North of England XI against the Royal Australian Air Force, a team which was making much of its chances and which, of course, was the base of the Australian 'Victory' Test XI of 1945. Six of them, in fact, played in the Old Trafford 'Victory' Test that summer.

Before the match, the ashes of Cecil Parkin, chief jester of pre-war cricket, were spread on the wicket, and, as a kind of final ghoulish joke, they blew about and into the faces of the mourners. He had died in 1943, but had made this last rather grim request. Of the Australians, Keith Miller was already creating news, especially as a batsman, while the wicket-keeping of Sismey was also properly admired. The day, however, was Washbrook's for, after Sutcliffe, now aged fifty, had departed for three, the Lancashire opener sped to an exhilarating 133, and the North won by five wickets. It is no mean memory that, on my first formal visit to Old Trafford, Cyril Washbrook scored a century. Learie Constantine also made an impact. In the field, he was the epitome of concentration, long, slender fingers spread wide and forward in patient waiting. Running in to bowl at a fine pace, he indulged in the intriguing habit of glancing up at his raised right arm, just prior to the final wheel. He batted with sublime impertinence. We were sitting at square leg, when he effected that cheekiest of shots: the ball tucked away to the on-side under a raised left leg, and we saw fully both that piece of classic impudence and the flashing grin that accompanied it. And then, my next visit, the summer of 1945, and the huge crowd gathered to watch Hammond's England and Hassett's Australia celebrate the war's end in a most refreshing contest.

So wartime cricket, like every other phase of cricket, recruited adherents to the game, locked them in for life as *aficionados*, and now deposits them, in later middle-age, to ponder affectionately on those happenings. However, there is more to the story than that. First, cricket, like every other facet of national life, had to make some accommodation with the totality of World War II. From one angle, cricket had a 'good' war, one of which it might rightly feel proud. As Lady Kemsley's star-studded teams demonstrated, there was a two-way benefit, one being morale, and the other charity. Second, the very exclusive absorption of the war, in turn, affected cricket as, again, it did every other national feature, and whether cricket's response to that challenge was for good or ill is a moot point. Third, there were the losses accrued by cricket during the war: most tragically, in life itself, then, quite sadly, in men's time and experience, with players, great and promising, losing a yawning stretch of their careers and, beyond that, most seriously and yet under-described in the literature, the six-year absence of a training- and proving-ground for very young cricketers.

Last, and very important, was the actual cricket itself, where it was played, and by whom, for what reason and for what purpose, and, naturally, with what results. Because what purports to be 'first-class' cricket disappeared almost entirely and because first-class cricket is obviously the be-all and end-all for the statisticians, literati and administrators, wartime cricket, much of it of decent, some of it of high, and almost all of it of entertaining standard, has rarely been captured in anything like its entirety by historians and writers. A brief interlude of a section in the major histories: a few paragraphs in appropriate biographies and autobiographies (one honourable exception being a most judicious chapter in Gerald Howat's estimable biography of Wally Hammond); and a narrow shelf of slim, squat *Wisdens*, together with the miraculous sustenance throughout the war of *The Cricketer*, the former often looking to the future, and the latter as often to the past: these have been the combined weight of coverage of six out of the 81 seasons there had been since 1864 when a champion county was officially declared for the first time. It is very light indeed. Quite recently, Gordon Andrews has produced the *Datasport 1940–45 Cricket Annual*, a two-part log of the playing record and chief figures of wartime cricket, and this has proved a most useful statistical compendium. Otherwise, it is a thin field.

Here is an attempt to collate the chief facts and figures about cricket during the war, alongside some discussion of its social and cultural context. It is, at one and the same time, résumé, record and reverie.

ONE

The Anxious Preliminaries

On Friday 1 September 1939, the British government issued its warning to Adolf Hitler, demanding that he cease his attack of that morning on Poland. Two days later war was declared.

On that same Friday, first-class cricket in England ground to a halt, and it was to be nearly seven years before it resumed in 1946. Those six seasons constitute the longest gap in first-class play in the hundred years since that concept was unofficially acknowledged.

By a series of accidents, just one match remained to be finished. A handful of fixtures scheduled for the early days of September were automatically cancelled, so that the games played on Wednesday 30 August, Thursday 31 August and Friday 1 September were the last pre-war matches. There were six of them. However, three ended in two days, with Middlesex beating Warwickshire, Somerset accounting for lowly Northants and Worcestershire defeating Nottinghamshire. The Leicester and Derbyshire game was abandoned because of heavy rain.

Up at Old Trafford, Surrey were playing Lancashire in a game switched to Manchester because the Oval had already been put to military use. Lancashire had had the worst of the struggle. They had been left the whole of the last day to score 352, a tall order. When the players foregathered on that dismal Friday morning, it was immediately decided to abandon the game because of the international situation. The Lancashire batsmen, having scored only 211 in the first innings, may have felt that, in peace as well as in war, discretion is valour's better part, but, of course, the Surrey players were doubtless anxious to return to their London-based homes, for, naturally, the sounds of war were more insistent around the capital than elsewhere.

All this left Yorkshire, now to be clear champions, to rout Sussex at an exceedingly and unseasonably damp Hove. It was the benefit match of James Parks, member of one of those cricketing families on which Sussex appears to thrive. The crowds, in part because of this, had been good. There were holiday-makers a-plenty still in Brighton, and Yorkshire were most attractive visitors.

Cricket correspondents there present have written, of the unreal atmosphere at Hove, and of how the game 'somewhat lacked conviction', progressing its due and planned course because no one really knew how to stop it. Others were only too glad of a final sight of the much-loved game before war, now seemingly inevitable, darkened the vision. The Yorkshire captain was also generously keen for Parks to have a full benefit match.

The first two days had witnessed a close exchange of high scores. Sussex had scored 387, for which George Cox (from another of those families) with a masterful 198 had been chiefly responsible, abetted by 60 from John Langridge (representative of yet another Sussex kin-group). Yorkshire just topped that with 392, with Len Hutton (103), Arthur Mitchell (67) and Maurice Leyland (64) ending their seasons in typically substantial manner. A future England captain, Norman Yardley, then only twenty-four, was, however, Yorkshire's leading scorer with an entertaining 108.

Then the rains, which ended the match at Leicester, came, and left the Hove pitch a spiteful trap for batsmen. Sussex were brushed aside for 33, and no one reached double figures. It was a pitch made to measure for classic left-hand spin, of which Hedley Verity was a supreme exponent. In six overs he took seven Sussex wickets for nine runs. It is said that, unlike most bowlers, Verity did not relish the chance to obtain comparatively easy victims on a viciously turning pitch. His quiet and contemplative pleasure lay in the higher science of procuring success in ideal batting conditions. Nevertheless, it was a masterly piece of bowling, and Yorkshire needed only 30 for victory.

Len Hutton was caught behind for a single, by S. C. Griffith, later to become Secretary of the MCC, off the slow bowling of James Langridge. Hutton was perhaps not too disappointed, having scored a hundred the previous day, and his older colleagues, Wilf Barber and Arthur Mitchell soon gave the champion county a resounding nine-wickets win. Thus to James Langridge, and not Hedley Verity, fell the curious honour of taking the last first-class wicket to fall in England for the duration. Hedley Verity had enjoyed a remarkable season. He had taken 191 wickets at an average of 13.13, and his 7 for 9 was a dramatic finale to his fruitful summer. He was never to play first-class cricket again.

In his autobiography Neville Cardus describes the scene at Lord's on that Friday, with some desultory cricket in play, with a sole barrage balloon lowering gloomily overhead, and with workmen removing the bust of W. G. Grace. 'The noble lord at my side', wrote Cardus, 'watched their every movement; then he turned to me. "Did you see that, sir?" he asked. I told him I had seen. "That means war," he said.'

As Middlesex had summarily dealt with Warwickshire inside two days, there was, in point of fact, no play at Lord's for that resigned peer to have watched and, as Neville Cardus was himself in Australia at the time, the story is, of course, symbolic rather than factual. Neville Cardus assumed that literary authenticity should often be preferred to mundane, scientific precision. For cricketers, the curtailment of first-class play did mean war and very soon the sporting metaphors flourished. 'England has now begun the grim Test Match with Germany,' intoned Sir Home Gordon in his weekly front page commentary for *The Cricketer*, and he approvingly quoted Flt Lt A. J. Holmes, the Sussex captain, who reckoned the Germans had as much chance of winning 'as a snowball would in hell'.

Of course, the war was not wholly unexpected. The diplomatic events of the 1930s, culminating in the false-bottomed Munich agreement of 1938, had forced people to accept, if only half-consciously, that the probability of war was not remote. R. C. Robertson-Glasgow, reviewing the 1939 season, said that, 'as is customary when great issues hang in the balance, men set themselves to quiet but determined enjoyment.'

It had been a pleasing season, and its success made it a wholesomely representative one. Yorkshire were champions, and their two chief bowlers, Hedley Verity and their opening bowler, Bill Bowes, led the national averages. Walter Hammond commandingly topped the batting averages, with a formidable 63.59, while Len Hutton, Denis Compton, Joe Hardstaff and Herbert Sutcliffe were in close order behind him. The England selectors today would be happy to pencil in seven such names.

The University match had been watched by close on 16,000 paying customers, and the Saturday audience, with members, had been estimated at 9,000. Here were the young amateurs of the morrow: R. Sale, E. D. R. Eagar, J. Stanning and D. H. Macindoe of Oxford; F. G. Mann, B. D. Carris, P. M. Studd, P. J. Dickinson and A. C. Shirreff of Cambridge. Dickinson made a century, and it was the first freshman's hundred since Eustace Crawley in the 1887 match. Some of these were to be 'names' in years to come; others were to fade into the shadows. P. J. Dickinson, for instance, was to play for Surrey, but not eminently. Six seasons were to take their toll.

The West Indies had been the visiting tourists, captained by R. S. Grant, who was also a Cambridge blue. They drew two and lost one of their three-match rubber. Their leading players were George Headley, nicknamed 'the black Bradman', J. H. Cameron, another Cambridge blue who also played for Somerset, E. A. Martindale, the fast bowler, that most exciting all-rounder, Learie Constantine, and the leg-spinner C. B. Clarke, who was to have such an impact on wartime cricket in England.

Headley was just thirty but, although he played in three home Tests after the war, he never again toured England. He did, nevertheless, score 1745 runs in that 1939 season, with an average of 72. Constantine and Martindale, both established northern league professionals, never played Test cricket again. The elegant and prolific Headley bid farewell in grand manner with a century in each innings in the Lord's Test. Hutton, in his début against the West Indies, replied with a fine 196. At the Oval he scored 165, sharing with Wally Hammond (138) in a record third wicket stand of 264. K. H. Weekes foreshadowed the exploits of more famed Everton with the only other century of the series, 137 at the Oval.

These splendid doings gave way to alarums and excursions as war threatened. The Kent secretary, G. de L. Hough, told the West Indies management on 24 August that their fixture beginning on Wednesday 30 August might need to be cancelled, and, more or less assuming this to be the case, the West Indians hurriedly packed their bags and sailed for home on Saturday 26 August. This meant the cancellation of the games against Kent and Sussex and ended hopes of the West Indies playing in the traditional end-of-season festival matches at Skegness, Folkestone and Scarborough.

'Indignation', according to Sir Home Gordon, 'was profoundly excited' in Sussex at this cancellation. The somewhat gung-ho A. J. Holmes wired the West Indies on Friday 25 August, 'Essential to play match tomorrow. Keep the flag flying.' But the West Indians were already preparing to evacuate, and few could blame them in the circumstances. Hundreds of miles from their homes and families, they were naturally fearful of being, in *The Cricketer*'s word, 'stranded', and, indeed, their journey on the *Montreal* out of Glasgow, with submarines about and with recalls to port and turnings about, was a minor epic in itself. Lest readers might cast aspersions on West Indian valour, the same journal reminded them of the 'large contingent' of troops from the West Indies which had fought in Palestine in the 1914–18 war.

Sussex made do with a President's XI and a Captain's XI, and kept the flag flying as best they could. Cardus, as so often, stated a truth within his fiction, and the pictures and treasures of Lord's were soon removed to an unknown place of security. The Yorkshire players, after their savage routing of Sussex on the day following the makeshift replacement of the West Indian fixture, found travelling home difficult. They were not permitted to use cars south of Birmingham, and trains were difficult because of the evacuation schemes by now in full swing. A coach was eventually hired to transport them back to Yorkshire. A couple of days earlier, travelling to Manchester, the Surrey team had suffered a long delay of three hours at Crewe, with troops and evacuees already beginning that crazy maze of seemingly endless journeys which was so characteristic of the home front during the war. Doubtless this uncomfortable experience steeled them to forgo that last day against Lancashire.

Certainly, by the time war was actually declared on the Sunday, 3 September, all county cricketers were safe in their houses, with the cricket season moribund, and with thoughts turned to warfare and how one could, as the saying was then, 'do one's bit'. At least the cricket authorities were fortunate that it was, in any event, the season's end. They had time to draw breath and consider the possibilities for next summer. The forthcoming tour of India was, naturally, cancelled and soon the planned South African visit of 1940 and the MCC tour of Australia in the following winter were abandoned.

The winter sports were faced with an immediate quandary. Football was just beginning its season as war threatened, and players were reporting for training in a most unreal atmosphere. Three sets of matches were played, the last of them on Saturday 2 September, but the crowds were well down on normal times. With the outbreak of war came an automatic ban on the assembly of crowds and, on 6 September, the Football League put an end to the League competition. Nevertheless, almost immediately new arrangements were put in train, with every effort being made to encourage football in the services. On 14 September it was announced that friendly games would be allowed, even in evacuation areas, provided police approval was obtained. A week later the FA, after consultation with the Home Office, lent its support to all kinds of fixtures, so long as there was no interference with the war effort. The number of spectators was limited in the interests of public safety. On 16 September, a fortnight after the outbreak of war, 120,000 people watched thirty-one Football League friendlies. Pools were reintroduced, in the face of public demand, in October.

On 21 October a regional competition was begun, with ten mini-leagues based on geographical propinquity, and not status. Crowds were scanty at first, and the first winter of the war was one of the severest on record. However, with the help of a liberal measure of representative games and the, at first, grudging acceptance of the wide deployment of guest players, there were improvements, and the Football League was emboldened to launch its War Cup scheme, with home and away ties. The sixty-four first round matches attracted half a million spectators. So it was that, in a relatively short time, football had organized a systematic and sensible replacement for both its divisional league and FA Cup structure, and, below this top-class enterprise, plenty of non-league and services soccer was being organized. The cricket authorities, who always kept an eye on the rival sport and its activities, could not help but be impressed.

Over these months preceding the season of 1940, with football apparently finding its feet, there was considerable debate about what shape, if any, cricket should take. To understand that discussion it is necessary to sense the general atmosphere nationally in these early months of the war.

Reactions to the Munich settlement in the autumn of 1938 had been mixed. There had been impatience about Britain becoming involved in a quarrel about 'a faraway country', to wit, Czechoslovakia, and yet people were ashamed at that acceptance of Czech dismemberment, especially as the moral revulsion against Hitler had steadily grown. Men and women were, understandably enough, glad there was peace but many saw it as unreal, at best as an extra time for preparation; indeed, it has been estimated that had all the German bombing of 1940–1 occurred the previous year, Britain would probably have been defeated. For instance, we had twenty-six fighter squadrons in September 1939, compared with a meagre six squadrons in September 1938.

Thus there was a year of rearmament, marked by evacuation schemes, air raid precautions, the erection of shelters and the distribution of gas-masks. By the summer of 1939 the government had made an alliance with Poland – an unprecedented act for the British in peacetime – although it was obvious that little could be done directly by way of military assistance to that country. In diplomatic terms, the Conservative goverment was feebly stuck between sympathetic reconciliation with either Germany or Russia, neither of whom it trusted. Drifting a little, the government made friends with neither and, to its unpleasant surprise, it was Russia and Germany who joined forces. Behind the ideological veneers, the age-old power struggle continued: buffeted by its larger neighbours, Poland was again to be partitioned, its recurrent fate since the eighteenth century.

This was in August. Britain, with little or no alternative, stood by its Polish policy, signed the Anglo-Polish treaty and passed an Emergency Powers Act. Hitler postponed his scheduled attack of 25 August, and Sir Nevile Henderson, our ambassador in Berlin, and Lord Halifax, the Foreign Secretary, pressed the Poles to accept Hitler's demands for negotiations. Hitler, anticipating that France and Britain would stay on the sidelines as they had with Czechoslovakia, eventually invaded Poland. At first, Britain issued only a warning; with Lord Halifax still hoping to arrange a conference, no legal ultimatum was actually issued until 9 a.m. on the 3 September. On Saturday 2 September there had been a crucial debate in the House of Commons, followed by an equally critical late-night cabinet meeting. In both of these forums the reluctant government was urged toward war, and, at 11 a.m. on the Sunday, Neville Chamberlain made his historic broadcast. At 5 p.m. that afternoon France also declared war.

These protracted diplomatic exchanges and martial preparations created a mood of resignation. The public accepted war without any complaint and with scarcely a word of argument. Conversely, it was a quiet, almost docile acceptance. There was none of the exuberance that marked, for instance, the French decision to take up arms against the Prussians in 1870, when Paris rang with warlike cries and slogans, or, for that matter, the war fervour that gripped Britain in 1914. There was some grim determination and a dutiful, often cheerful, willingness to join the war effort, but there was no wild rejoicing.

Then there was nothing. The horrors of war, which had struck ferociously and immediately in 1914, did not materalize. It was the Bore War.

The Poles were soon vanquished and, as with Austria and Czechoslovakia, Hitler was able to point to Germanic minorities who welcomed the hegemony of Berlin. On the one side, the Allies, who had given Poland precious little assistance, were anxious not to provoke Hitlerite aggression, being particularly apprehensive of heavy bombing. On the other side, the Nazi government hoped Britain and France would call off the war once Poland was defeated, and peace overtures were made. Hitler was already looking slightly over his shoulder at his erstwhile ally in Moscow.

Neither side was keen for much of a fray and, leaflets and some sporadic fighting apart, it was stalemate. It is a remarkable fact that no British soldiers lost their lives until 13 December when, fifteen weeks after the onset of war, there were fatal casualties on the Maginot line.

The British government at this point had no purposeful policy except, if it may be termed purposeful, that of procrastination. Time seemed to be on its side and complacency was rife. In the first eight months of the war, only men up to twenty-seven years of age had registered for military service, an exceedingly slow rate, while rationing – in spite of a genuine public belief in its merits – was tardy in implementation. When it was organized in January 1940, it was established on the awkward and labyrinthine principle of registering for each product with a retailer, instead of permitting a freer distributive pattern as the commercial experts had advised. Soon there would be one rationing officer for every four hundred households. The system worked competently enough in a dilatory way, but the later introduction of both clothing coupons and a 'points' system for tinned and other groceries demonstrated how much more efficient a customer-orientated system was than a retailer-orientated scheme.

Perhaps the phoniest aspect of the phoney war was the discreet absence of the promised *Blitzkrieg*. There was a real terror of massive bombing, a profound dread which owed something to the aerial assaults on Warsaw and, prior to that, in Guernica during the Spanish Civil War, and even more to the woeful exaggerations of the pundits. It was calculated that 100,000 tons of bombs would rain on London in a fortnight, a figure never reached, such was the margin of expert error, throughout the entire war. It was confidently predicted that a multiplier of fifty casualties for each ton of bombs must be utilized, whereas the actual figure was between fifteen and twenty. Some commentators had anticipated a quarter of a million casualties in the first week of a new war.

The fear was endemic. As a seven-year-old I lucidly remember the first-ever night-time alert. Roughly awakened, we filed, white-faced and shivering, into the back-garden and down into the Anderson shelter, the stomach-churning sound of the siren wailing about us. Children and adults alike believed the end was nigh, and that Armageddon had arrived.

Then, nothing. Raids continued to occur, the bombs were sometimes dropped but, often enough, it was just the odd enemy plane, miles away, that led to a, perhaps over cautious, warning being sounded. The blackout was ubiquitous and all-embracing, unlike the practice in some other countries where only air raid alerts acted as the signal to douse the lights, so that an unending gloom persisted, despite the enemy's lack of attention. The anticlimax was welcome, even if the atmosphere remained oppressive.

People grew blasé. It had been planned to evacuate four million people, but only a million and a half did leave their homes, although perhaps a little more than that number also found their own safe billets privately. Such was the complacency bred by the quiet opening phase of the war, that a million official and many thousands of the 'private' evacuees had returned home by January 1940.

Against this background, the discussion about the 1940 cricket season varied freely from one extreme to the other. There were still the diehards who believed that practically any cricket was distasteful, and they represented the view held during World War I that while young men perished it was odious for their contemporaries to enjoy this best of games. This almost theological stance found two pieces of rather more practical support. With the threat of air raids and the hazards of war-time travel, the assemblage of crowds might have proved not only disruptive but dangerous. Then it had to be recalled that games might prove a distraction and, by luring workers and soldiers away from their gainful employment, cricket might, it was urged, ruin the national war effort. Some football matches kicked off at peculiar hours to avoid this temptation, while some other sports, such as horse-racing, were frowned upon as wasteful and demeaning.

Sir Home Gordon, writing his accustomed leading article in *The Cricketer* at this stage, claimed to be 'one of a minority who desired every form of cricket, except county matches'. He invoked the spirit of Francis Drake, recalling how, as legend had it, he 'continued to play bowls after he learned that the Spanish Armada was sailing – to destruction'. Robertson-Glasgow shared this view, and noted his 'general feeling that the game can and should be kept going wherever possible'. He realized that a prime difference between the two wars was that, this time, the nation as a whole would shortly be under arms. This meant that there was 'no room for the charge of scrimshanking', such as had been furnished by the first war. For instance, the military registration of undergraduates was different. They were recruited only on a fair basis which tried to take account of their studies. In the first war, service in school OCTU's had enabled teenagers to obtain immediate commissions and, sorrowfully, to become subject to the heavy death-rate of subalterns in the trenches.

Robertson-Glasgow argued that cricket was 'good for national morale' and Home Gordon claimed it would be 'good for the stamina' of the players, and a 'distraction' for their 'elders' watching. 'Cheerful and vigorous batting' must, in his view, be attempted. Doubtless encouraged by the curiously diffident and uncomplaining way Britain had slipped into a mighty war and the discovery that this mighty war was something of a damp squib, the cricketing authorities agreed that cricket must be organized in some manner. There was little cause to think it, as some did, 'improper ethically' so to indulge. 'There was no reason', wrote Robertson-Glasgow, 'or gain in wearing sackcloth and ashes in advance.'

That other purpose for cricket – the raising of charitable funds – was soon invoked, football having already charted that path. For instance, as early as 18 October 1939 a ten thousand crowd at Aldershot watched an FA XI play a 'camp and town' select and raised £364 in receipts and collections. Early in May 1940, Stanley Christopherson, President of MCC and cricket's representative on the sports subcommittee of the Lord Mayor's Red Cross and St John's War Appeal, wrote in *The Cricketer*. He appealed to cricket organizers to arrange matches for charity, a request to which many responded. This call for assistance was based on an overall campaign to raise £10 millions for the two voluntary casualty services because a three-year war, calculated against the experience of World War I and the lethargic introduction to World War II, was now anticipated.

So there were authoritative voices calling for cricket to be played. However, these tones were modified by a traditional view about what kind of cricket mattered. There were some who, far from wishing to see cricket obliterated, were anxious to see some form of first-class play sustained. Given the relatively peaceful opening to the war, there were those who flirted with the notion of a county championship. It is instructive that both *Wisden* and *The Cricketer*, twin founts of cricket's political science, were as opposed to such schemes as they were in favour of cricket actually continuing. It was 'wildly impossible' to conceive of a county championship,

said *Wisden*, while *The Cricketer* espoused everything but
county cricket. It was right that members should continue to
pay subscriptions to keep county clubs in business, but it
was, according to Robertson-Glasgow, 'cloudy thinking and
an over-generous flow of sentiment' which led some to think
that the counties should not only stay in business but, in
fact, do business, and play against one another.

There was a suggestion that one three-day match a week
should be attempted but Robertson-Glasgow, in a significant
passage, urged that, in the best of circumstances, three-day
cricket had been 'scarcely maintaining the public interest' in
the late 1930s. He expected that, in the hurly-burly of war,
such an experiment would fail. Two-day cricket had been 'a
dreary disaster' when tried in 1919, so there seemed to the
authorities little merit in renewing that option. The Lancashire county club issued a plan for a regional competition,
with the counties split four ways according to geographic
proximity. The Lancashire officials had noted how briskly
the Football League had moved to construct a regionalized
scheme which, after a poorish start, had started to prosper. A
more localized system to some extent overcame a critical
difficulty of World War II. Transport in wartime was unre-
liable in the extreme, as the Yorkshire and Surrey players
had discovered in those nervous days just before war was
declared. Obviously, the priorities had to be military and
freight requirements, with much less scope for leisure travel.
District public transport was not too bad: it was possible to
journey to and from a nearby ground. It was the long-
distance railways, fast and exact, which had made possible the
development of first-class cricket in the second half of the
nineteenth century: now it was their very uncertainty which
forestalled any hope of a national cricketing scheme.

A regional system seemed like a rational compromise.
Wisden's judgement was that the Lancashire plan was 'carefully thought-out, if perhaps over-ambitious'. The *coup de
grâce* was delivered on 12 January 1940, when the MCC
Advisory Committee declared that it was not prepared 'at this
stage' to organize such a scheme, or indeed any other. It

would leave it to the counties to resolve matters as best they might, but it appeared that the sole remedy lay in 'the improvising of one day matches whenever and wherever possible'.

This remained the position throughout the war, no change being advocated or requested. The decision, or absence of decision, is understandable. Home Gordon pointed to the 'melancholy, half-hearted apathy' of the last first-class matches at the end of August, 1939, inferring that it would be difficult to summon up the necessary energy, skill and spirit for high-grade cricket. The MCC was struggling to maintain a skeleton organization, and only forty members attended the Marylebone club's annual general meeting in May 1940. The task of promoting a wartime competition must have appeared unduly arduous.

Alternatively, that uneasy compromise – play as much cricket as you like, but without any system or competition – may be interpreted as yet another manifestation of cricket's age-long dilemma. Cricket, in its formal robes, is a definitive product of Victorian England, and has never fundamentally been altered, in spite of a number of marginal changes. The classic two-innings encounter, usually over three days, became and remained the purest exposition of the sacred game. Only in that format could true art be exhibited and, as significant, true artists be trained. Less than that was tolerable, for it was wholesome enough and could be entertaining. But it was not cricket, at least in a first-class sense and, once it was clear that a regular pattern of three-day matches with a regular supply of three-day players, would be hard to develop, then a complete halt was called.

Before and since, the cricket authorities have been caught in this trap, in which their duty to the game, as an art-form, conflicts with their understanding of cricket as a public entertainment. The war was to demonstrate that there was a hungry demand for cricket, and crowds were vastly pleased with the cricket they watched. If, as Robertson-Glasgow had claimed, the public was apathetic about three-day cricket, had the cricketing leaders some obligation, especially in wartime, to shape cricket according to public taste? The war, in an exceptional way, underlined the poser that was, in later years, to be pressed by financial urgency: was cricket a branch of aesthetics to be preserved for its own sake, or was it an aspect of public culture, to be packaged and marketed accordingly?

There is just a suspicion that cricket, to borrow a phrase from Neville Chamberlain at that period, missed the bus. There is just a hint of condescension in the view that, as the ideal was unattainable, there was little point in pretending or settling for second-best, and thus a somewhat *comme-çi, comme-ça* air prevailed. Everyone was left to his own devices. A regional scheme of one-day games, with some provision for guest players, might well have strengthened the ability of cricket to fulfil its wartime role as fund-raiser and morale-booster. It could have added an extra edge to what proved to be an attractive distraction.

Of course, not every county would have been able to participate in every season. In the Football League there were many variations, with twenty-one clubs dropping out in the awkward 1941/42 season. None the less, the regional league and the cup competitions were maintained and, by the 1945/46 season, only Hull and New Brighton excluded themselves. Non-league clubs helped fill the vacancies, Lovell's Athletic, Aberaman and Bath City among them. Similarly, counties in trouble might have combined (as occasionally happened for charity matches) or other elevens could have been mustered: a combined Oxbridge side might have been a possibility, and a Dominions XI a near certainty, while, given reasonable ground-rules, the Army and RAF could have joined the cricketing fray. Again, the cricketing imagination was none too venturesome.

There is no doubt that the mood, in general, was to keep playing cricket and ensure it remained alive. At another level, cricket, as a precious cultural form, was taken, rather like the valuable artefacts from the Lord's pavilion, and buried for the duration. It is a most curious paradox. Top-class football retained something of the illusion of its pre-war structure and benefited thereby: top-class cricket rejected any suggestion that its essence could be qualified. The best was probably the enemy of the good.

Some of this might be explained by lack of preparedness. In June 1938, that is three months before Munich, the Department of Air Raid Precautions, under the tutelage of the Home Office, had considered what would happen to entertainments should war occur. Closure was mooted, but re-opening after one week, dependent on the intensity of the expected air raids and the judgement of the police, was visualized. In the September of that year, plans were laid by the football authorities about what should happen in time of war. It was this foresight which enabled football's War Emergency Committee, composed of representatives of both the Football Association and the Football League, to meet within days of the outbreak of hostilities.

It was assuredly a more workmanlike approach than that of cricket, which appears to have had few contingency schemes to fall back on. This was, in part, an indication of the more business-orientated principles of the football clubs, each of them, legally speaking, commercial entities, as opposed to the subscriber-membership base of each county cricket club and the ruling body of the MCC. It also reflected the less ambiguous belief of association football that its job was to provide the public with entertainment. There was a much woollier view extant in cricket, where the first priority was the preservation of county clubs, for and on behalf of the members, with the populace a long way behind in the reckoning.

It is instructive to remark the parallel of the theatre, which like cricket is no stranger to philosophic debate about the respective demands of art and entertainment. In the summer of 1938 discussions were already informally in being about the role of theatre in wartime. By April 1939, an outline of what would be required and, importantly, the place of government in ensuring a co-ordinated national theatrical service had been submitted. Mainly because of the obsessive zeal of its chief progenitor and director, Basil Dean, the

Entertainments National Service Association (ENSA) began its work by 25 September 1939. By March 1941, and despite many obstacles and much criticism, ENSA had organized 350 companies performing each week for troops and war-workers, involving more than 2,000 shows a week, live and cinema. Thirty-four garrison theatres and 185 garrison cinemas had been built, converted and equipped, and well over 32 millions had attended performances.

Show business had been able to build on its experience in the all-too-recent First World War, and several of those involved were to the fore. Basil Dean had been an original pioneer of the garrison theatre. Now in the initial shock of war, sport and theatre might necessarily have been thrust from the centre of consideration, and rightly so. One might argue too, that variety acts and soccer were avowedly more popular than cricket, and deserved prior attention. It has to be said, however, that, in other facets of the entertainment world, there were shrewd and farsighted organizers who judged, first, that morale would be a key factor in the war, and, second, that an opportunity existed to protect and then enhance the fabric of their profession.

Cricket's reaction was slower, more naïve and more spasmodic. It was patriotic enough. As in the first war, one immediate response was to urge well-known cricketers to set an example by following the flag. But, as sometimes has been the case with cricket, there was an amateurish character about the response and an absence of rational drive. Compared with the theatre and football, cricket had eight or so months – near the entirety of the phoney war – to construct some programme, exactly at a time when people were that much more relaxed and hopeful of some normality. It might, like the theatre, have learned a little from the minor successes of cricket during the later summers of the 1914–18 war. This it signally failed to do.

The request was for 'improvising', and this is the crucial word, one-day games, and that these should be held 'whenever and wherever possible'. It is intelligible enough. Cricketers were being mobilized and cricket grounds put to military use; cricket, of any description, takes longer to arrange than a football match or a music hall concert. None the less, it does seem that a slight chance was missed to produce something a little more durable and regular. It may seem carping to labour the point, but this was a critical juncture. Social organization is frequently inhibited by the impetus of its start. Once a concept or an arrangement has been accepted, it is extremely difficult to shift it. The distinct structure of wartime theatre and football had been engineered within weeks of the war beginning and, fundamentally, it was never revised. The same is true of cricket. It began with a sporadic approach, and this never changed, although, truth to tell, much splendid cricket was soon to be on offer. Not for the first time or the last in its fascinating history, those in control of cricket took it too seriously in one direction, and not seriously enough in another.

The distinction between attitudes to cricket in the two World Wars is basic to any understanding of this issue. To begin with, the time-scale is significant. When the Great War started in 1914 it was a hundred years since there had been any threat to English soil or any major continental hostilities that had drawn in the British. The furies of war had been distant echoes, faintly sounding from the Sudan or South Africa. Suddenly war was adjacent and furious. Within weeks of the arrival of the British Expeditionary Force – the true 'Old Contemptibles' – on the Continent, there was extremely heavy fighting and the retreat from Mons was under way. Belgian refugees flooded into a shaken and anxious Britain. It was the first time in living memory that warfare had crept so close.

We sometimes forget now that the second World War was a mere twenty years after the first, scarcely a generation. Many fought in both wars, and the nation, save for those of about twenty-five and under, had some memory, however vague, of the previous conflict. For instance, Frank Woolley, the famous Kent and England left-hander, born in 1887, played eighteen times for his country before the First World War, in which he served as a naval coxswain, obtained a further forty-six caps thereafter – and played several innings when in his fifties in charity matches during the second war. Patsy Hendren was born two years later. This gifted Middlesex batsman played in fifty-one Tests between the wars, in the first of which he served as a private soldier and then, like Frank Woolley, he joined enthusiastically in wartime cricket in the early 1940s.

Shattering although the blow of warfare was in 1939, there was a real sense in which men and women were rather more attuned to the possibility and character of a European war than they had been in 1914. To that degree, they were rather more relaxed, and keen to preserve some normality in life.

Cricket is essentially a Victorian game. In the hands of W. G. Grace and his confrères, and with the encouragement of church and school, its combination of discipline and ritual had reached profoundly into the national consciousness. It was at once a ceremonial and a proving ground, to the point where it might be argued that the game's cult actually altered the terms of Christianity: in life or in death, 'He marks not that you won or lost but how you played the game.' Henry Newbolt's poem 'Vitaï Lampada' relates how 'the voice of the schoolboy rallies the ranks' with the cry of 'play up, play up and play the game', when 'the sand of the desert is sodden red'. It was the same words that had helped when there were 'ten to make and the match to win', and the same words which are etched on the carving on the outside of the Lord's perimeter wall.

In 1914 a similar challenge was mounted to those 'who played their game in the fields of France'. Cricket had been the preparation for the battle of life. It was a taxing and intense commitment and, once war came, there was no place for two such weighty alternatives. There was not space for both first-class cricket and a patriotic war, and cricket had to be, and was, sacrificed accordingly. Unlike most other sports, cricket has not changed markedly in style and structure since the late nineteenth century. W. G. Grace would recognize and would adapt quickly to modern cricket were he, happy thought, to be reincarnated. In 1939 the same ritual was pursued, but it was perhaps not quite so solemn and overriding as in the intensive formative years. Playing cricket did not seem to many in 1939 (although it certainly did to a few) to be quite the blasphemy that it had in 1914.

The 1914 cricket season was, of course, still in session when war was declared on 4 August, and first class matches continued fitfully. The elder statesmen of the game moved to extinguish the spluttering embers. The mood was one of, in Benny Green's phrase, 'hysterical idiocy'. Lord Roberts made a stirring speech which included 'a spirited reference to people who went on playing cricket at such a time', and Archie Maclaren, England's captain, used the pages of *World of Cricket* to denounce the Kaiser as 'that crowned madman' and 'that hog in armour'. Most poignant and probably most effective of all was the action of W. G. Grace. In one of the very few times of his life that he directly published his own thoughts or sought to intervene in a political issue, he wrote on 27 August as follows to the *Sportsman* – and not *The Times*, as several authorities have suggested, for it was his sporting acquaintance he intimately addressed – in an attempt to halt cricket.

There are many cricketers who are already doing their duty but there are many more who do not seem to realise that in all probability they will have to serve either at home or abroad before the war is brought to a conclusion. The fighting on the Continent is very severe and is likely to be prolonged. I think the time has arrived when the county cricket season should be closed, for it is not fitting at a time like this that able-bodied men should be playing cricket day by day, and pleasure-seekers look on. There are so many who are young and able, and are still hanging back. I should like to see all first-class cricketers of suitable age set a good example, and come to the help of their country without delay in its hour of need.

Surrey were awarded the championship, despite the cancellation of matches and their having had to play Kent and

Yorkshire at Lord's because the army had occupied the Oval. 'Never before', said the *Wisden* of 1915 dolefully, 'has the game been in such a plight.' The 1915 season was, in effect, the first time there had been no first class cricket played in England since that concept had been recognized some fifty years previously. Sydney Pardon, *Wisden*'s editor, pointed out that 'public feeling against the continuance of first class cricket during the war, having been worked up to rather a high pitch', there was no realistic option. In a severe but applauded move, Yorkshire made enlistment of players in the forces or employment on munitions 'a strict condition of their continued engagement'. 'Cricketers', said *Wisden*, 'have made a splendid response to the call to the colours.'

The impact of war was felt immediately and fiercely. On 11 November 1914, Lt A. E. J. Collins of the Royal Engineers was killed. He had, aged thirteen, distinguished himself by amassing the highest ever recorded score, 628 out of 836, in a junior house match at Clifton in 1899. The non-publication of *Wisden* was 'seriously considered' in 1916: 'as regards the future, the outlook is dark enough'. But the demand of the obituary columns was sufficient reason. By 1916 no less than 2112 MCC members were in the forces, and 69 of them had perished in the previous year. Lord Hawke reported that 75 per cent of first-class cricketers were now in either the Army or the Navy, and many were killed or wounded on active service. Dozens of pages of obituaries dominated the slim volume of *Wisden* for 1916.

The 1917 *Wisden* was 'a mournful volume', for 'the outlook for the game is as dark as possible', and its 'chief feature is a record of the cricketers who have fallen in the war'. No less than sixty pages logged the deaths of some 440 young cricketers. They included university and public school players, as well as minor county and major club members. About half a dozen current first-class performers were killed, including M. W. Booth of Yorkshire, J. Moon of Middlesex, F. B. Roberts of Gloucestershire, K. L. Hutchings of Kent, W. B. Burns of Worcestershire, and, from Warwickshire, the bowler

Percy Jeeves, whose surname P. G. Wodehouse celebrated in that most dignified of butlers.

There was another 'appallingly long list' of obituaries in the 1918 edition, forty-two pages in all, including well-known names like Odell of Leicester, G. L. Jackson of Derby, Raphael of Surrey and, 'in unknown circumstances', Hunt of Middlesex. The greatest loss of World War I, comparable to that of Hedley Verity in the following war, was the death of Colin Blythe, the renowned Kent and England player. Like Verity, he was a studious left-hand spin bowler. A sensitive man and a competent violinist, he found the idea of war abhorrent, but fought as bravely as anyone. He reached the rank of sergeant before being killed at Ypres in November of 1917. Colin Blythe was aged 38 and had won nineteen caps. He was regarded as unlucky to have been a contemporary of Wilfred Rhodes, and many judges placed him in the highest rank of spin bowlers.

There were a final thirty-seven pages of deaths in the 1919 *Wisden*. A. H. Hartley (Lancashire) Jennings (Kent) and Colbeck (Middlesex) were among the most notable, but the rolls of honour also exhibited the way the Empire had come to Britain's military assistance. Major R. O. Schwarz MC, one of South Africa's quartet of pioneer googly bowlers was killed, as was G. C. White, another South African player, while A. Cotter, a famous Australian fast bowler with 21 Tests to his name, was also lost in action.

Famous cricketers were among the first to flock to the colours. A. N. Hornby, Lancashire and England, was in charge of army remounts, while his team mate, the majestic Reggie Spooner, was wounded with the Lincolnshire Regiment. Frank Chester, the Worcestershire player, badly injured an arm but survived to become one of the most notable umpires ever. Major Troughton, the Kent captain, won the Military Cross in 1916. The transference of loyalty from cricket to warfare was solid and uncompromising. It has been estimated that 3,000 young cricketers were reported dead in the principal wartime *Wisdens*.

At first practically every description of cricket stopped.

Some attempts were made to keep 'cricket alive', but such games, said *Wisden* disdainfully, 'were of no importance'. The MCC requested the counties not to organize matches against each other, and the order was sedulously obeyed. A duty was recognized to the public schools, whose scores are the only ones reported in the early wartime *Wisdens*. In 1915 the MCC, conscious of the need to preserve cricket's premier training ground for amateurs, raised teams to play forty-four matches against schools, twenty-eight of which they won. One curious effect of the war was to force schools to play one another, rather than top-level clubs, most of which suspended activities. Winchester, for instance, normally only played Eton but, in 1915, the school XI met Harrow for the first game since 1854, the time of the Crimean War. In the following seasons, the MCC normally organized some twenty-five or thirty matches against the public schools.

The Butterflies, Herts Club and Ground and Notts Amateurs were conspicuous among the very few clubs that played regularly. Among army teams, the London-based Artists' Rifles was by far the most successful, in terms both of consistency of fixtures arranged and of games won. In the summer of 1916, for instance, they won 16 of their 26 matches, and lost only one, while Sgt D. J. Knight, the Surrey batsman, scored 1478 runs for them. The fixtures were chiefly with schools and other regiments.

League cricket was maintained. It was the mainstay of English cricket during the war and, after some early misgivings, it was sustained for the benefit of war workers in the north. Such audiences benefited from the appearances of first class cricketers, among them Jack Hobbs, and also Sydney Barnes, who took 404 wickets at an average of 5.5 in the Bradford League during the war years.

There was a little desultory cricket in France. Robert Graves has written of how, at Vermelles in June, 1915, officers played sergeants barely three-quarters of a mile from the front line. They played, with a splintered piece of rafter for a bat, a knotted rag ball and a bird-cage, containing, with a Pythonesque flourish, a deceased parrot, until the French troops evacuated the bombarded village. It was a far cry from the university match or Harrow versus Eton at Lord's. Robert Graves wrote movingly of spending leave in London, and finding it unreal, such was the intensity of experience in the trenches, almost to the point of feeling relieved at one's return to the truer reality. It was difficult for ordinary cricket to find any place or meaning in that remorseless grimness.

As happened in the 1939–45 war, cricket grounds were, in any event, employed for military purposes. Lord's was put to a number of such uses. A territorial artillery battery, an Army Service Corps transport unit, a Royal Army Medical Corps outfit, a wireless and cooking instruction centre: Lord's was kept extremely busy. Some nearby premises belonging to the MCC were utilized for the training of 400 officers, while the staff and members made haynets for horses. In 1916 they produced 18,000 of these storage bags for the many horses then on military duties. Old Trafford was a hospital for 500 patients and Trent Bridge housed a hundred military wounded. The Derby pavilion was a hospital for the Royal Garrison Artillery, while the Leicester ground became a rifle range and horse remount depot. The Northampton ground was also taken over by the army.

Gradually, matters improved. The war dragged on and people became habituated to it. The notion that cricket was a sinful pastime was less urged. In 1916 the Oval and Lord's witnessed some irregular games between military teams based in and around their environs, while one or two counties – Lancashire, Derbyshire and Yorkshire – arranged a couple of matches for the Red Cross and the Wounded Soldiers Fund. Essex was the most active of the counties, providing some thirty games mainly for the benefit of military personnel in the area.

By 1917 opinions had changed even more. *Wisden* felt that the MCC had taken 'a sensible view of school cricket', comparing this with the anxious 'feeling shown in the early days of the war'. The 'propriety' of playing cricket was now rather more generally accepted. There had been, claimed *Wisden*, 'a great change of feeling'. It now seemed 'illogical' and even 'absurd' to ban cricket, a view 'diametrically opposed' to the abolitionist opinion in the first summer of the war. *Wisden* reminded its readers that, in the summer months of 1915, net practice at the Oval had been stopped as the players were 'being jeered at by men off the tram cars' as they rattled past the ground.

Racing had been stopped, but not billiards, boxing or football. The music halls had soon started up again in 1914. *Wisden* acknowledged that it had not been 'unwise' to halt cricket 'in the first shock of the catastrophe', but it argued that more cricket could have been organized in the first two seasons of the war. *Wisden*, in the person of its editor, Sydney Pardon, was arguing, sometimes in contradictory style, with itself. It was keen to justify both the playing and the non-playing of cricket. Slowly, the adjustment was being made and, as long as the emphasis was on entertaining war-weary troops or raising money for war charities, then cricket could be ethically justified.

Thus two matches were organized at Lord's in 1917 and they raised £1300 for charity. One of them, on 14 July, and foreshadowing similar fixtures in World War II, was between the English Army and the Australian Army. Macartney and Kelleway appeared for Australia, whilst the English team was a star-studded one. The team included J. W. H. T. Douglas, Plum Warner, Patsy Hendren, Ernest Tyldesley, Harry Makepeace and, in his final appearance at Lord's just months before his untimely death, Colin Blythe. Yorkshire ran four charity games, Essex managed another thirty or so club and ground fixtures, against schools and regimental sides, and at Canterbury, in the very heart, of course, of the training and transit nexus for France, no less than 119 games were organized.

There was a further shift upward of gear in 1918. Yorkshire played seven matches for charity, including the county's first appearance of the war at Sheffield, where an attractive Yorkshire Council side were the visitors on Whit Monday and Tuesday. There was another two-day match at Dover, the chief embarkation port for France. Pelham Warner's XI played the United Services, and these two-day fixtures were to influence some of the early post-war planning of cricket.

Four successful charity matches were played in London in that last Great War season. After a Dominions XI had drawn with a West Indian XI, an England XI confronted the Dominions XI before 10,000 spectators. A substantial amount was raised for the Lord Roberts Memorial Workshops and the King George V Fund for Sailors. The peculiar distinctions of rank which were later to be discovered in World War II prevailed. The England team fielded Cmdr C. B. Fry, RN, Major L. H. Tennyson, Lt P. G. H. Fender and Lt Col Johnny Douglas, alongside L/Cpl George Gunn, Coxswain Frank Woolley and Private Patsy Hendren. The amateur and professional dichotomy was maintained on the parade ground as it had been in the pavilion.

A third match at Lord's in aid of the Chevrons Club drew another sizeable crowd of 8,000. Col F. S. Jackson's XI and Capt. P. F. Warner's XI were the combatants on this occasion, which was graced by what *Wisden* judged 'the finest display of the season', Air Mechanic Jack Hobbs's 86 for Jackson's team. Finally, there was the first major game at the Oval since before the war, when 9,000 watched another confrontation between England and the Dominions. These were all one-day matches.

There were even reports of cricket in France. At Étaples, on matting wickets, the likes of Johnny Douglas and H. S. Bush travelled far to obtain some cricket, and Reggie Schwarz played there, not long before his unfortunate death in the last months of the war. The summer following the armistice in November 1918 saw the resumption of the county championship on a somewhat rickety basis and, in scenes again presaging the 'Victory' summer of 1945, the Australian Imperial Services team undertook a tour of England. Captained by C. Kelleway and H. L. Collins, they won 12, lost 4 and drew 12 of their 28 first-class fixtures.

This gradual recovery of cricket is as interesting as its virtual oblivion at the beginning of the war. Given the short gap between the two wars, it meant that the game's administrators and senior players of 1939 well understood the manner in which continued cricket could be justified. Sir Pelham Warner, as he afterwards became, was a crucial figure in this, for he acted as MCC Secretary throughout the second war, having captained 'charity' teams in the first.

Although World War II was 'total' in a literal and practical sense, World War I, exploding as the first continental conflagration to engage Britain since Waterloo, was 'total' in its psychology. Jingoism expected an absolute commitment: hence the white feathers handed out or mailed to supposed cowards and backsliders; hence the jeering tram car passengers overlooking the Oval practice nets. One could not combine the serious business of war with the serious pleasure of cricket for, as hundreds perished in the trenches, enjoyment was interpreted as an obscenity.

There were differences between the two wars which help to explain this attitude. Fighting a four-year war, largely on the Western front, the British Empire suffered the savage loss of over 900,000 killed and over 2,000,000 wounded, that is, almost 40 per cent of those mobilized became casualties in that most senseless and bloodiest of conflicts. On the 1 July 1916, the British Army at the Battle of the Somme had 58,000 casualties in that one staggering day of butchery. For all manner of reasons, technical and otherwise, the human damage in World War II, tragic and despairing though it was, turned out to be much less severe. Six years of war, in several theatres, resulted in 373,000 dead and 475,000 wounded; carnage enough, but less than a third of the Great War casualties.

This created a very different domestic atmosphere. Right from the onset of the war in 1914 the casualty lists were lengthy and sorrowful: every family and every street made its sacrifice and, in several cases, the manhood of a village or a township was destroyed. The slaughter was non-stop and unavailing. Subalterns leading platoons into dangerous action are said to have been especially vulnerable. Often they were ex-public schoolboys or university graduates, the very stuff of which school and club elevens had been constituted.

Those slim volumes of *Wisden*, testifying to the mournful passing of many hundreds of young cricketers, many barely weeks out of school, were avidly purchased by sorrowing families, naturally anxious to preserve some memorial of a lost son. Now they are collectors' items.

Apart from the happily reduced numbers of killed and injured, the rhythm of the Second World War for the British was also different. It was more spasmodic. There was the phoney war in the pre-Dunkirk phase. There were longueurs before D-Day, and so on. The fighting was patchier and it tended to concentrate in one theatre rather than another periodically. It was, therefore, that much easier to adjust to possible distractions, such as cricket, without quite as much feeling of guilt about one's fellows at hourly and mortal hazard.

By and large, the trenches were all there were in the First World War. That was the reality of war. If you were not in Flanders or on the Somme, you were not at war. There was a clear and black and white distinction about it which was not paralleled in the subsequent conflict. Particularly after the retreat from Dunkirk, the entire nation was on a war footing. Of course, there had been serious blockading and consequent food shortages in the 1914–18 war, but the terrors of total war added a new dimension for an island kingdom which, unlike many of its continental neighbours, had not had warfare carried to its doorstep in any shape or form since the Jacobite Rebellion of 1745. With its army driven home from France and Belgium, Britain became its own fortress, and so it remained until 1945. Of course, the position eased after the successes of the Battle of Britain and the eventual end of the Blitz, although the rocket missiles in the closing stages of the war produced a late and very nasty terror. None the less, Britain acted as a fort, initially as a sternly defended bastion, latterly as the armed platform for attack.

As a result, the great majority of the armed forces including those from overseas, spent substantial periods of time closeted in the United Kingdom, whereas, in the 1914–18 war, the forces were principally embattled in France and Belgium. Next, the nature of war, mainly because of aerial bombardment, meant that the civilian population shared the same dangers as these landbound troops and a necessarily home-based air force. Indeed, the citizens of the East End of London, or of Coventry, or Plymouth or Merseyside were frequently at greater risk than the military. The deaths of 93,000 civilians bear witness to that. They include civil defence workers and fire fighters, home guards, merchant seamen and service women, and they amount to as much as a quarter of the military dead. Civilian casualties in World War I were negligible by comparison, with only perfunctory Zeppelin and clumsy aeroplane attacks to disturb the calm. Only about a thousand civilians lost their lives in the First World War.

This sense of a common threat ensured that the near-hysteria of the 'white feather' brigade was not repeated. A splendid illustration is the case of Raich Carter, the famous bustling inside forward of Sunderland, Derby County, Hull City and England fame. He served two years in the Auxiliary Fire Service, in which he became seriously interested. Then, his fitness affected by the arduous work and unfairly taunted, as were others, that he stayed in the fire brigade to avoid the armed forces, he joined the RAF. Henceforward he enjoyed the comparative comfort and safety of being an air force physical training instructor, instead of being subjected to the explicit risk of fire service duties in the Blitz.

Naturally, there were accusations that some were shirking their civic duties just as, equally, there were those who did dodge the column but, all in all, the climate was less tense. A much more definitive schedule of deferred occupations and the draconian pursuit of legislation appertaining to the direction of labour assisted the process, for it all helped maintain the feeling that we were all in the same boat. It has been pointed out that Germany, purportedly totalitarian, never achieved the same degree of commitment to the war effort as the British did under the benign despotism of that classic parliamentarian, Winston Churchill. Men and women were rigorously channelled into war-orientated occupations, just as factories and firms were obliged to construct their quota of this or that product. Those playing cricket were, as everyone knew, doing so in the intervals between flying on extremely dangerous bombing operations or as a break from a remorseless stint in an aircraft production workshop.

Both war and cricket were regarded if not less seriously, then certainly less solemnly in 1939 and this augured well for the sustenance of cricket. There was perhaps a greater awareness of the causes of the Second World War and, because of that, a profounder understanding of its import. Men stand now aghast at the futility of the Great War. They cannot fathom why and how it happened. It was a chauvinist war, and a highly nationalistic affair, so much so that many marvel now how the 'donkeys' managed to lead so many 'lions' to the ultimate sacrifice. Yet nearly fifty years on there are few who question the necessity of the second war. They may query its occasion and its internal strategies, but the sense that it was a just war, a struggle for inalienable rights, has persisted. The evil of Nazism had to be suppressed. If it were a fight to preserve the freedom, for example, to play cricket, then playing cricket at moments of relief from the war itself appeared rational enough.

Cricket was, then, relatively prolific in the second of the great wars and, in so being, it was at one with the overall attitude toward sport and recreation. The lessons of the last couple of years of the first war – that cricket did no harm and indeed did morale and charitable causes a little good – were remembered, and the same was true of many other similar features. This was due, in part, to a more sophisticated grasp of the human psyche. The abrasive and unyielding approach of World War I was deemed to be counter-effective. The value of relaxation was realized. One did not have to be a fervent and active patriot twenty-four hours a day to prove one's macho loyalty. Just as the problems of cowardice under fire or of what, in the trenches, was called shell shock were more sympathetically reviewed, so were more determined efforts made to provide genuine respite from the rigours of war. There were as many as 60,000 conscientious objectors, but the difference of mood, 1914 to 1939, is most lucidly shown in this instance: bitterness and a wickedly nasty response in the former; for the most part, a decent tolerance in the latter year.

The whole cultural dimension of World War II testifies to this more broadly humane approach.

TWO

The Formative Year

Just as the plots of Hardy's novels often unfold in parallel with seasonal and climatic changes so, uncannily, did World War II coincidentally evolve in kilter with cricket seasons. The war started as cricket ended; it faltered and almost ground to a halt during the close season. On 4 May 1940 Lord's mounted its opening match of the summer. In a fixture that was to be characteristic of the Lord's programmes during the war, the City Police played the London Fire Service. The firemen shot out the policemen for a paltry 98, and then scored 214 for 8, before the City Police, in a second innings, struggled to 43 for 5. The fire service were deemed to have won by 116 runs for, as yet, there was no regulation to cover a result where a team batted on beyond its opponents' total.

On 9 May Winston Churchill became Prime Minister, following hard on the German invasion of Holland and Belgium. With a numbing suddenness the Bore War was ended and there was a comprehensive and stark realization that total war had arrived. Abruptly, the notion vanished that warfare involved the set-piece of the battle or the static containment of the trenches. With it disappeared the equally long-held convention that Britain could fight a continental war at arm's length, that is, by forwarding troops to engage the foe on someone else's soil. Only the shades of the Spanish Armada of 1588 and Napoleon's flat-bottomed barges of 1805 nebulously hovered to remind the British dimly that invasion and occupation were not out of the question.

There were a couple more matches at Lord's in May. St Mary's Hospital beat Hampstead CC by four wickets, while the Balloon Barrage beat the BBC by only 36 runs, Michael Standing taking 3 for 19 for the broadcasters. The MCC had no fixtures of its own at Lord's in 1940, but they created a scratch programme of ad hoc matches, many of them involving civil defence or service sides, or teams drawn from hospitals or agencies, like the BBC, with a relevance to the war effort. It was, obviously, a delight and a tonic for club players of this level to use the Lord's facilities and step carefully on the sacrosanct greensward.

Several matches were, in Robertson-Glasgow's phrase, 'wiped-out' at Lord's, because of the disruption consequent on the fearful passage of events. Down at Hove, Sir Home Gordon reported the abandonment of a Sussex and Surrey match and a game between the under- and the over-thirties, following the 'dastardly invasion' of the Low Countries. On 25 May he watched A. E. R. Gilligan's XI play RAF Hastings at Lewes, whilst, above him, he watched planes 'being rushed up to devastate the ponderous German tanks' – a sentiment worthy of Alan Bennett's satire in its gullible optimism.

Two days later the epic retreat from Dunkirk was under way, and, by 3 June, 399,000 men, shattered and fatigued, had been safely brought home. During June a further 192,000 were evacuated from the Bordeaux and Somme areas, the great majority into the south-east of England. Over the 27 and 28 May, Churchill made the decision to fight on, somewhat to the surprise of Hitler, who had expected England to seek terms after the surrender of France, which, rapidly and inevitably, occurred on 22 June. Later in the summer, on 19 July, Hitler indirectly offered peace in a major speech but this was by no means acceptable. The idea that this was an old-style conflict of nation-states, to be settled after some bloody sparring by armistice and diplomatic bargaining, was no longer tenable. The focus was on Hitler. He was now, in a pithy phrase used to summarize the situation, 'a devil or a joke', a monster with whom it was impossible to negotiate through the civilized channels of tactful diplomacy. Adolf

Hitler, baffled by such intransigence, proposed the invasion of Britain and the Luftwaffe began its attacks. The story of the 1940 cricket season must, therefore, be related against the infinitely more dramatic tale of the Battle of Britain, during a period when, however unruffled and determined the British remained, the odds against victory looked long and forlorn.

As the Dunkirk evacuation proceeded, there was cricket at Lord's. On 1 June, the soon-to-be famed British Empire XI played at Lord's for the first time. They beat the London Fire Service by 144 runs, 290 for 6 declared to 144. Hugh Bartlett, the popular Sussex player, scored 82; L. F. Parslow, a club cricketer who made something of a wartime name, opened the innings with 75; and Ray Smith of Essex turned in a pleasant all-round performance, with 55 and 3 for 42. On that Saturday the trains, packed with worn-out soldiery from the Dunkirk beaches, wound their way past cricket match after cricket match on rural meadows, and people remarked on that strange contradiction. The same day West Ham beat Blackburn Rovers one-nil at Wembley in the War Cup Final, with Dunkirk survivors among the 42,000 crowd. It is said that seamen, fishing corpses from the Channel off Dunkirk, found the radio broadcast of that final gratuitously offensive but, overall, few really believed that all work and no play was any sort of recipe for, as Churchill put it graphically at that time, 'victory at all costs'.

Home Gordon spoke of the 'overpowering anxiety' at these dismaying events, and he praised in *The Cricketer* the 'superb embarkation' from Dunkirk's beaches. Aged 69, that doyen of cricket statisticians and commentators had become staff captain for the Brighton LDV. That was the Local Defence Volunteers (familiarly known to scurrilous youth as 'look, duck and vanish') who were, a month or so later, to be transformed into the Home Guard. Not unlike another Home Guard captain on the Sussex coast, Arthur Lowe's fictitious Captain Mainwaring in BBC's 'Dad's Army', Sir Home Gordon was given to the mildly unctuous metaphor. Hitler 'has captured the first two wickets with his express grubs', he opined, 'but our best bats have still to go in'. The cricketing figure of speech was to be a staple of wartime prose and oratory, as Montgomery's famous hitting of Rommel for six recalls. How England's openers, Hutton and Sutcliffe, interpreted that critique is not known: along with Verity and A. W. Carr, the Notts captain, they were engaged in cricket at the Catterick camp about that time.

Later in June questions were raised in the House of Commons about the continuance of horse racing which, although it had remained active in the first war, was regarded as wasteful and slothful by some in the second. It used much-needed transport, it took considerable time and, as ever, it had its shadow of disreputable seediness as well as its aristo-cratic sheen. Cricket was not so abused, for it involved 'the healthy distraction of a keen game'.

Cricket struggled on. What Home Gordon rather euphem-istically termed 'the rapid transformation on the Western Front' created minor havoc and led to the cancellation of 'all the big games'. Apart from an end to some fixtures pro-grammed for Lord's, several districts in the south were labelled 'defence areas', with an embargo placed on public assembly for outside entertainment.

All in all, twenty-six matches were played at Lord's, a creditable record in the circumstances and given the lack of forward planning. Many of them were fixtures which, in peacetime, would have been laughed out of court at head-quarters. Hampstead ARP, St Marylebone ARP and Padding-ton ARP fielded sides, while the fire service made six appearances. Three of the traditional public school fixtures were completed: Oratory v Beaumont; Stowe v Tonbridge; Haileybury v Marlborough, the last two being finely fought two-day games. A Lord's XI also routed a Public Schools XI, which included Trevor Bailey in its number. Ken Farnes took 10 for 87 in the match with quick and fiery bowling.

A goodly handful of quite distinctive matches were, how-ever, on offer. Just after the Dunkirk evacuation, on 8 June, Eton Ramblers defeated the Forty Club, with such notables as G. O. Allen, who took 9 for 23 and scored 35, Hubert

Ashton and Lord Tennyson on display. Then on 13 July there was the click of the turnstiles for the first time at Lord's during the war. A sixpenny entrance was charged for the first of what became an eagerly anticipated series between the London Counties and the British Empire XI. Arthur Fagg (40) Joe Hulme (78) and Arthur Wellard (45) helped the London Counties to 259 for 8, and then the off-breaks of Durston, the Middlesex professional (4 for 51) cut a swathe through the middle batting of their opponents who managed no more than 155. Sergeant Denis Compton mustered a solitary single for the losers but, of great import, was the size of the crowd. It was 8,000, of whom 6,425 paid, and a Red Cross collection netted £120. It was the beginning of a lengthy line of sizeable crowds, and it is worth noting, in this regard, that over 2,000 watched Oratory play Beaumont.

On the following Saturday 5,000 watched Eleven of Lord's, including eight under-twenties, score 214, with W. R. Watkins (75) and Leslie Compton (72) monopolizing the run-making. In reply, the last pair hung on for fifteen minutes to enable Eleven of Middlesex to sneak a draw at 189 for 9, with Denis Compton contributing 51. There was a marvellous game on the first Saturday in August, watched by 6,000 (4,521 paid) which meant a healthy donation to King George VI's War Fund for Sailors. It was a draw, but over 500 runs were scored and fifteen wickets fell. The RAF were 300 for 7 declared, with Cpl H. W. Parks of Sussex on 78, Aircraftman P. R. Sunnucks of Kent on 72, and Flt Lt Robins of Middlesex on 96. The strong London Fire Service response was 216 for 8. D. Kelly scored 93, and a certain Cpl Alec Bedser finished with 4 for 42.

The highlight of the summer was the second fixture between the London Counties and the British Empire XI, which ended with the London side's first-ever defeat. Well over 13,000 were in attendance. 10,326 produced receipts of £258 which, together with a collection of £145, meant a decent contribution to the Red Cross and the Cricket Friendly Society. It was a day of contrasts. The young club cricketer, Parslow, scored his first century at Lord's, as the British

Empire amassed 308 for 4. Compton (60), Nelson of Northants (44), Bridger of Cambridge University (40) and
J. G. W. Davies of Kent (51 not out) were the other scorers;
indeed, no one failed. It was veterans who led the charge of
the London Counties. Arthur Fagg, Andy Sandham, Joe
Hulme, E. W. Brooks of Surrey and, aged 53, even Frank
Woolley, shared in a valiant effort which, at 255, fell 53 runs
too short. Interestingly, it was the 'chinamen' of Denis
Compton which were the chief menace. He took 6 for 81 as
that high summer's Saturday was graced by over 550 runs.
Frank Woolley must have been pleased with his 38 runs and
with bowling out Denis Compton.

The next Saturday another crowd of over 8,000 turned up
in aid, once more, of the Red Cross, and neither charity nor
audience was disappointed. 540 runs were scored in under
seven hours, as Sir Pelham Warner's XI beat the Cricket
Club Conference by 3 wickets. They did so chasing 269 for 8,
with just five minutes to spare and with a pyrotechnic display
by Compton, who scored 101-in fast time, to establish that
winning position. This was Kenneth Farnes's last appearance
at Lord's. A few days afterwards there were over 7,000
present to watch Sir Pelham Warner's side easily beat a West
Indian XI. They scored only 146, in reply to 263, with
Hutton and Compton being the chief scorers.

The Battle of Britain raged on but, until about this time in
August, its chief location was over the Channel. Henceforward
the German air force turned its attention away from shipping
and the English coast and concentrated attention on the
south-east, in particular on RAF stations, as Hitler's anxiety
about mounting and, more meaningfully, sustaining an
invasion daily grew. Matters did become more difficult. On
31 August the match between the Buccaneers and the British
Empire XI was profoundly disjointed by the stratagems of
the air battle. There were late arrivals, rejiggings of the
batting order and an early finish. In between times Freddie
Brown, pressed into service as an opening bat, made 77 out
of 268 for the Buccaneers, and then took all six wickets to fall
as the British Empire wobbled to 141 for 6 and a drawn

match. The West Indian leg-spinner, Clarke, who had taken 5 for 68 a week earlier against Pelham Warner's team, now enjoyed the splendid analysis of 6 for 97.

Suddenly, the Battle of Britain took its third and final twist. On 7 September, constrained, it is said, by a rather lightweight British bombing of Berlin, Hitler felt obliged to attack London, for the arch-propagandist Goebbels had promised the German nation that their capital would never be bombed. Whatever the reasoning, it was tactically misplaced, for the heat was reduced on the Kent and other airfields, and Britain's aerial defences survived and regrouped. Invasion seemed at its most imminent around the first week of September. Hitler procrastinated, chose dates and then postponed them, troubled by the inadequacy of his air supremacy. Although it was October before Operation Sealion was finally abandoned, the chance of invasion had in reality been lost by the middle of September, as more wintry conditions loomed, the Luftwaffe failed to clear the skies, and another cricket season ended.

On 7 September, the very day the Germans began their air raids proper on London, a Middlesex XI were playing a Lord's XI. The match had what *Wisden* described as 'a strange and dramatic end'. The long air raid closed down the game for a considerable time, but a 'strict rule' had been issued by Lord's that time should be played out if at all possible. Middlesex had scored 152, with Patsy Hendren, aged 51, top scorer with 45, and his club colleague, Sims taking 4 for 59. As the autumnal twilight frowned over this last match at Lord's, Laurie Gray swept aside the opposition. He took 6 for 24 and the Lord's XI were all out for 120.

Military and social historians have dilated on the clear blue skies and shimmering warmth of the summer of 1940. Amidst the grimmer and more tragic ironies of men circling in those translucent skies to outwit and kill their foes lurked a tiny sporting irony. After some of the rainy summers of the 1930s, here was a perfect cricketing summer with no first class play. Of the twenty-six games at Lords, only one match, that between Oratory and Beaumont, was spoilt by rain. Twenty-one matches resulted in outright victories, although the conventions of club cricket (that is, declarations, sporting, astute and challenging, rather than set periods of time or numbers of overs) were utilized. That left just half a dozen drawn matches, at least two of them very exciting and nail-biting ones. Some 13,000 runs were scored, at an average of about 440 a day. It had been an enthralling summer's cricket at Lord's.

A critically central figure was, of course, Sir Pelham Warner. When World War II began, the Secretary and Assistant Secretary of the MCC, Colonel Rait Kerr, and R. Aird disappeared on military duties. With the once-weekly counsel, as a kind of acting Secretary, of W. Findlay, who had been MCC Secretary from 1926 to 1936, Pelham Warner became Deputy Assistant Secretary for the duration. He was steadfastly encouraged by the President, Stanley Christopherson, despite some failing of health in the later years of the war, for as in the first war, MCC halted its strict annual rotation of that office. Following the precedent of Lord Hawke, in office from 1914 to 1918, Stanley Christopherson remained at post until 1945. Toward the end of the war, Lieutenant-Colonel H. A. Henson, the Secretary of Gloucestershire, was invalided out of the army and offered sterling assistance, and Colonel Rait Kerr was also more readily at hand in those later years. The Chief Clerk, James Cannon, persevered until 1944, when he retired after giving an amazing 65 years service to the club. The Head Groundsman, A. Martin, served with the Metropolitan Police throughout the hostilities, and his predecessor, H. Gladwell, returned from retirement to the ground on which he had first worked in 1896. In turn, all these were aided by devoted secretaries and other workers, while A. Fowler and G. Beet performed a significant war service by umpiring, in Warner's phrase, 'in match after match', uncomplaining in their day-in, day-out arbitration of, it is recorded, an unwavering excellence.

Pelham Warner organized his ageing crew with assurance and dedication. He was born in the West Indies in 1873 and,

aged 14, saw his first match at Lord's – MCC against Sussex
– 1887. Two years later he played there for the first time,
representing Rugby against their old rivals, Marlborough. He
went on to play for Oxford University and Middlesex, and he
played fifteen times for England. He led the first MCC tour
to Australia in the winter of 1903–04 and, on his return, he
joined the MCC committee to which he gave lengthy years of
service. He scored 60 centuries in a highly competent first-
class career, over half of them at his beloved Lord's.

He was now 66 years old, one of cricket's elder statesmen,
in the line of Lord Hawke, Sir Stanley Jackson and Lord
Harris. He had been a successful player, and he had captained, helped select and managed Test teams. His pedigree
was immaculate. To say that cricket was his life is a cliché
which happens to be authentic: he held the game in awe as
his credo, and his familiarity with its every detail bred no
contempt whatsoever.

As an officer in the Great War, he acknowledged that the
playing of cricket then would initially have been 'unseemly',
but as that dulling battle of attrition settled into its lengthy
term and the boys were not home by Christmas, he realized,
like others, that it was 'illogical' to ban the sport. In the last
two years of the war, he himself participated in one or two of
the sparse handful of charity games that were permitted, and,
in fact, was the only man to have an eleven 'named' after him
at Lord's in both wars.

Thus Pelham Warner was ideally placed to judge the mood
and implement the apt practice. It is often argued that the
military leaders and political masters of World War II had
witnessed, often as junior officers, the crass and disastrous
folly of the generals and that the improved treatment of the
soldiery, not least the vastly less horrifying casualty lists,
stemmed in part from this previous salutary experience. In
the minor key of sport, Pelham Warner also reflected this
phenomenon. He clearly saw and knew that cricket, far from
being some offensive blasphemy in the face of battle, was, as
he put it, 'a healthy and restful antidote to war stress'.

There was another salient factor. In so far as cricket was

some kind of institution, a recognizable element of the national heritage under assault, then Lord's was, self-evidently, the temple of the cult. It seemed, therefore, that cricket needed to be maintained, not only to boost British and Empire morale, but also to reduce that of the enemy. 'If Goebbels', wrote Warner, 'had been able to broadcast that the war had stopped cricket at Lord's, it would have been valuable propaganda for the Germans.'

The choice of the verb 'broadcast' is informative for, of course, the ubiquitous wireless had made it possible for nation to speak forth unto nation in a manner unimaginable in World War I. Plainly, the Germans could scarcely have been told, much less have cared, about the absence of cricket in the First World War, but, in the succeeding war, these exchanges of self-congratulatory statements assumed some prominence. Whether the propaganda contest was quite so meaningful in the bellicose scheme of things is perhaps debatable, but what is certain is that, on both sides, it was deemed to be so. In Sir Pelham Warner, the quintessential man of Lord's, cricket could not have found a more conscientious protagonist of its merits.

With regard to Axis gloom about the English disporting themselves at Lord's, Pelham Warner himself recorded the anecdote of one Gordon Johnson. He was elected a member of the MCC in 1942 although at that time a prisoner in Italy. Such matters of prime cultural significance require epic measures, and the news was conveyed to him through the good offices of the Vatican. Rather than use what might have been suspected of being a military or secret acronym, the missive congratulated Gordon Johnson on being elected to Lord's, not the MCC. The untutored Italian authorities imagined he had been elevated to the peerage, and proceeded to treat Johnson and his companions with a little more generosity. Whatever that tale tells us about the aristocratic susceptibilities of republican Italy, it does give cause to wonder whether cricket was the worthwhile propaganda ploy some believed it to be.

Nevertheless, Sir Pelham Warner, within his own lights,

conducted the affairs of Lord's and the MCC with some aplomb and E. W. Swanton has paid genuine tribute to his 'courage and unquenchable enthusiasm' throughout the war.

It is by way of comparison, not of complaint, that the advantages of a different approach are considered. Sir Pelham Warner, one of cricket's proud clutch of knights, was by background, training and inclination, a banker rather than a gambler. His self-appointed task was to secure the assets of cricket in the vaults until the good times came again, not to risk them in some brave attempt to update the game for the last half of the twentieth century. Truth to tell, he might not long have enjoyed the confidence of the cricketing establishment had he been of such a temperament. It did mean, however, that, at this crucial juncture, cricket lacked the kind of maestro or social innovator who, in other fields, was looking excitingly ahead rather than yearningly behind.

No William Beveridge, no Nye Bevan, no Arthur Rank, no Billy Butlin, no Frank Whittle, no Basil Dean, no Bernard Montgomery, no Ernie Bevin emerged from cricket, like one of Thomas Carlyle's 'great men', to transform and modernize cricket. War often acts as a catalyst for social and technical change. Aviation, medicine and broadcasting are but three instances of tremendous changes brought about under the stress of war. Cometh the hour: cometh the man.

Cricket was not to benefit from any such flair for social and cultural exploration. Sir Pelham Warner performed his job nobly, but he was a keeper of the fort, not a raiser of the siege.

Although Lord's was, properly, the focus of English wartime cricket, there were other developments. Some cricket organizers had not dillied and dallied over the winter months of 1939–40, and two major initiatives were successfully undertaken. As Robertson-Glasgow reflected in *Wisden*, given the situation, 'entertainment, therefore, was left largely to enterprise', and the two chief exponents were to be the London Counties XI and the British Empire XI.

The originator of the London Counties XI was C. J. E. Jones of Swanley and a leading light of the Forest Hill Club, where he had efficiently arranged matches for professionals' benefits in pre-war seasons. Therein lay a significant aspect of the venture. Professional cricketers were, on balance, better paid than professional footballers in those bygone days: it is said that the young Hammond loftily turned down an offer to play football for Southampton, as his wage from Gloucestershire was so much better. Compared with the ordinary worker, they were, of course, well-off, and so the arrival of war struck them peculiarly. Given their social and educational backgrounds, the majority of professionals could find work only in the lower echelons of the armed forces, civil defence or other types of war work. They became war reserve police constables, store clerks and the like, and several of them, in terms of their accustomed standard, began to feel the pinch quite quickly. It depended to some extent on the way in which the counties treated their players during the long close-down, but few counties, needless to say, were in a position of such financial strength as to be able to pay decent retainers on their contracts.

Thus a meeting was held on 21 February 1940 at Andrew Sandham's cricket school, with the purpose of discovering how 'to augment the depleted incomes' of cricketers. It was a very serious undertaking. Jack Hobbs attended to advise the players, and he became the President of the London Counties Club. Apart from Sandham, Frank Woolley (who occasionally played) and Patsy Hendren were also present to offer words of sagacity and encouragement.

There was a hint of acerbity. The aim was to find 'the best possible substitute for competitive cricket' when other important officials 'could not be persuaded to make an attempt'. The refusal of the MCC or the counties to organize anything like a programme irked many of the older professionals. From their viewpoint, they were, so to speak, locked out, in that they were prevented from pursuing their calling and practising their trade. The fragilities of form are such that, for many, summer after summer of idleness might mean a complete loss of ability and, consequently, of livelihood. Not every cricketer was automatically swept into the armed forces, especially in those slow-moving early months of the war, and the idea of keeping one's hand in and earning a little honest money was attractive.

It is to the credit of these very dedicated professionals that they saw their first duty as the preservation of ancient standards. They established a touring team which travelled in the outer environs of London, playing local clubs, often on village greens, carrying good practice to what they called 'the cradle of cricket'. The adopted 'the decision always to play the game seriously, however weak or strong the opposition', and this remained the abiding principle of the London Counties XI. No 'true lover', the organizers urged, would want second-best, and so there were no cheap runs to be offered by way of shallow entertainment, nor wild runs sought in the same cause. 'Slack fielding' was sternly eschewed: all was aimed at the near-maintenance of first-class values.

It is scarcely surprising that this puritanical zeal enabled London Counties, throughout the hot summer of 1940, to bury most of their opponents without trace or mercy. They won 23 of the 26 fixtures played, drawing two, and losing just one, in their second encounter at Lord's against the British Empire XI.

Arthur Fagg opened for London Counties, and his was a classic case. A sufferer from rheumatic fever, he was not going to be called to the colours, and yet the chance to ply his trade was denied him. He scored 1,098 runs for an average of over 57 in those games, while his Kent colleague, L. J. Todd, scored 745 runs before joining the RAF. Joe Hulme, the Middlesex favourite, scored 849 runs. Jack O'Connor of Essex and F. S. Lee of Somerset, also batted strongly, with the chief wicket-takers being Arthur Wellard (70), A. Watt of Kent (62) and J. Durston of Middlesex (61).

They were, then, a case-hardened band of veteran stalwarts, and very popular they proved. Apart from earning a little for themselves, they were also able to raise substantial amounts for war charities, in particular the Red Cross. Their exploits are reminiscent of that fascinating era in cricket's history when Exhibition elevens were the rage. William Clarke, one-eyed, calculating and patriarchal, was the main figure. He organized the All-England XI which, six days a week, five months a year, tirelessly journeyed to the oddest of places to play local teams, usually against odds and frequently odds of twenty-two. This was in the mid-nineteenth century and, once more, it was a time when county cricket was at something of a low ebb. At one time, seven of these cadres were in the field, including the United South of England XI which W. G. Grace himself organized. There was a hint of syndicalism about them and, like the early tours to Australia, they were chiefly established and managed by and for professionals.

Their valuable impact on the game was missionary-like. Those pre-Packer professional circuses demonstrated the wonders of cricket in all manner of obscure locations, and they contributed hugely to the creation of a national following. The London Counties XI emulated them in this respect also. First class cricket had long been a question of seventeen counties playing one another on no more than thirty different grounds. Now the mountains came to Mahomet. Household names suddenly appeared on one's own doorstep, and, to some degree, revitalized an affection for high-class cricket in the localities.

The British Empire XI had something of the same propensity, for it, too, attempted to keep well-known cricketers 'before the public', and journeyed unceasingly to that end. The club owed much to 'the unbounded enthusiasm' of nineteen-year-old Desmond L. Donnelly. This youthful entrepreneur found a taste for cricket administration when he arranged a local match for the Red Cross, with a barrel of beer as a sidestake. It was against Rosslyn Park at Wimbledon. The British Empire Club won by six wickets and rightfully claimed the ale. It was 5 May, oddly enough, the same day that London Counties played their first match, beating West Wickham by 116 runs. This British Empire XI played no less than 37 matches, winning 22, losing 9 and drawing 6. Over 80,000 watched these matches, and some £1,200 went to the Red Cross in consequence. Donnelly, according to Sir Home Gordon, had 'a flair for raising cricket sides'.

It was an august outfit. Pelham Warner was President, and the captain was Hugh Bartlett, the giant Sussex cricketer, described by Donnelly as 'a source of inspiration'. There were solemn overtones. Donnelly's ambition was that the British Empire club would help solder the links of friendship across that commonwealth of nations. It was strongly imperial in sentiment. Rightly enough, Donnelly and his colleagues recognized both that the Dominions were lending their support in the war, and that cricket was a cultural denominator among them. Non-indigenous players were not too plentiful in that opening season, but the wish was everpresent that Dominions players would swell the ranks.

L. F. Parslow, of Chingford CC and the Essex Club and Ground XI, opened the batting with solidity and effect. He scored 900 runs for an average of 45 and, of all club cricketers, he was definitely the 'find' of the war. W. M. F. Bebbington, who had originally played for Darjeeling, kept wicket. He had been invalided out of the Army but, apart from his prowess as a keeper, he also scored 809 runs. Another success was R. P. Nelson, the Northants and Cambridge University amateur, who scored nearly 300 runs in relatively few games in the brightest of styles. He was commissioned in the Royal Marines and was unlucky enough to be killed shortly afterwards. Denis Compton, J. G. W. Davies of Kent and J. R. Bridger, the Cambridge batsman, also played for the British Empire XI, but their most triumphant colleague – and the finest advertisement for their devotion to the Empire – was C. B. Clarke, the West Indian leg-spinner. He hd toured England with the 1939 West Indies team and, indeed, returned post-haste with them when they beat a hasty retreat as the war-clouds gathered. He returned to Britain very soon afterwards, in order to secure his medical studentship, and, come summer, he was eager to play. He took 83 wickets at just over ten a wicket, and that marked the beginning of a seasonal exposition of some brilliance from the sporting young

West Indian. He was, in fact, to prove the most spectacular bowler of wartime cricket.

The British Empire XI, with its avowed political flavour, was strictly amateur, playing for love of cricket and love of Empire. They operated the same methodology as the London Counties club, in that they played a busy programme of one-day games against local clubs and service sides. It is interesting, however, to remark the difference. It is intriguing that just two major initiatives were adopted, the one as forthrightly professional as the other was steadfastly amateur. The division of pre-war cricket was retained and, as players, officials and public recognized, when these rivals clashed at Lords, it was a wartime carbon-copy of the annual 'Players' and 'Gentlemen' fixture. On the first occasion they met in July 1940, there was a great assembly of paying customers and, said *The Cricketer*, 'the enjoyment of the crowd was patent to all'.

Should the MCC have 'done more to encourage and foster' cricket during the summer of 1940? *Wisden*, in the person of Robertson-Glasgow, took up the question which had been on the minds of several, including the management of the London Counties club. Robertson-Glasgow defended the MCC stoutly and with some justification. The counties, he claimed, had been given their chance to operate some kind of programme, with the Lancashire regional scheme as a focus for that discussion but they had 'decided that such a thing would be impossible'. All attempts to run a county competition 'inevitably failed'. Robertson-Glasgow pointed to the 'satire' of county finances, for several counties found it easier to keep afloat with no fixtures. Sparsely attended games required a certain amount of expenditure on wages for players and gate-men and so on, as well as many other overheads. The ludicrous situation had been reached where it was cheaper for a cricket club not to play cricket.

This certainly had an effect on harassed county secretaries and committees. The financial risk of playing a cricket match in peacetime was risky enough, the English summer being notoriously fickle and the English public not always easily moved. The tendency was to remain cautious and pessimistic.

At the same time, the counties had to keep their grounds and their bank accounts in trim, and there was a portentous concentration on the future. Loyalties were appealed to, as members were asked to keep up their subscriptions so that everything would be in place for a fresh start once victory was assured. By Christmas of 1940, for instance, both Hampshire and Kent had received over a thousand subscriptions each, while Middlesex and Surrey offered a half-subscription to members – a guinea rather than two guineas in the case of Middlesex – because there was no cricket.

A round-up of the seventeen counties in the first season of the war reveals this general mix of lethargy and harassment, and serves also to provide a profile of the fate of county players.

Derbyshire played and drew their one game of the summer, against Notts at the Whit weekend, but they were unable to raise a team for the return match at Ilkeston on August Bank Holiday. The reason given is interesting. Practically all the Derbyshire professionals were playing in the Bradford League and were not available. Buxton, Richardson, A. Rhodes and T. S. Worthington had joined the Royal Artillery, which embraced, of course, the anti-aircraft gun defences and often meant players were still stationed locally. All the other players were on war work and were available as the admittedly heavy demands of such jobs permitted. What is striking is that it was cricketing, not martial, duties which denuded the ranks.

Glamorgan arranged and then scrapped three fixtures, and decided wholly against any games in 1941. Four of their players held commissions. The captain, Maurice Turnbull, Wilfred Wooller, the rugby international, and J. Mercer were lieutenants and their capped bowler, J. C. Clay, was a captain. H. G. Davies was an army sergeant, and A. J. Watkins, P. Clift and P. F. Judge were in the RAF. Glamorgan was to be one of the most passive counties throughout the early years of the war.

Gloucester had witnessed a veritable exodus of players into the armed forces and they, too, showed few signs of cricketing activity in 1940 or indeed, later. The players serving were Flt

Lt Wally Hammond and Pilot-Officer Charlie Barnett, 2nd Lts B. O. Allen, G. W. Parker, E. D. R. Eagar and A. H. Brodhurst; together with Aircraftmen A. E. Wilson and Jack Crapp and Privates G. E. Lambert and C. J. Scott. Tom Goddard was in the Observer Corps; R. A. Sinfield and W. L. Neale divided their time between agriculture and the ARP, and Monty Cranfield was in the Auxilary Fire Service. The entire Gloucester squad had gone to war.

Hampshire played no cricket in 1940, although some club matches were arranged at Southampton. 'Considerable damage' was done to the Southampton ground by bombing, for, of course, the port was a prime military target. C. G. A. Paris, G. Hill, R. C. Court and G. E. M. Heath had joined the Army; G. R. Taylor, P. A. McKenzie and A. McLeod were in the RAF; N. McCorkell was the lone Hampshire representative in the Royal Navy, while John Arnold, another footballer-cricketer, was in the Auxiliary Fire Service.

The larger south-west region fared badly. Worcester, like Somerset, Gloucester, Hampshire and Glamorgan, found war conditions difficult. They tried for three but managed only one match, a drawn match against Warwickshire. A crowd of 2,000 at New Road should perhaps have been salutary. The Hon. C. J. Lyttelton was in the Royal Artillery, E. Cooper, Roly Jenkins and B. P. King were with the Army; and R. Howorth, P. F. Jackson and Hugo Yarnold were RAF physical training instructors. Opening bowler Reg Perks was treading a different beat with the police. Somerset was a complete blank. A nil return in *Wisden* 1941 tells that curt doleful story.

Most of the Leicester players were recorded as having joined the forces, and just three games were completed in 1940. They beat Northants twice, by eight wickets at Barwell and by 68 runs at Spinney Hill, Northamptonshire, and drew with Notts at Trent Bridge. Sussex, perhaps the worst placed geographically for cricketing events apropos of the enemy across the Channel, managed a few matches as A. E. R. Gilligan's XI and then, as the news darkened and France was conquered, these were abandoned.

Warwickshire made no real attempt to organize a fixture list and, apart from the drawn game at Worcester on August Bank Holiday and a few club matches on Saturdays at Edgbaston, there was little cricket. P. Cranmer and R. E. S. Wyatt, the leading amateurs, were in the forces, and Tom Dollery, later to be Warwickshire's professional skipper, was in the Army. Warwickshire were genuinely inhibited by air attacks, for Birmingham was often under severe assault in the first year of the war. Edgbaston was damaged several times and the bowling shed was destroyed. Birmingham was, of course, a crucial armaments centre, and Birmingham Football Club's ground, St Andrews, was hit no fewer than eighteen times.

Lancashire suffered in the same kind of way. First, Old Trafford was taken over by the army, and at the MCC's annual meeting, P. T. Eckersley, the former Lancashire captain and Member of Parliament, gave 'a graphic account' of the military use to which the ground had been put. It was rumoured that Lt Eckersley was earmarked to captain Hampshire, but the tale arose simply because his naval duties had taken him to Southampton. Sadly, he was killed on active service on 13 August, aged 36. Next, the Old Trafford ground was bombed and there was extensive damage. Thus Lancashire, despite being advocates of a regional league, found themselves unable to muster any sides. On the other hand, there were plenty of players available. The Lancashire professionals seemed equally divided between the armed services – with Cyril Washbrook and Norman Oldfield in the RAF and Dick Pollard in the Army – and essential war work, where Winston Place and Eddie Paynter found themselves. With plenty of soldiers and airmen located in the north-west and with plenty of war industry in the Manchester area, there was always a superfluity of class players on hand, and, as the seasons passed, there was a considerable amount of high-class cricket played.

Across the Pennines, Yorkshire watched almost its entire staff disappear into the forces, led by their secretary, J. H. Nash, who was in the Royal Signals. Brian Sellers, Hedley

Verity and Herbert Sutcliffe were soon army captains;
Norman Yardley and Bill Bowes a pip behind as full lieutenants. Like a parody of some Cardus essay, those tough
professionals, Maurice Leyland and Frank Smailes, became
sergeant-instructors in the Army Physical Training Corps.
Paul Gibb, C. Turner and E. P. Robinson went into the
RAF. Again, many of them were posted handily, especially
with Catterick barracks acting as a major training and staging
post. Several of these players were available for three successful games at Sheffield, Leeds and Bradford for the Red Cross.
All drew crowds of six to eight thousand. The first two were
pick-up games, with Captain Sutcliffe's XI taking on Sergeant
Leyland's XI and then Major Ferrand's XI. Hutton scored
56 for his old opening partner against Maurice Leyland's
team. The third match was against the Bradford League, for
whom Constantine scored exactly a century out of 259 for 7.
Sutcliffe scored 127 in the Yorkshire reply of 209 for 6. 1940
also brought the sorrowful news of the death of Pilot-Officer
George Macaulay, an old white rose protagonist. He was
killed on 14 December at the age of 43.

Essex, like Sussex and Kent, were victims of invasion
fever, with some of their grounds in the specifically labelled
'defence areas'. They had also lost players to the war, princi-
pally through commissions to D. R. Wilcox, T. N. Pearce,
F. St G. Unwin, T. P. B. Smith and A. B. Lavers. J. W. A.
Stephenson was an army captain, and Flying Officer R. M.
Taylor distinguished himself by winning the DFC in 1940.
R. M. Heaven was in the Royal Navy; F. H. Rist and F. H.
Vigar were in the RAF; M. S. Nichols was an army PTI and
T. H. Wade was a military police sergeant. A varied collection
of martial careers, but, not withstanding these difficulties,
Essex exhibited great valour in playing six matches under the
creditable title of 'an Essex XI'.

Near neighbours Kent lost an entire team to the services.
B. H. Valentine, P. G. Foster, W. H. V. Levett and
J. G. W. Davies became army lieutenants, while D. V. P.
Wright, N. W. Harding, Carter and Godfrey Evans joined
them in khaki. F. G. H. Chalk and Leslie Ames were pilot

officers, with L. J. Todd, P. R. Sunnucks, R. R. Dovey and
T. W. Spencer also in the Royal Air Force. C. Lewis was
employed on naval construction. The country was saddened
by news of the death on 21 November of Lt-Cmdr G. B.
Legge, RNVR, their one-time captain and a former Oxford
captain. Cricket was played, despite all hazards, in profusion
at Canterbury. The St Lawrence and Beverley clubs organized
thirty-five fine matches, many of them involving army units,
on the county ground, and this established a hopeful precedent for the rest of the war, especially in an area of some
military concentration.

In the London area, Middlesex, as a county club, contrib-
uted little, the chief onus falling on the Lord's authorities to
organize that battery of games which, naturally enough,
engaged many Middlesex players. The list of Middlesex men
on war service is a lengthy one. Majors G. O. Allen and
H. J. Enthoven; Lieutenants Ian Peebles, B. D. Carris and
N. S. Hotchkin; 2nd Lts Jack Robertson, F. G. Mann and
W. H. Webster were the army officers, with A. W. Childs-
Clarke, G. E. V. Crutchley, A. W. Thompson, S. M. Brown,
Denis Compton and Laurie Gray as the other ranks. P. O.
Bill Edrich and Flt Lts R. W. V. Robins and W. R. Watkins
represented Middlesex in the RAF, while R. H. Hill, G. C.
Newman and G. T. S. Stevens joined the Navy. P. W.
Brooks was in the London Fire Service, Leslie Compton was
a police war reservist, N. E. Haig was a captain in the
Observer Corps, and F. T. Mann, F. G.'s father, and R. H.
Twining were in the Home Guard. W. F. F. Price, J. M.
Sims and C. I. J. Smith were employed on war work. Nearly
thirty players are thus logged by *Wisden* as being in some
part of the war effort, although it should be added that the
Middlesex connection with Lord's probably made it simpler
to keep track on all the players, and *Wisden* did not pretend
that its records were in any way exhaustive for the counties.
Middlesex also played fairly by the professional staff, to
whom grants were made in lieu of retainers, a generous
enough gesture at that awkward time.

Over at the Oval, Surrey were another county to suffer war

damage early on in the war but, determinedly, they resolved
to play nine matches on club grounds on Saturdays, winning
five and drawing and losing two each of the others. Later the
Oval was to be transformed into a gigantic prisoner-of-war
cage. The Army claimed several players, Major E. R. T.
Holmes, Captain H. M. Garland-Wells, Lieutenants F. R.
Brown and P. J. Dickinson among them. Alf Gover and
E. A. Watts became physical training instructors, while a
talented quintet – T. H. Barling, R. J. Gregory, J. F. Parker,
H. S. Squires, E. W. Whitfield – donned air force blue.
F. Berry and Laurie Fishlock were, as the wartime phrase
went, 'on munitions'.

Northants tried hard to keep interest alive, although they
did not use the county ground in 1940. They played one or
two games at Spinney Hill and, a modern-sounding device,
these were sponsored by local industry. They also established
something of a precedent by agreeing to play the London
Counties XI, the first county to do so, and it was a worthwhile
experiment. It was played over two days, 18 and 19 May,
with the crowd allowed in free of charge on the second day,
which was a Sunday. Some 3,500 took up the opportunity
and were privileged to watch 523 runs scored. London
Counties amassed 365 for 6 declared (Frank Lee, 90) and 181
for 1 declared (Fagg, 100 not out). Northants did well in the
first innings with 280 for 4 declared (Snowden, 100) but
collapsed in the second innings for 138, losing by 128 runs.
Importantly, it was one of very few two-day, two-innings
games played that summer, and it worked well enough. Apart
from the loss of R. P. Nelson, on 29 October, their gallant
young captain, Northants also suffered the blow of Sub-
Lieutenant E. J. H. Dixon's death during service with the
Fleet Air Arm. W. Hawtin, a one-time Northampton player
and latterly the Wigan professional, was killed in a munitions
accident in the South Lancashire area. W. E. Merritt, V.
Broderick and Philips had joined the Army; A. G. R. Binson
and Newton the RAF, together with R. J. Partridge, Denis
Brookes and H. W. Greenwood who were air force PT

instructors; C. W. S. Lubbock was in the Navy, and P. C. Davis was in the AFS.

Pride of place must go to Nottinghamshire for, of all the counties, they were the one which bravely decided to keep a decent and rational county side in the field. The Notts officials spotted the fact that many serving men were close at hand. Several had been in territorial units with localized head-quarters, or had joined nearby regiments at the onset of war. Others were retained at recruitment centres as physical training instructors. Thus, with relative ease, Notts arranged a sane little programme of six matches, three of them against the strong RAF team, one against Leicestershire, one against the Notts and Derby Border League Select, and a two-day game with Derbyshire, one of only a tiny handful of such games attempted. It was played at Whitsun. Notts responded with 334 for 9 declared to Derbyshire's first innings total of 239. Then Derby made 201-for 6 before declaring, leaving Notts too short a time to score the hundred or so runs required, and the match was drawn.

August Bank Holiday saw a goodish crowd of 2,000 at Trent Bridge, and they enjoyed a high-scoring game with Notts comfortable winners by seven wickets. The RAF accumulated 257, but Notts passed that score easily and progressed to 286 for 3, the day producing 543 runs. Guesting for the RAF, Joe Hardstaff, with 183 against his erstwhile chums, enjoyed the season's highest individual score. According to *Wisden*, 'particularly noteworthy' were the performances of a young man employed by the police, named Reg Simpson. Apart from an earlier 65 and 71, he now impressed the observant critics with a gifted display of 134 not out against the RAF, G. F. H. Heane, the Nottingham captain (108) joining him in one of the war's highest partnerships. It is perhaps no coincidence that the debonair Simpson was one of few batsmen of his immediate generation to establish an international reputation in post-war seasons, for Nottingham at this time were giving him more chances of good-class play than other counties seemed able to offer.

What is, in general, clear is that the counties made up their

individual minds in 1940 and held to their decisions. A pattern
was established for six years, ranging from an ambitious Notts
to a reluctant Somerset.

The cricket leagues of the north and midlands were the
happy beneficiaries. Curiously, the Lancashire League, often
deemed in those days the premier competition, cancelled all
professional contracts, with disastrous consequences. There
was 'a noticeable fall in the attendances on all grounds'. Gates
were down from £250 to £14 for the normally exciting
encounter between arch-rivals, Burnley and Nelson. Church,
assisted by Cecil Parkin's son, Reg, and Tommy Lowe, the
Lancashire junior player, won the competition. The East
Lancashire League and Bolton League were less rigorous.
Achong, the West Indian spin bowler, Charlie Hallows, the
England and Lancashire bat and his county colleague, Len
Warburton were professionals in the former, and the Lancashire opening attack of Dick Pollard and Eddie Phillipson
and their wicket-keeper comrade, Bill Farrimond in the latter
competition. Sydney Barnes, a stoical sixty-seven year old,
was wheeling astutely away for Stone in the North Stafford-
shire League, in the area where he had played much of his
earlier cricket. He took 4 for 12 in one of their matches about
the time of the Dunkirk embarkation.

The Birmingham League prospered. Notable amateurs
returned to club cricket, among them R. E. S. Wyatt, who
topped the league averages with 516 runs for Moseley; C. H.
Palmer, the Worcestor and Leicester bat, who totalled 514
for Old Hill, and the last of Worcester's famed Fosters,
M. K. Foster, who scored 328 runs for Walsall. The pros
were also out in force, with Eric Hollies catching the eye with
his 99 wickets for Old Hill, at an average of just under ten.
Tom Goddard, F. R. Santall (Warwicks) and R. Howorth all
played in the Birmingham League, while Reg Perks took 94
wickets and W. E. Merritt, of Northants and New Zealand,
had a bag of 80 and 878 runs, an unprecedented all-round
performance, for Dudley.

It was, however, the Bradford League which really attracted
the stars and, in turn, attracted the crowds. It was reminiscent

of the 1914–18 seasons when Jack Hobbs, George Gunn and Frank Woolley had acted as professionals in the northern leagues. *Wisden* spoke wistfully of, 'the talent which migrated to the Bradford neighbourhood'. Despite the exigencies of war service and war work and the troublesome nature of public transport, practically all the Bradford clubs fielded Test and county personalities, and sometimes two or three of them.

There were some devastating all-round performances. Learie Constantine took 76 wickets and made 366 runs – including a century in less than an hour – for Windhill and Derbyshire's George Pope had 88 wickets and 641 runs for Lidget Green. Wilf Barber, of Yorkshire, scored over a thousand runs in league and cup games for Brighouse, including a hundred in thirty-six minutes against Bradford. The custom of taking a collection for a fifty or a five wicket haul was maintained during the war and Wilfred Barber set a splendidly patriotic example by donating his several subventions to the Red Cross. D. Smith (Derby and Lidget Green) A. Mitchell (Yorkshire and Baildon Green) and L. G. Berry (Leicester and East Brierley) were three more local heroes. G. W. Brook, the Worcester bowler, took 87 wickets for Ecclesfield, but Verity's deputy, Arthur Booth, Yorkshire's substitute left-hand spin bowler, had the most wickets, just beating Pope and Brook with a tally of 89.

Len Hutton returned to his home township and opened the batting for Pudsey St Lawrence with his brother, George. He scored 133 not out. Winston Place, Washbrook's opening partner with Lancashire, was also among the runs: 745 for Keighley. However, it was Eddie Paynter who took the chief honours, also playing for Keighley. He scored 1040 in league matches alone, a feat only performed once before, by Oldroyd for Pudsey in 1933. It marked the beginning of what, for Paynter, was to be a remarkable swan-song, as he deployed the war seasons in a festive riot of runs.

There is no doubt that the leagues in wartime provided infinitely more crowd appeal than they did before or after. Every Saturday one could watch three, four, sometimes five established first-class cricketers, alongside a decent sprinkling of excellent club cricketers, ambitious to keep pace with the maestros.

So cricket, at various levels, continued. The MCC arranged 39 games with schools, in conscious imitation of the chief contribution of that club to the scarce cricket of the Great War. Another nine fixtures had to be cancelled. Eton played Harrow in an exciting one-day game, although it was not at Lord's. Oxford and Cambridge fielded sides, but just failed to play the traditional university match. What they did, however, was to maintain the ritual of the three-day match, a convention many believed to have been forgone until 1945. In May Cambridge scored 518 for 5 declared, with centuries from E. R. Conradi, J. R. Bridger and J. R. Thompson, in a three-day fixture with the recently-formed British Empire XI. This was the only major innings of the war to top 500 in England. Their opponents managed but 159 and 251 (Yardley 138) and perished by an innings and 108 runs. It was not, of course, a first-class match. Oxford's final trial in 1940 was a three-day affair, and three more games in Oxford – two trials, including the Freshers' trial, in 1941 and another in 1942 – just about completed the handful of three-day fixtures until the summer of 1945. Incidentally, and just following the British Empire club's Cambridge débâcle, they were routed by Oxford in a two-day game. Oxford University reached 491 for 3 declared, with S. I. Phillips (178) and N. T. A. Fiennes (157) the heaviest scorers. Their 295 for the second wicket was to remain the record for any wicket during the war period. The British Empire's response was 229 and 308, and they lost by a great margin. That match was also notable for the 657 runs amassed on the first day. The British Empire soon got into its stride, and suffered few defeats during the rest of the season.

One or two minor counties kept up their activities, notably, in that first wartime season, Bedfordshire, Durham, Northumberland and Devon. When Devon played a side led by Walter Hammond at Torquay there was a record crowd –

another instance of the drawing power of class cricketers outside their conventional habitats.

Club cricket was sustained by doughty ancients and eager striplings, with plenty of services and civil defence elevens to add to the fixture lists. Apart from keeping decent community amenities in existence, the smallest clubs were able to emulate the highest in the land by providing, at their appropriate level, leisure opportunities for bored or weary soldiers and airmen. Among the senior clubs, the Cryptics, the Optimists, the Buccaneers, the Forty Club and the Eton Ramblers were in the van. Some suffered. The Gentlemen of Cheshire had their ground confiscated for war use in what one historian has called a fit of 'inverted snobbery' and they never recovered their playing-field. Some of the confiscations of important sports grounds were reminiscent of the insistence on removing Stanley Baldwin's wrought-iron railings from Bewdley for salvage; a kind of reminder, almost cruel in some cases, that the rich had to suffer as well as the poor.

The Club Cricket Conference had itself emerged in World War I, partially in response to the needs of clubs to find succour in times of despair. Many clubs were to enjoy contact with the Club Cricket Conference in the last war and the Conference gave sterling service.

Of course, the war intervened in the most direct way. Sir Home Gordon, visiting Lord's on 24 August, 1940, enjoyed seeing a sizeable crowd there, 'although not a tithe of the spectators carried a gas-mask'. Yet not even his nonchalance in face of danger could mask his view of 'the hovering balloons', 'the blue-clad wounded' and the nurses collecting for charity. His stiff upper lip was again in evidence at a match in Sussex at the end of the summer, as the Battle of Britain touched its climax. A dog-fight raged overhead but, despite this and the hurried departure of two Home Guards, 338 runs were scored in three and a half hours, and a result was obtained: 'what an illustration', the Brighton Home Guard staff captain enthused, bluffly, 'of the failure of blitzkrieg!'

Others were a little more realistic. A Club Cricket Conference official announced on 7 September that the patriotic cricketer 'regards it as a duty to stop playing immediately on alert', and that, naturally enough, was the governmental line, far removed from the rather fruity heroics of some. As it was, by a combination of good fortune and some discretion, cricket contrived to survive that air-torn summer without any casualty during a match.

Cricket grounds might just pass muster as air landing strips and, on 3 August, it was decreed that all cricket fields had to be rendered 'useless for enemy aircraft landings'. This was secured at Lord's, as elsewhere, by 'placing obstacles all over the ground when a match is not in progress', and thus it was that no Heinkel nor Dornier ever despoiled the sacred sward of St John's Wood.

Plenty of grounds received the bombs, if not the actual planes. Typical of the gritty but self-conscious reaction of many British people in that hazardous year was a notice posted outside a South Coast cricket club which had been badly mauled by aerial assault. 'Local cricketers,' it ran, 'are as pleased as you. Each peardrop which falls on this ground saves lives and property. We shall carry on. Nothing which falls from the skies will deter us, except RAIN!' That was characteristic of nervy, jokey England in 1940, as a society under risk of invasion overtly demonstrated that 'Britain can take it!'

Inevitably, the companionship of cricket was tragically marred by deaths. Mention has been made of George Macaulay, Peter Eckersley, G. B. Legge, E. J. H. Dixon, R. P. Nelson and W. Hawtin. Oxford lost others, apart from Legge. R. E. C. Butterworth, also of Middlesex, Captain Rucker and M. H. Matthews, a wicket-keeper, were three other dark blues to lose their lives. G. B. Legge had toured twice abroad and won five caps against South Africa in 1927 and four against New Zealand in 1929. Macaulay had played in eight tests, spaced sporadically between 1922 and 1933. Legge and he were the first internationals to be killed in World War II. *Wisden* records the deaths of twenty-two cricketers in that first year, only a few of them active at the first-class level in 1939.

So the first summer of the war ended. It had been a poignant combination of martial alarums and cricketing excursions, and it provides a critical peak from which to make an interim judgement about wartime cricket.

A flicker of doubt crosses the mind. It concerns cricket's essential conflict between art and leisure. On the one hand, one must marvel admiringly at the sturdy and brave efforts of cricket-lovers from Lord's to the minutest village green who struggled to organize some kind of cricket with the German bombers overhead and an invasion fleet poised across the English Channel. On the other hand, one must compare these highly personal endeavours with the more concerted essays of alternative sources of entertainment. It is apparent from the histories of other bodies – the theatre; the BBC; the football authorities; in some degree, the cinema – that the appalling crisis of the summer of 1940 actually rallied them. Half a million troops were back on British soil and, for untold years ahead, the continental land war was postponed. It was no longer a question except in the relatively small campaigns in the middle and far eastern theatres, of sending comforts, shows and other entertainments to the boys overseas. The boys were right here, with a vengeance, and here they were, in the main, to stay for four years.

It is when the crisis is at its height that the issue of morale may be most important and so it is at this time that sport, wearing its show-business hat, needs to be to the fore. It must seem churlish to cavil, nearly fifty years on, about such might-have-beens, but there is a sense in which the doubt springs from cricket's fruitfulness, not its barrenness, at this dreadful time. It is because so much happened in *laissez-faire* fashion, that, from the admittedly smug hiding-place of retrospect, one is prompted to ask whether, with a little more co-ordination, something more attractive and compelling might not have been arranged.

It was already apparent that, for obvious reasons, many sportsmen would be deployed at training depots as physical training instructors. This occurred for three reasons, two saintly and one a little sinful. First, footballers and cricketers, given their professional backgrounds, did often genuinely make excellent tutors. Secondly, and this belief increased as the war drew on, there was an acceptance by military leaders that sportsmen, like actors and singers and comedians, might play a more useful role in the battle for high morale. Thirdly, there were always commandants – and this was to endure throughout the post-war years of national service – keen to clutch on to a sporting star that the regimental or station team might lick its rivals and fill the commanding officer with pride. Furthermore, many cricketers were involved in civil defence or war work in or around their home areas.

On examination, it would appear that eleven counties, even in 1940, could, on a reasonably regular basis, have fielded virtually first-class sides for one-day matches, had they set their mind to it and come to terms with the temptations of league cricket for their contracted players. These were Derbyshire, Essex, Gloucester, Kent, Lancashire, Leicester, Middlesex, Northants, Notts, Surrey, Warwicks and Yorkshire. The list may seem optimistic but it is composed of counties who did manage some show of cricket in 1940. Or it might have been possible to have drummed up half a dozen of these alongside a Bradford League XI, a Birmingham League XI, the British Empire XI, the London Counties XI, a West Indian or Dominions XI, the RAF, the Army, an Oxbridge XI, groupings of minor counties, a civil defence, fire service and police XI. With any luck, four groups of four might have played home and away (or those with no 'home' on two separate grounds), leading to four winners playing off semi-finals and finals. Without too much worry about eligibility and a liberal use of guest players, according to the accident of player's location, an interesting little tournament might have emerged.

It would have been, to borrow a German wartime coinage, ersatz; some games would have been cancelled because of lack of personnel and others ruined by air raids, but it might have been worth a try. What is significant and slightly depressing is that the only competition contemplated was something like a full-scale county championship, and once that idea, rightly, was jettisoned, that was the end of the thinking. As far as one can judge, it occurred to no one to break the mould and conceptualize afresh. It is worth remembering that, during the following winter of 1940 and 1941, when the Blitz was at its most alarming and disruptive, the Football League ran a northern and southern league, with thirty-odd teams in each, playing as many matches as possible (no fewer than 38 in the case of Bury) together with a League Cup, won by Preston, and two subsidiary cup tournaments.

The point is underlined by the lack of press coverage of the cricket matches that were arranged, several of them interesting and even dramatic. *The Cricketer* complained acidly about the quality papers advertising the fixtures, but declining to publish the scores. The heavy restrictions on newsprint, which reduced newspapers to a most sketchy size, account partially for this, but perhaps the press accepted cricket's own valuation of what it managed to provide. The press delights in sport with a competitive edge and, had there been more body in the cricket, it is likely they would have had some space for the scores. Cricket relies very much on its newspaper-reading public and the fillip of finding out how one's local heroes had performed would have been available. Football certainly received relatively generous treatment.

A general assessment, then, would be that though, at this opening stage of the war, cricket managed to produce much of value, it failed, perhaps, to take full advantage of its opportunities.

THREE

The Mid-war Summers

While Don Bradman accumulated a record 1,200 runs in the Sheffield Shield competition some thousands of miles away, Britain spent the winter of 1940–1 under fire. The end of the cricket season and the onset of a gloomy autumn initiated this ordeal by incendiary and high explosive bomb. London was raided 57 times, and 13,500 tons of bombs were dropped on the metropolis. All things, even bombing, are relative. A hundred-ton bombing raid was then regarded as par, but, a couple of years later, the British would unleash sixteen times that amount in a single raid – and something like 13,500 tons would be a weekly total.

Many now believe that saturation bombing of this kind was not crucial in the war, and that men and resources were wasted in the most profligate style with only marginal effects – losses of only one or two per cent on some estimates – on the German economy. Certainly, if the massive destruction of German towns was to have such slight effects, the comparatively limited assaults of the Luftwaffe must have been tragically insignificant.

It is one thing to analyse dispassionately the military inadequacy of the Blitz and another to recall the death and destruction it wreaked. Because, and for the first time for centuries, the civilian population and its property were under frightening attack, the story of the Blitz is now a vivid folk-memory. Its proximity made it so, even if its effect was not so fundamental: for example, during the London Blitz, three out of five people slept regularly in their own houses. It was other factors, less intrusive but insidiously menacing, which, together with the bombing, created the characteristic conditions of the next two or three years. One such was the heavy strain on a railway system which, because it had been unplanned and left to private adventure, was now both sprawling and decrepit. Another feature was the consolidation of the U-boat blockade which, in spite of the ceaseless valour of the merchant navy, led to considerable unease. Hitler's aim was to blast and starve out the British and, with acid irony, the end of invasion fear introduced what were, in material terms, the worst and hardest two years of the war.

The key word was shortages, in part the result of German action, in part the result of people and resources being siphoned off to combat that activity. The news was often bleak and depressing, as the war in the Mediterranean faltered and the war in the Far East collapsed catastrophically. British imports in 1942 fell to under 25 million tons and exports had declined by over two-thirds. American Lend-Lease was introduced, but it was slow to build up and very costly. In terms of shortages, the summer of 1942 was probably the worst of the war.

The British response was an extraordinary demonstration of concrete national unity, judged by some historians as greater than at any time in British history and as potent as ever was attained in any other country. It was, however, not just a collective mood of *pro patria*. It was powerful enough to tolerate, even to demand, the practice of a wide-ranging collectivism which, even at this distance, startles when its parameters are recalled. No other nation – assuredly not Germany, with its rather superficial reputation for jackbooted efficiency – drew together the sinews of war with such zeal and assiduity. Every person, every scrap of material, every conceivable human activity had a bearing in the war effort, and this common doctrine informed the whole enterprise. From the seeming lethargy of the autumn of 1939, the nation was galvanized into an elaborate form of War Socialism, in which the good of the Commonwealth was the sole and model touchstone.

It was much more effective than the botched mess of the first war and was, of course, partially a reaction to that régime. Suddenly, magically, no one believed any more in *laissez-faire*. Civil servants and trades unionists, employers and workers, all endeavoured to work together in the most effective way possible. Both resources and personnel were co-ordinated. Every morsel of food or piece of clothing, every artefact or service, was under centralized scrutiny, with the emphasis on standardized production directly or indirectly for the war effort. It was the age of the 'Utility' principle. An intricate mesh of boards and councils ruled over everything, from potatoes to fizzy drinks, and tried to ensure that firms were organized so that only useful objects were produced. There were 20 types of biscuit, rather than 350; only 22 prescribed articles of furniture were allowed; from carpets to pencils, everything was standardized.

As for people, the direction of labour and the conscription of women completed the systematic recruitment of all to the common cause. Much of it was accomplished tactfully but it could scarcely have been contemplated without the good will of the citizenry. By the middle of 1941, amazingly, half the people employed were on government work of some kind. Sir John Anderson introduced a manpower budget, every bit as important as the fiscal budget, for, as he remarked in a strangely Marxian turn of phrase, 'labour lay at the root of all wealth'.

If some Jungian exertion of the collective unconscious was at work, it was pragmatic rather than emotive. Of course, it was not total: there were scroungers, dodgers and shirkers as in any society, but, for the majority, there was a common cause and there was silent agreement that the solution lay in highly centralized planning.

This portrait of a nation, straitened by food and other shortages, buffeted by evil circumstance, but responding with a comprehensive display of Spartan control and civic diligence, is as heartening as it was largely unexpected. It affected every aspect of British life, and that included cultural and leisure activities. The newspapers and, crucially, the wireless were the fount and the expression of the mood. The nine o'clock news became almost as sacrosanct as holy communion, and the news readers – Alvar Liddell, Bruce Belfrage *et al* – were received as the spokesmen, almost the high priests, of the people.

Cricket rather missed out on this togetherness and on this surge of approval for overall planning. The die was cast in 1940 and that, bar a marginal alteration, was that, until peacetime. It is interesting that the 1942 *Wisden* focuses specially on the Tom Brown Centenary match. In 1841 Tom Brown or rather his creator, Thomas Hughes, had captained Rugby in the original fixture with the MCC. A side including R. E. S. Wyatt, E. R. T. Holmes, Gubby Allen and Jim Smith celebrated that happy occasion and much was made of it. The 1841 schoolboys had had the better of it, drawing with one wicket left and fourteen to win. Their 1941 counterparts were ignominiously bundled out for 31 and lost by 118 runs.

It is the backward-looking, pastoral approach which intrigues. This is not to deride that completely. The heritage of cricket is, in many respects, an inspiriting one and there was hopeful talk of the better days to come, when Rugby schoolboys and MCC members might go serenely about their peaceful occasions. But there was no balance. There was little or no sense of the present and what might be done now, what new scheme or national plan might be brought into being at what was, in a curious way, a most propitious time for invention and re-creation.

In the winter season 1941–2 the MCC complained about summer football, for the soccer authorities had extended their season until 31 May. It was a familiar grumble. These matters, felt the cricketing establishment, were immutable and not to be altered at a whim. It was, eventually, to be a vain complaint for, self-evidently, there was no reason why people shouldn't play or watch football whenever they wanted. Again, there is that feeling of defensiveness, of an unwillingness to move with what were stirring times.

The government was convinced enough. There was what

has been called 'a desperate need' for recreation. The previous summer Ernest Bevin, not a statesman normally associated with the mystiques of leg theory or the cover drive, had asked Sir Pelham Warner to arrange for a cricket eleven to visit the north in the aftermath of Dunkirk. 'Cricket', was the message, 'can take off some of the grimness'. It was not easy, and criticisms still occasionally were made about the frivolous nature of sport in wartime. Stanley Christopherson, President of the MCC, urged his colleagues to 'ignore those people who do not understand what we are doing'. What they were doing was to encourage improvisation and an indeterminate approach to often casual cricket. It was sensible enough after its fashion but it lacked flair and panache. After all, it *was* a time for heroics.

One practical feature illustrates this point. Sports equipment was, naturally enough, in short supply. The control over its production was tight, not to crush its manufacture out of existence, but to ensure, as with other commodities, that it did not lead to more urgently needed goods being forgotten. In short, the 'Utility' concept was applied. At the same time, because of that 'desperate need' for diversion, it was necessary to have a modicum of games impedimenta available, even if only of stereotyped design. Apart from the requirements of the armed forces and the schools, the allocation of sports tackle was delegated. In the case of cricket gear, the county clubs were requested to determine priorities among the local clubs. It almost harked back to late medieval days when the sheriff was the king's adjudicator in each shire. It all proceeded very tamely. No one appeared to spot the opportunity, created by shortage, to seize hold of cricket as a national organism, at a time when the need to think in national terms was generally accepted. Rowland Bowen has described this occasion as one which could have led to 'a central cricket organization'. Some county cricket associations did, in fact, develop during the war. By dovetailing local clubs with the county, first-class or minor, a positive network could have been constructed, and one with a reasonably

democratic foundation. The Club Cricket Conference continued its difficult work as best it could but a possible – by
no means a simple, but still a possible – moment passed in
which cricket's administration might have been transformed.

The Club Cricket Conference struggled manfully. Its 1941
report spoke of 367 active members including, surprisingly,
38 new recruits from among Britain's cricket clubs. Its
Emergency Fixture Bureau – a hauntingly characteristic 1940s
label – may have helped that expansion. The bureau arranged
783 matches out of 1243 applications for its brokerage, not a
bad record in those circumstances. More pertinently for the
years ahead, the organization was taking very seriously the
issue of post-war sports grounds. With grounds adapted for
military usage and some abandoned for lack of administrators
or players, and with planning for peacetime, especially in
relation to housing, already firmly set on the political agenda,
the Club Cricket Conference was to be congratulated for its
foresight. Its officials began to plan for the preservation of
sports grounds in post-war Britain, and sought allies of a
similar inclination.

This aid was to be urgently needed. For example, in 1944
the Wembley Borough Council attempted to requisition fifty
acres of land used for cricket for housing purposes under the
conditions of the 1935 Housing Act. The Club Cricket
Conference were able successfully to oppose what cricketers
regarded as a philistine decision. The dilemma is easy enough
to spot. As the war ended, the extensive damage caused by
the Blitz, coupled with the parlous state of much other urban
housing stock, created a vociferous call for new housing, and
building sites, especially in built-up areas like Wembley, were
by no means common. The struggle between land for homes
and land for leisure was an authentic one.

Otherwise, all was as before. Lord's was prepared for
another busy season, having survived some near-misses during
the previous autumn's bombing. On 16 September 1940
bombs had dropped in Wellington Road very close to the
ground, and on 1 November the synagogue opposite the rear
of the tavern was destroyed. An oil bomb fell thirty yards to

the left of the nursery and sight-screen (at 'deepish mid-on' according to Pelham Warner) on 16 October, and this device contained a German officer's photograph and his compliments slip. On 9 December a thousand-pound high-explosive bomb dug an enormous crater just short of the north-east stand. Once these alarming manifestations were over, Lord's was to run no further risk of enemy attack until the last months of the war.

Fifty-three matches were arranged at Lord's in 1941, and fifty-eight in 1942. From early May to mid-September two or three games were played each week and, when these were of any note, good crowds gathered to enjoy them. Just short of 90,000 paying spectators watched in 1941 and over 125,000 in 1942. In the latter year the concession of free entry to uniformed servicemen was abandoned and everyone paid sixpence. This was at the request of the military commanders and indicated a genuine acceptance that everyone, in uniform or 'civvies', faced a common threat and, frequently, a common danger. The price remained sixpence in 1943 and then, for the last two wartime seasons, it was increased to a shilling. The gates quoted do not include the many members who also attended. The siege socialism of the war was, as might be expected, far from all-pervasive and British and allied officers continued to be 'given the entrée to the pavilion' throughout the war. Paying crowds of five, six and seven thousand were normal and, for special occasions, this might easily rise to ten or twelve thousand. For the combined counties fixture at the August Bank Holiday of 1942, 22,000 packed Lord's on the Saturday, and a further 8,000 on the Monday. An average of between three and four thousand spectators was maintained over the two seasons, even though some of the fixtures were rather minor affairs involving local ARP and military units.

On 28 June 1941 Oxford and Cambridge met at Lords for their first wartime encounter. It was a one day match, with a 7,000 attendance. Both sides had played a dozen or so previous games, but Oxford University were handicapped by the loss of their ground, the Parks, because it was required for military purposes. Cambridge won easily by 7 wickets and a year later they repeated their victory, this time by 77 runs. Four Oxford wickets fell in the last ten minutes, and the Oxford captain was last out, caught off the seventh ball of the last over as the clock stood at seven o'clock.

On 3 July a highly-fancied anti-aircraft brigade eleven, bristling with talent – E. R. T. Holmes, Maurice Leyland, Doug Wright, Joe Hardstaff, Harold Butler, C. B. Harris, T. F. Smailes, G. F. H. Heane was vanquished by a Lord's XI. The anti-aircraft representatives scored 201, out of which Heane and Hardstaff had half-centuries. Charlie Barnett (102) and Jack Robertson (86) provided a convincing nine wickets win, the Lord's XI finishing on 295 for 3. A month later, on 16 August, there was a peculiarly low-scoring match when Pelham Warner's XI, having succumbed to Matthews of Glamorgan (6 for 31) and finished with a paltry 87, proceeded to oust the RAF for 61, Alf Gover and Maurice Nichols sharing the wickets.

On 6 September 10,000 turned up to watch the Army score 235 for 9, with Denis Compton 114 and Maurice Leyland 42. The Lord's XI scored 186 for 6, Todd managing a half-century, but the hero of the hour was Bill Edrich. Sqn Ldr W. J. Edrich, of Bomber Command, had just been awarded the DFC. He was cheered all the way to the wicket. When he had scored 4 his sparring partner, Denis Compton, dramatically caught him a foot from the pavilion boundary, and he was cheered home again by a delighted crowd.

The major opening match of 1942 was a two-day clash between the Army and Sir Pelham Warner's XI. The Army were 247 (Leyland 67) and 136 for 6 declared. Their opponents responded with 193 (Fishlock 87, Leslie Compton 62) and 149 for 1, going well but with neither side able to snatch the initiative. Alec Bedser played for Warner's XI. On 4 July the Civil Defence easily accounted for the RAF by 7 wickets before a crowd of 4,000. Like the RAF and the Army, it was possible for ARP and NFS teams to be very strong, and this particular eleven included John and James Langridge, F. S. Lee and H. P. Crabtree. The Navy, a smaller and necessarily disparate force, were not up to the standard of the other civil and military arms. On 11 July the Royal Navy played their first representative match of the war at Lord's and fell victim to a powerful Army side. Robertson (109) and Smailes (53) were the leading scorers out of a total of 275 for 8 declared, and then CSM Alf Gover took 5 for 30 and the sailors were dismissed for 102. Curiously, Ken Cranston, later a Lancashire captain and England all-rounder, was not invited to bowl for the Navy. The Army later beat a goodish Civil Defence Services XI on 15 August before a crowd of 9,000. The Civil Defence batsmen collapsed for 85 and, helped by Gubby Allen's 62, the Army passed that total easily and accumulated 209 for 3. Batting again, the Civil Defence were much improved. They scored 156 for 2, F. S. Lee 90 not out.

On 12 September the Royal Australian Air Force team made a spectacular wartime début at Lord's. They scored 236 (Sheridan, 122) and left an RAF XI reeling on 59 all out; but it was, said *Wisden* 'the magnificent fielding' which was most remarked.

The armed forces contributed much to wartime cricket at Lord's and elsewhere, just as the Army and the RAF were the central core of soccer during the war. In 1941 a four-match tournament was organized which led to what *Wisden* felt to be 'spirited cricket'. A crowd of 15,000 enjoyed the first match of the tourney at Lords in June, when the RAF won by five wickets, over 500 runs were scored, including 127 not out from First Lieutenant Leslie Ames. In July the Army avenged this defeat at Trent Bridge, winning by the same margin of five wickets, with almost identical scores. L. A. C. Gibb of Yorkshire, scored 102 for the airmen, but Sergeants Harris and Hardstaff steered the Army to victory on their home ground. At the beginning of August the Army won by eight wickets at Harrogate, this time with Sergeants Hutton and Leyland weighing in with half centuries in their home county. Then at Aigburth, Liverpool, later in August, the RAF squared the series, winning by seven wickets. A two-day match at Sheffield, at the end of August, was an additional fixture and the RAF won by 77 runs, after the Army eleven collapsed for 90 in the second innings.

It is interesting to note the military ranks of the players in the Lord's match in this mini-series. Many of the professionals were non-commissioned: Pte Cooper of Worcestershire, Sgt Instructor Denis Compton, RAF Sergeants Washbrook, Gregory (of Surrey) and Charlie Oakes, LACs Judge and Nye, Cpl Todd. That might have been expected and, with few exceptions, had been the case in World War I. Major G. W. Parker (Gloucester), Major Brian Sellers and Major J. W. A. Stephenson (Essex) were latter-day instances of amateurs, as in World War I, being officers. The exigencies of the later hostilities created some pressure for preferment to be on merit as well as status. There were opportunities for likely candidates, simply because jobs had to be done, and done quickly by the best qualified person available. That particular Army and Navy game demonstrates this. Second Lieutenants J. D. Robertson, T. P. B. Smith and T. F. Smailes, Captain Hedley Verity, Flt Lts. Leslie Ames and H. S. Squires, were all 'professional' officers. It does indicate that, between the wars, the lot and the character of the professional cricketer had improved and men like Robertson and Verity were confident, articulate and unafraid of responsibility.

As one or two commissioned 'players' have since commented, the social whirlpool of army and air force life was to prove significant in the post-war years. Having exhibited powers of command and having enjoyed the social perquisites associated with such powers in the military field, and having perhaps developed more sophisticated social skills, professionals of this type, already a little jaundiced by the vagaries and indeed the cant of the divide between the paid and unpaid, were to be very reluctant to accept it again. War has a tendency to shake up ossified structures and, in this minor form of the divisiveness of players and gentlemen, it had its effect. It was not immediate or even very marked, but the murmurings of change were there; it was never quite the same after the war, although the attempt was made to maintain the divide. The wonder is that it was 1963, eighteen years on, before the distinction between amateur and professional was abolished. Less surprisingly, the introduction of the professional captain, such as Tom Dollery at Warwickshire, came quickly after the war and was probably hastened by it.

This exciting and popular tournament was not repeated in 1942. As the balance of the war shifted, personnel moved – to the Middle East, for instance – and administrators changed posts. Patterns of fixtures were not always easy to sustain, but there were two splendid and well-attended games at Lord's. The first, in June, resulted in an RAF victory. The Army suffered early shocks, before Major S. C. Griffith rallied them with 81. Cpl L. J. Todd, of Kent, took 5 for 70. The RAF had little trouble in amassing 243 for 3, with Washbrook on 102 and R. E. S. Wyatt on 70. Early in September, and despite the competition with football fixtures (after complaining about summer football, cricket was now encroaching well into the football season) 14,000 turned up for the return fixture. The Army almost obtained their revenge. They scored 291 for 3, with the NCOs, Harris (115) and Compton (56) as well as the officer, Capt. Gubby Allen (69) joining forces. Leslie Ames (70) led a perky response but wickets fell, and the last two held out at 266 for 9 in what *Wisden* termed 'a tremendous finish'. The Army and RAF could normally field high-quality and exceedingly well-balanced teams and the matches were almost invariably watchable, combining both talent and excitement.

Elsewhere, cricket continued in much the 1940 vein. Double British Summertime created problems, for it meant that an eleven o'clock start was unnaturally early, with heavily dewed wickets and misty dawn-like conditions making life difficult for the early batsmen. Double British Summertime – with the clocks forward two hours – was designed to help the war effort by aligning the daylight hours with most people's travel and work. There was always mild controversy about the measure and opening batsmen joined farmers in protesting against it. Similarly, attempts to finish games later at 7.30 p.m. were also found to be unsatisfactory, partly because of travel difficulties both for players and spectators. After some experiment, the practice of ending play at 6.45 p.m. was resumed. The eight-ball overs were the normal rule for one-day play, and the MCC had also ruled that where a winning side, batting second, continued its innings, the victory should be described for posterity by the runs scored and wickets fallen at the very moment of triumph. The authorities did not want the statisticians of the future to be foxed by the natural wish of cricketers – and spectators – to continue play while time allowed.

On the county front, an interesting development was the combining of the shires when, at August Bank Holiday weekend, Middlesex and Essex joined forces against a Surrey and Kent select eleven. Unluckily, 1941 was a damper summer than 1940 and rain interfered after a packed house at Lord's had thrilled at the sight of runs galore. Middlesex and Essex galloped to 412 for 6. Edrich (102), Robertson (85) and Compton (56) led the race, but A. V. Avery, the Essex batsman, betokened his county's presence with an engaging 96. Surrey and Kent were 65 for 3, and struggling, and rain was their disappointing saviour.

The same fixture, at the same time, in 1942 produced one of the war's classic contests, fortunately played out before massive gates and raising over £400 for the King George Fund for Sailors. The Kent and Surrey innings was an occasion for two post-war celebrities to show their youthful skills. Trevor Bailey, who had made something of a name for himself as captain of Dulwich and the public schools representative eleven, created a zestful sensation. He took three wickets in his first over and ended with 4 for 36. Resistance was provided by one Sgt Evans, and by no means for the last time in that cheerfully belligerent career. His 55 enabled the south of the Thames combination to reach 193. Middlesex and Essex made 281, of which Nichols scored a sound 51. Kent and Surrey improved on a second showing, a century from E. R. T. Holmes permitting a declaration at 277 for 6, leaving their opponents a target of 190 in a hundred minutes.

After a sluggish start, Compton and Edrich, in a sunlit prelude to their achievements in 1947, manufactured 68 in 35 sparkling minutes. Edrich was the leading scorer with 73. With five minutes to go 26 were required and Compton contrived to take his team within reach. Four was needed off the last ball. Compton, cavalier as always, attempted the grand slam for six. In another prescient moment he was stumped by Godfrey Evans off the bowling of Alec Bedser for 57. *Wisden* spoke of 'the sensational incidents, and a finish that compensated for the inconclusive result' after such a 'glorious effort' at victory. Compton, Edrich, Bailey, Bedser and Evans had exhibited their sporting qualities, like a trailer for the post-war scene, and thousands had been enthralled by a wellnigh impeccable match.

Of these four home counties, Middlesex proffered little else beyond the two combined matches of 1941 and 1942 although, predictably, many of their players were represented in the heavy Lord's programme in both seasons. The Kennington Oval had been badly bombed, leaving the pavilion and ground in impoverished state. With an eye to peacetime, Surrey concentrated on its colts, for whom it organized a score of games each summer under the tutelage of Andrew Kempton. The names of Alec Bedser, Bernard Constable and A. W. H. Mallett figure prominently in the lists, but other promising apprentices – B. O. Wildbore, P. H. R. Hawkes, B. D. Wix, P. Wingate, W. B. McAlister – were never to achieve the same degree of familiarity. Essex still suffered from the location of its grounds in prohibited areas, although odd games were played at Southend and Chelmsford. At the latter venue, in 1942, Lt P. Smith's Army XI played Brian Sellers's XI, and R. Smith's Essex XI played the British Empire.

Despite its similar problem of closeness to the coast, Sussex was a trifle more ambitious. Five games were arranged in 1941, involving three losses to the RAF, a draw with the Brighton and Hove Cricket Association and a draw, over two days, with Cambridge University. Five more fixtures, including a two-day drawn game with a United Services XI, followed in 1942. All this in the wake of bombs at the Hove, Eastbourne and Hastings grounds and the transformation of Worthing, the square apart, into allotments. Cricket grounds were vulnerable to the 'dig for victory' campaign. Sussex, skippered by Captain Maurice Tate, a billeting officer, made their first appearance at Bognor and raised £300 from a 4,000 crowd for the Coast Regiment Fund. Alf Gover's XI were the opposition. At Chichester Denis Compton led an eleven against Sussex, and Trevor Bailey took 6 for 29 for the visitors. Hove also provided hospitality for a two-day fixture in which a combined Navy and RAF side comfortably thrashed an Army eleven by over 200 runs. Eric Bedser scored 134.

Even more helpfully, Sussex organized the Sussex League, utilizing Wednesday half-day closing and Saturday afternoon for the purpose. Navy, Army, Air Force, ARP and NFS and other relevant teams were engaged in an imaginative venture and one which might have been promoted elsewhere, on either a regional or even a national scale.

Several counties remained in gloomy purdah. Derbyshire managed one match each year, against the effervescent Notts; Gloucestershire tied with the British Empire in 1941 (one of the few recorded wartime ties; Tom Goddard took 4 for 56) at Newnham-on-Severn, and lost to an RAF team in 1942: otherwise the county lay in *Wisden*'s graphic word, 'dormant'. Glamorgan and Hampshire, their port HQs highly militarized, were equally torpid and arranged nothing in either year. Somerset was a little better, for R. J. O. Meyer organized some games at Taunton. Somerset Services drew with Gloucester Services at Bristol and then won the return match at Taunton by 184 runs, Meyer himself contributing 76 and taking 3 for 10. The South of the Thames beat the North of the Thames by four wickets, and Harold Gimblett smote 54 in 65 minutes. This was in 1941. The next year a game between R. J. O. Meyer's XI and Southern Command was the only major fixture in Somerset.

Warwickshire were severely incommoded by bomb damage at Edgbaston but did manage a few weekend games there.

R. E. S. Wyatt led an eleven against a Worcester eleven on
August Bank Holiday in 1941, and the recipe was repeated
the following summer. In the holiday week of 1942 Warwick
played and lost to Worcestershire, enjoyed a well-fought draw
over two days with a tough Civil Defence outfit, R. E. S.
Wyatt scoring a magisterial 171 not out, and welcomed the
Birmingham League XI and the Coventry and District XI
to test each other, the Birmingham League being rather
unmercifully whipped.

The context for this – as for several other such programmes
– was the government's 'Holidays at Home' campaign. In
part, this was to offer solace to workers and their families
where jobs made holidaying difficult but the chief reason was
the anxiety over the railways being clogged up by trippers
and the coastal districts, already inundated with servicemen,
overrun. Throughout the war, and it is significant in terms of
conveying cricketers, transport was always a worrying issue.
The campaign was only partially successful, but many local
authorities exerted themselves to plan a week or fortnight of
lively entertainment. Fêtes, fairs, parades, concert parties,
competitions, brass bands and events of all kinds were formu-
lated in an endeavour, enthusiastic more than authentic, to
bring the tang of Blackpool's Golden Mile or Brighton's
Regency frolics to the municipal park of war-torn Coketown.
Many people insisted on making an attempt to travel, often
to visit relatives in perhaps the only chance of the year so to
do, but even a limited success was worthwhile.

Warwickshire's programme was a feature of Birmingham's
'Holidays at Home' drive and, according to reports, 'big
crowds made a successful return'. Cricket, the ideal summer
sport, was tailor-made for such campaigns. It underscores the
potential cricket had as a wartime activity. It is the natural
counterpoint to the argument, often used in World War I
and occasionally in World War II, that frivolous sports
diverted soldiers and munitions workers from the path of
stern duty. There had to be breaks and leave, if only for
human batteries to be recharged, and what better metabolic
regeneration than a few hours at Edgbaston watching the

county captain, R. E. S. Wyatt, score 171 not out? Men and women would work harder and produce more if their arduous shifts and duties could be tempered by relaxation. Not merely out of altriusm, but more out of a realistic sense of optimal effort, the government practically insisted that activities like cricket matches were on offer.

Some counties seemed to play only if stirred into action by others. Worcestershire played a match each year against Warwickshire but nothing else. A. F. Lane raised the team in 1941 and generously met the expenses. That apart, the Worcester ground was chiefly deployed for school, club and service cricket. Leicestershire and Northants improved a little on this, playing each other twice each summer. Northants also played the British Empire XI and, in 1941, London Counties. Leicester, with both ground and finances in a poor condition, also played Notts and, like Warwick, organized a group of fixtures as part of the local 'Holidays at Home' drive.

Lancashire staged some glittering contests. As late as 21 September 1941 they drew with a gifted West Indian XI at Fazakerley, near Liverpool. A crowd of 10,000 were rewarded by Constantine who belted 39 in 30 balls. The match was drawn. The Lancashire team was a vintage one, including Charlie Hallows, Winston Place, Cyril Washbrook, Bunny Oldfield, Jack Iddon, Eddie Paynter, Frank Sibbles, George Duckworth and Eddie Phillipson. Old Trafford's war damage had been estimated at £60,000, a formidable figure by the values of the 1940s, but the county were encouraged by an increase in subscriptions from £1,814 in 1941 to £2,269 in 1942.

A considerable breakthrough in the north-west came in 1942. A. D. Procter, well-known in Manchester cricketing circles, found himself in charge of the Welfare Section of the Ministry of Labour and National Service in Manchester. His task involved raising funds for appropriate welfare schemes and he decided cricket was to be the method. With so many cricketers in the services or on war work in the north-west, and with a large population to provide the audiences, it was an astute stroke, and Mr Procter went about his self-appointed job with a workmanlike application missing in many other areas. Elsewhere, the charity aspect had been a little casual, almost a subsidiary to the pleasure of playing. A. D. Procter worked strenuously to provide top-rate entertainment. He did not, British Empire-style, form an exhibition eleven but rather concentrated on assembling juicy clashes. In the summer of 1942 this resulted in the raising of £3,500 for charity. Some 125,000 spectators attended the twenty or so matches, an average of 5,000 a game.

Six of these matches merit a brief mention. Aigburth witnessed a 500-run thriller, with Lancashire, helped by a Cranston hundred, beating a full Army side (C. S. Dempster, 89, and Denis Compton, 73) by four wickets. At Longsight, Manchester, E. H. Eytle's half-century just failed to bring the West Indies a win in a drawn match with Lancashire, for whom Cyril Washbrook scored 53. At Didsbury, Manchester, Lancashire hung on to their last wicket to draw an exciting game with the strong RAF team. An Empire XI amassed 385 for 5. Eddie Paynter, Norman Oldfield and Winston Place, born and bred in the County Palatine, may have been startled to find they were licit members of the British Empire, and they celebrated that status with 60 apiece. A North Wales XI could summon up only 151 in reply. Then, at Blackpool, an England XI beat the West Indies by 70 runs. This pattern of entertaining games, spread throughout Lancashire and into North Wales, was one of the most successful initiatives of the war, and it is right to emphasize that they were government-sponsored.

Yorkshire, for once, took something of a relatively rear seat. E. F. Holdsworth raised a white rose eleven in 1941 to play the Bradford League, for whom, in a drawn game, Paynter raced to 54 in 50 minutes, including 21 off five balls. This was at Bradford on 11 August and, the following day, Yorkshire were vanquished by a strong British Empire XI. Wyatt and Crabtree scored half-centuries. In 1942 an England XI defeated a Combined Counties XI by 24 runs. Bradford was the chosen venue, for Bramall Lane, Sheffield, had been damaged by bombing. Meanwhile, J. Appleyard, the Leeds and District League secretary, was busily organizing Sunday matches for charity, raising, for instance, over £1,000 for a cricketer's bed at the Leeds General Hospital. He arranged matches at Wakefield, Sheffield, Leeds and elsewhere in the broad acres, gathering together crowds of 5,000 to 8,000, and recruiting strongish teams, seasoned with lots of county players. Often they were based on service teams, such as Northern Command versus Western Command.

Kent eschewed a county side in the main. During 1941 and 1942 there was only one such match recorded, when a Kent XII beat S. C. Griffith's XII by over a hundred runs, C. H. Knott scoring 75 and 2nd Lt J. W. Martin taking 9 for 52. However, Kent continued its 1940 practice of organizing a multiplicity of matches at Canterbury. There were 72 in 1941 and a bewildering 132 in 1942. This was more the other side of the medallion. Where some were motivated by the charity aspect or the need to offer relaxation to large crowds, Kent devoted its resources to the servicemen and others who wished to play cricket in decent surrounds. It was an equally respectable argument. The pleasing converse of Lancashire taking something like first-class cricket to Fazakerley or Colwyn Bay was Kent inviting deserving rabbits to enjoy the experience and the memory of playing on one of England's most lovely grounds.

Notts throughout remained the champion county with respect to their wartime programme, lauded annually by *Wisden* for their undoubted flair and organization. Ten high-class matches were planned for 1941 and eleven for 1942, so that practically every weekend first-class cricketers paraded their talents at Trent Bridge. Reg Simpson scored two centuries in 1941, and C. J. Poole (an eighteen-year-old from Notts Amateurs) and Joe Hardstaff had one hundred each. Poole, Simpson and Harris averaged over 50. Harris and Butler who, with Hardstaff, voyaged out to India before the start of the 1942 season, were the leading bowlers. F. C. W. Newman, of Surrey, guested efficiently in 1942, and J. S. Hodgkins proved 'a capable all-rounder'.

The county played matches against old rivals like Derbyshire and Leicester as well as newer combinations like the
British Empire and London Counties teams, the RAF and
the Army. They also played the National Fire Service and,
lest it be thought that might not have been very daunting,
the cricketing firemen included Harold Gimblett, James Langridge, John Arnold, Bill Farrimond and Arthur Mitchell,
Test cricketers all, together with John Langridge who was
very unlucky never to have won an England cap.

Not content with this, the Notts secretary, H. A. Brown,
yearly tagged by *Wisden* as 'energetic' or 'enterprising' or,
deservedly, both, arranged other fixtures, such as Northern
Counties versus an Army XI, containing Lieutenants
D. V. P. Wright and T. F. Smailes. The Northern Counties
performance was notable for a century by the New Zealander,
C. S. Dempster, and for the appearance of George Gunn, the
England and Nottinghamshire veteran. At the age of sixty-
two, he must have made Frank Woolley, Patsy Hendren and
Joe Hulme feel chicken-like.

In another attractive coup, an August Bank Holiday crowd
of 4,000 found that well-known civilian, Harold Larwood, in
harness once more with Bill Voce. They contrived to represent
the Other Ranks against the Officers. Sgt Leyland's 78 and,
from Essex, Cpl S. Proffitt's 53 not out meant a daunting
total of 288 for 7. The Officers barely escaped humiliation,
subsiding to 104 for 8. Voce took 2 for 14 and Larwood, who
had not bowled a ball for two years, took 2 for 13.

Here was another approach to wartime cricket. Nottingham
insisted that a county could remain in business and its
headquarters could remain an effective focus. From the
playing point of view, a batsman such as C. J. Poole, like
Reg Simpson, was being introduced into a good class of
cricket.

The kind of enterprise which Nottingham showed was
exhibited outside the formal county scene, by the British
Empire and London Counties elevens. They illustrated that
it was possible to extend the concept of high-grade cricket
beyond the conventional first-class scene, however harsh the

circumstances. W. M. F. Bebbington took over as secretary in 1941 from the zestful D. L. Donnelly, who had been called to the colours, and he had the satisfaction of leading the amateurs to nineteen victories out of forty matches played, at which £2,000 was raised for charity. The playing record was even better in 1942, when twenty-three out of thirty-four games were won, but only £1,500 was raised for war charities.

The winter of 1941–42 did witness a mild palace revolution, when the club 'underwent practically a complete reorganization'. Authoritative figures came to the fore. Sir Pelham Warner, S. F. Rous, Secretary of the Football Association and the principal official of the Red Cross Sports Committee, Ray Smith, of Essex, as captain, and A. C. L. Bennett, of Surrey, as team manager, became the supervisory quartet. *Wisden* was slightly cool about the change. Although the new régime 'functioned smoothly', it 'seemed regrettable that D. L. Donnelly and W. M. F. Bebbington . . . took no part in any of the activities'. Certainly, fewer games were played and less money made in 1942, and 'it could only be deplored', said *Wisden*, that the London Counties fixture was dropped. In 1941, on 9 August, the Empire XI had defeated their professional rivals by 67 runs at Reading. This was in addition to the Lord's clash, a month earlier when, on a rainy Saturday, the professionals had been all out for 194 (F. S. Lee 45, A. Fagg 44 and Frank Woolley a modest 14) and the Empire batsmen were on 34 for 3 when the match had to end. Now, in 1942, and for whatever obscure reason, this mock version of Players and Gentlemen did not take place.

A change in control did not alter the general pattern, however. Nearly seventy players were used each season with C. B. Clarke the outstanding bowler each summer – in 1942 he took 129 wickets at an average of 10.7. *Wisden* applauded his 'intense enthusiasm and natural ability'. A. V. Avery, H. P. Crabtree, the Essex player, and A. C. L. Bennett were the most consistent trio of batsmen in both seasons. R. E. S. Wyatt averaged 82 in his six 1941 innings, and Ray Smith performed satisfyingly in 1942. It was said of Trevor Bailey that he 'tired quickly' but that he 'should develop into a more than useful county player'. A good example of their charitable effort was at Slough, on 3 and 4 May 1941, when they met the local club in aid of the Slough War Weapons Week, a game at which A. V. Alexander, First Lord of the Admiralty, announced the successful evacuation of Allied forces from Greece.

The players were not all Empire-born, as had been the express desire of the founders, but there was a fair spread, encompassing New Zealand, West Indies, Australia, India, Canada, Ireland, Malta, and even Holland and Argentina. Learie Constantine occasionally played – he was no longer playing league cricket, but was at the start of his impressive administrative career as a welfare officer for the Ministry of Labour and National Service, looking after the needs of West Indian seamen and other migrants from those islands. Writing in the *Spring Cricketer Annual*, Desmond Donnelly proposed that the British Empire club should tour England in the first post-war season, rather like the Australian Imperial Forces XI in 1919, or if the MCC decided not to tour India then, he suggested, the Empire side might make the trip, captained by Norman Yardley. He hoped to maintain the concept of an annual match at Northampton in memory of R. P. Nelson (two of which they had already played), to develop fixtures with the two universities, and to arrange a seaside festival – all in an effort 'to bind closer in peace the bonds that unite our great empire'.

Thus did the British Empire XI proudly uphold their idealism across much of the south-east, with occasional forays elsewhere. In 1942, for instance, they visited New Malden, Slough, Southgate, Edmonton, Spinney Hill, Winchmore Hill, Tunbridge Wells, Richmond, Hornsey, Trent Bridge, Chigwell, Peterborough, Birmingham, Sudbury, Coventry, Harpenden, Imber Court, Finchley, Uxbridge, Catford, Reading, Colchester, Ashstead, Addlestone, Teddington, Woodford Wells and Dulwich Hamlet.

Here was no casual bunch of peripatetic socialites. If the philosophy was a little jejune, it was entirely sincere and, in their own worthy fashion, the London Counties club was equally in earnest. They played, like the Empire XI, nearly forty games in each of the 1941 and 1942 seasons, winning well over half, and losing only four over both summers. They were captained by Jack O'Connor, one of their leading batsmen until he broke an arm late on in the 1942 season. Gover, A. E. Watt, Boyes, of Hants, and Young were the main bowlers, while the Compton brothers, Fagg and Lee were the chief run-makers. In 1941 Arthur Wellard performed several huge hitting feats and took 8 for 17 against Bexley Heath. They, too, experienced a change of government in 1942, when the founder, C. J. E. Jones, resigned 'through circumstances outside my control'. Captain W. H. Folkes of Hoddesdon became president, and W. M. F. Bebbington switched secretaryships from the British Empire to the London Counties. At this distance, it is impossible to tell with what degree of equanimity or otherwise that transfer was made but, in 1942, the London Counties, as well as having no British Empire fixture, never played at Lord's. *Wisden* felt the public were the losers on both counts.

The London Counties were a little more mundane in their philosophy than their amateur rivals. They espoused no profound political cause such as British imperialism. Their mission was, cricket-wise, evangelical. Their self-appointed task was to exhibit good quality cricket in what rather theatrically was termed 'the hinterland', those vast tracts of British terrain unmarked by the studs of first-class cricketers' whitened boots. They made money for charity – about £1,500 a year – and they made money for themselves, for that was another of their aims; the financial upkeep of the journeyman professional. But they travelled widely so that the public might have 'a rare glimpse of almost legendary celebrities'.

They were very popular. Over 10,000 turned out in June 1941 for a two-day match, arranged by Courtaulds, on behalf of the city hospital, in badly blitzed Coventry. Coventry, strengthened by the likes of Ames and Wyatt, won a high-scoring encounter by one wicket, just reaching the London Counties score of 359. Leslie Compton and R. E. S. Wyatt scored centuries. In 1942 there was a 20 per cent increase in attendances, as the cricketing public flocked to see the 'almost legendary celebrities' and created several local record 'gates'.

Ambition was as vaulting with the London Counties as with the British Empire. Writing in *Wisden*, Norman Preston felt 'there can be little doubt now that there will be scope for such an organization when the last trumpets of war have died down'. The opportunities this formula offered for revealing local talent and for spreading the virtues of cricket were such, he believed, that the intention to carry on after the war must be taken seriously.

It is precisely such initiatives as these which should have given some direction to the future of the game, for they proved that the county dogma was not sacrosanct. Nevertheless, that dogma appeared, in peacetime, to be insurmountable, and the two great exhibition clubs of the war years collapsed without a murmur.

Of the minor counties, Durham and Oxfordshire were chief among those organizing matches, while the MCC arranged its usual series of about thirty schools matches. Areas of troop concentration produced significant cricket. Aldershot District services had a fine side which played many matches and warranted inclusion in *Wisden*. Blackpool Services, chiefly RAF, were led by W. H. R. Andrews of Somerset and, in 1942, they won the Ribblesdale League. Soccer fans will recall how well both Aldershot and Blackpool performed in wartime football and for exactly the same reasons. Some clubs made a magnificent contribution. One instance is that of Epsom CC which, under the tutelage of its secretary, L. D. Heaton, raised £1,000 for charity in 1942. Epsom had a quality fixture list, including London Counties, the British Empire, Cambridge University Crusaders, the RAF (a game watched by 3,000), and the club provided the venue for interesting matches, such as the British Empire versus Brian Sellers' XI.

The Leagues prospered throughout 1941 and 1942. Thirty-nine county players, including thirteen internationals, were logged as appearing in the Bradford League. There was much muttering and a meeting or two to complain about the alleged and, for those times, fabulous £25 paid to Learie Constantine weekly. His club, Windhill, won the 'A' Division and Jim Smith of Middlesex was also within their ranks. Paynter, for Keighley, and Barber, for Brighouse, excelled again, with averages over fifty. A. V. Pope and Copson, the Derbyshire bowlers, took 130 wickets between them for Saltaire, ensuring the 'B' Division title for that club. Parks, Hollies, Goddard, Dempster and Wyatt were seen to advantage once more in the Birmingham League and Don Kenyon, attached to Stourbridge, was a name to watch for his future career with Worcestershire. In 1942, Eric Hollies took 61 wickets for West Bromwich Dartmouth while, in the Bradford League, T. B. Mitchell, A. H. Dyson (Glamorgan) and B. P. King (Worcester) had good seasons, helping Lidget Green to the 'A' Division championship. The Pope and Copson combine moved to Windhill to help compensate for Constantine's disappearance on welfare work. They were runners-up. Keighley regained the 'B' Division title and, in a remarkable flow of consistency, Eddie Paynter had a third brilliant season, including 158 against East Brierley. He averaged an unbelievable 122. The West Indian, E. A. Martindale, was his co-adjutant. The Lancashire League still excluded professionals: Church, in 1941, and East Lancashire, in 1942, were the winners.

Doughty deeds had illuminated the two mid-war summers. Arthur Wellard hit fifty in eight minutes for London Counties against Hoddesdon, one of the quickest ever half-centuries. E. H. Spooner, son of the Lancashire and England bat, Reggie Spooner, hit 113 for Eton against the British Empire, while C. B. Clarke took all ten wickets for the British Empire against the Metropolitan Police. Jack O'Connor completed 1000 runs for London Counties in 1941 and, in July 1942, he scored 208 against Peterborough, one of only two wartime double-centuries in one-day wartime cricket. On the very day he broke his arm, the openers for the rival British Empire team, Crabtree and Avery, established the war's record first wicket stand of 241. The same month, George Cox smashed his way to the war's fastest century outside the leagues – forty-five minutes – for A. D. Procter's XI against C. Hallow's at Radcliffe. In June 1941 the wartime record for a one-day total was attained: it was a massive 613, an Empire XI 324 for 5 and Sir Julian Cahn's XI 289 for 5, at West Bridgford.

There was news from the front line, too. It was reported that various cricketers were prisoners of war. Capt. F. E. Hugonin of Essex had been captured, while the Essex secretary, Lt-Col B. K. Castor, was taken at the fall of Singapore. Lieut. Wilf Wooller was posted missing in June 1942, but was later reported a Jap POW. L/Sgt L. Muncer, along with E. W. Swanton, was also in Japanese hands, while another Middlesex player, Lieut. B. D. Carris was a prisoner in Italy. Lieut. Freddie Brown and his Surrey colleague, G. J. Whittaker, C. G. Toppin, of Worcestershire, and Bill Bowes, Yorkshire and England, were also imprisoned in Italy. Several players won medals for valour, among them Major R. Aird, who was awarded the Military Cross for bravery in the Middle East, and Flt Lt P. A. McKenzie, who received the DFC. Both were Hampshire players. R. M. Taylor, of Essex, was also awarded the DFC.

Inevitably, deaths overshadowed these more lively activities. *Wisden* gravely recorded eighteen obituaries in 1941 and thirty-seven in 1942. L. C. Eastman, the Essex all-rounder, who captained London Counties on their first appearance at Lord's, died, aged 43, after suffering severely from bomb blast experienced whilst on ARP duties. D. F. Walker, a young Oxford, Norfolk and Hampshire batsman whose best season had been 1939, was killed on active service, a fate that also befell C. P. Hamilton, the Kent and Army player. E. J. H. 'Budge' Dixon, like D. F. Walker a former Oxford captain, was killed in 1941. In 1942 Capt. R. H. C. Human, Cambridge and Worcester, R. G. Tindall, an Oxford blue, Ross Gregory of Victoria and Australia and A. B. C. Langton, the South African cricketer, and Flt Lt D. Frank Walker, Oxford's captain in 1935, were all killed. Claude Ashton, Cambridge and Essex and a noted footballer, lost his life in a dual tragedy, for R. de W. K. Winlaw, of Cambridge, died in the same flying incident. Ian Peebles was nastily injured in a London air raid in the September of 1941, but resumed cricketing duties the following season.

In cricketing terms, the most mourned loss of these mid-war years was that of Kenneth Farnes, the Cambridge, Essex and England fast bowler. He had trained for night flying in Canada but, four weeks after returning to the UK to undertake that task, he crashed on 23 October. He was 30 years of age. Tall, accurate and committed, he had become England's main quick bowler by 1939 and had taken nearly 700 first-class wickets. It was to be expected that, in this phase of siege-like attrition, fatalities in aerial combat or other aerial exercise would be unpleasantly common, and many young Oxbridge cricketers had bravely chosen that path, rather as their Great War forebears had found themselves at high risk as subalterns in the trenches. Pilot Officer Farnes was the first household name from the cricket field to die in World War II, a name, that is, familiar to those whose interest in the game was but cursory. His picture and other details appeared in the news columns of the daily papers: boys had his cigarette card likeness, for he had achieved that lofty eminence. One gazed at the image and one had the news item pointed out by a cricket-conscious father. He was missed sorely immediately – and he was to be missed in the first post-war years for, although he would have been in his mid-thirties, his height and strength enabled him to generate some pace off a shortish and not too tiring run. He might have responded somewhat to the bidding of Lindwall and Miller.

Somehow the most poignant death occurred on 23 July 1942. Andrew Ducat, the Surrey and England batsman and a cup winning captain of Aston Villa and international footballer to boot, had been born in Brixton in 1886, and was now 56. He was the Eton coach. He was playing at Lord's for the Surrey Home Guard against the Sussex Home Guard. Andy Ducat moved quickly to 29 not out. He played a ball from Eaton, the Sussex bowler to mid on. Eaton was preparing to bowl the next ball when Andy Ducat fell forward and collapsed. It was perhaps strangely fitting. A veteran cricketer could ask little more than to die at Lord's, 29 not out and representing the Home Guard, that symbolic expression of patriotism in older age. The story soon eerily circulated of how Andy Ducat had, just prior to this game, dreamt three nights in a row that William Beldham, the Surrey cricketer of even earlier, almost pre-historic vintage and whose fine portrait graces the Long Room at Lord's, had beckoned him to follow him.

While England and English cricketers were busily coming to terms with hostilities, there was cricket overseas to be considered, and the mid-point of the war is possibly a helpful point from which to glance cursorily at cricket outside England and offer an overall sketch of what happened elsewhere.

It was 'the express wish of high government officials' in Australia that the Sheffield Shield competition be continued to the end of the 1939–40 season. Huge crowds watched a grand tournament, dominated as ever by Bradman and won by New South Wales. The following year the contest was suspended and only eleven first class games were played, ten inter-state games and a match between Don Bradman's XI and Stan McCabe's XI. Without the spur of rivalry for the shield, crowds dropped, although 75 per cent of the take went to charity. New South Wales again did well, winning six out of seven games. This curtailed season is notable for the emergence of players who were later to become vital cogs in the post-war Australian machine. Sydney Barnes of New South Wales scored a thousand runs in a handful of games, for an average of 75. Arthur Morris made his début in spectacular style, with a world record of a century in each innings for New South Wales against Queensland. Cec Pepper, Colin McCool and Ron Saggers were other young successes, but 'Tiger' O'Reilly was still demonstrating that his lethal bowling talents must command respect. It is interesting that Australia's post-war opening pair did, in effect, play one and a half seasons into the war, which must have been excellent experience for them. In this respect, the Australians followed their own example in the first war, when they played the Sheffield Shield for one wartime year and then stopped it.

New Zealand, where only two seasons had been completely dislocated in World War I, always played some good class cricket in World War II. New Zealanders served overseas, of course, especially in the Middle East, but, as also in Australia because of the Jap danger, many stayed at home. New Zealand forces cricket was to be tolerably good throughout the war.

India had suffered few effects during the Great War and, indeed, several English professionals had obtained jobs there for the duration. In the last war the shape of Indian cricket changed little. The even tenor of the Ranji Trophy and other important matches was continued in the placid surroundings of the subcontinent's cricket grounds. There were tours to Ceylon, and English servicemen joined in the entertainment, most cheerfully, Denis Compton, who delighted the crowds at Bombay and elsewhere. One of cricket's curiosities is that Reg Simpson, after some lively innings for the wartime Notts XI, actually made his first-class début for Sind while serving with the RAF in India.

The West Indies, far from the fury of battle, enjoyed little break in their first-class experience, although the Inter-colonial Tournament was stopped and never resumed as such. Names like Frank Worrell, Clyde Walcott and Jeff Stollmeyer began to appear on the score-cards of first-class games like Barbados against Trinidad. The origins of the great West Indian sides of the 1950s were quietly being nurtured during the war.

The most epic presaging of this coming greatness was in February 1946 when Clyde Walcott (314 not out) and Frank Worrell (255 not out) added 574 for the Barbados fourth wicket against Trinidad at Port-of-Spain. The Trinidadians were no slouches, for a double century from G. E. Gomez and a century from K. Trestrail enabled them just to save the game. 574 was the then world record for any wicket, beating the 555 of Percy Holmes and Herbert Sutcliffe for the first wicket, Yorkshire against Essex, in 1932. A year later the new record was just overtaken by V. S. Hazare and Gul Mahomed, with 577 for Baroda against Holkar.

South African and Rhodesian cricket was non-competitive during the war but there was a substantial amount of cricket played, not least with the support of dozens of RAF trainees. South African cricket spilled over into the East African and Middle Eastern theatres of war. For instance, at Christmas, 1941, Transvaal played the RAF at Johannesburg. Walter Hammond was in dominating form. He took 5 for 77 and scored 130 out of 350. There was a little first-class play; for example, in the 1941–2 season there was one such match, Western Province versus Transvaal.

There was an immense concentration of Empire troops in the Middle East: British, South African, Australian, New Zealand, Indian and every other imperial group of servicemen were represented. Cairo's Gezira Club soon became the centre of a wealth of cricket. Every Sunday there was cricket of, it has been said, 'virtually Test Match standard'. Hammond scored 129 for Gezira in one such game in 1942. It was from the Middle East that the first whispers began about the prowess of Jim Laker. The British Army played everywhere so that even Canada and, to some degree, the United States witnessed an increase in the amount of cricket played. There was cricket in Singapore, Malaya and Hong Kong until the arrival of the Japanese – and it was restarted in those areas as soon as the non-cricketing foe had been removed.

One of the most intriguing cameos of wartime cricket was the maintenance of the game in occupied Europe. It has been suggested that this exhibition of English tradition was a way of showing defiance. Recording events in *The Cricketer* of 25 August 1945, however, a Dutch official merely stated that cricket was permitted to 'go quietly its own way'. After a brief stoppage in the early summer of 1940, just after the occupation, cricket in Holland began again, with three regional leagues to avoid undue travel. The Dutch cricket journal continued to be published, under the title of 'Official Communications' for the Dutch Cricket Association, to meet German regulations. There was some damage to grounds because of German anti-glider precautions, but as matting wickets – the so-called Dutch wickets – were used, it was not too bothersome. When cricket balls were in short supply, a supply of hockey balls was procured and painted red. School-boy cricket was avidly encouraged. Several Dutch players helped the allies and, of course, after the Liberation, hundreds of matches were arranged with British forces teams. The civilizing effects of cricket were not total. The Dutch crick-eter, J. van den Bosch, joined the Dutch National Socialist Party and co-operated energetically with the Germans. 'There is', ran *The Cricketer* report, 'no further news of him.'

One should perhaps not read too many heroics into this gentle tale of cricket in occupied Holland. It is the story of cricketers insisting on pursuing their chosen pastime amid certain hardships, and of the occupying invaders not being especially concerned as long as the peace was kept. This applied even more in Denmark, which was left fairly intact by the Nazi conquerors, so that normal life, including the enjoyment of some cricket, continued without much hindrance.

It was, however, the British soldier who carried a cricketer's bat in his knapsack, along with his comrades in the air force and, for obvious reasons to a lesser extent, the navy. Abroad, as in Britain, there would be some military skulduggery to ensure teams were of good strength. Witness Harry Dalling, who lived at Trent Bridge from birth, as his father was ground superintendent, who occupies that role still today and is, as is well-known, the fountain of all lore about the famous Nottingham ground. He did absent himself from it for military duties, and tells the story of being stationed with the RAF outside Cairo. Along with another minor counties player, he raised a side which won a game against another locally based team. The following day the two entrepreneurs were paraded before an officer in the cookhouse, and asked whether they wanted to play cricket or do cookhouse fatigues. Not surprisingly, they decided on the former option, and proceeded to enjoy some weeks cricket for and on behalf of the catering officer, the proviso being that, once a week, they had to stand at the cookhouse door and distribute oranges to the queue of hungry airmen to prove that they were bona fide mess staff.

There were no lengths to which the enthusiastic cricketer would not travel. A late colleague and valued friend of mine, Norman Garner, found himself signals NCO in charge of a remote wireless location in Malaya. A useful club medium-paced bowler, he was missing his cricket. He set a task-force of Japanese POWs to work clearing a cricket pitch in the jungle. Then he created a makeshift side out of the few wireless operators and cooks with him in that lonely clearing, together with some members of the Black Watch who acted as the perimeter guard. One wonders what the Japanese imagined they were being asked to construct.

When prisoners themselves, British and Dominion cricketers insisted on playing some cricket, even in the direst circumstances, such as existed under Japanese supervision in the Far East. A well-known yarn concerns an article contributed to *The Cricketer* in 1943, describing the cricket played within a castle used for captured officers. It is said that, by delineating the local rules necessitated by the castle's architecture, valuable information on the site safely avoided censorship: there were references to 'the moat of a castle with splendid hazards and catching off buttresses; among tree stumps on a wicket of peat . . .' and so on.

About the same time Sgt Hooper of Hull sent *The Cricketer* details of a Test Match between England and Australia at Stammlager 383 in Germany, a game won comfortably by the Australians by almost 200 runs. Jim Ward, the genial and astute chairman of Nottinghamshire County Cricket Club, was a prisoner for much of the war and recalls a Test series contested at a POW camp near Munich toward the end of the war. With full equipment (with the exception of abdominal protectors) provided readily by the Red Cross and with a parole from the Germans to move outside the wires to a more suitable space, South Africa, Australia and New Zealand combined, and England played out a number of matches. It is ruefully recalled that the South Africans, with some high-level club cricketers, and the Antipodeans, as ever matching a tiny number from which to choose with an infinite competitiveness, had the better of these proceedings. In 1945 *The Cricketer* described a slate of matches at Luftwaffe 3 prison camp, where no less than 300 POWs played five matches each, on a pitch with 50 yards the longest boundary. It was, schoolboy fashion, 'six and out', for, the correspondent laconically remarked, 'it was difficult to retrieve the ball from outside the camp'.

E. W. Swanton, in *Wisden* for 1946, wrote an article entitled 'Cricket under the Japs', an impressive account of how, in those most bestial of conditions, men had kept up their spirits with some makeshift cricket and by continual talk about this most expansive of games. E. W. Swanton describes how, on his release from imprisonment, he found himself in a Thai village where, to his amazement, there was a wireless which was broadcasting commentary from the Victory Test at Old Trafford.

Toward the end of the war much of forces cricket was becoming quite serious, and a pleasant illustration might be the six matches played in Italy in the 1945 season, which were regarded as important enough to enter the official records. They were played at Caserta and Bari and two each at Eboli and Rome, between sides variously assembled: Army versus RAF; Western versus Eastern Italy; A. H. Hornby's XI versus Rest Camp Rome; Middle Eastern versus Central Mediterranean Forces. Teams were drawn from a wide region, two of the fixtures were two-day events, and the matches, played on matting wickets, were of high standard. Several talented players were on view, including Alec Bedser, Arthur Wellard, G. W. Parker of Cambridge University and Gloucester, W. E. Merritt, A. J. McIntyre, George Emmett, T. P. B. Smith, B. P. King, then of Worcester, Norman Yardley and Tom Dollery.

Playing cricket within sound or reach of battle is a well-established tradition. At the time of the Jacobite Rebellion in 1745, the Earl of Sandwich (who also gave his name to a

gastronomic item which has contributed greatly to the pleasure of cricket) was recalled to the Admiralty: 'I'll go to your
board', he loftily announced, 'when at leisure from cricket.'
The concept of finding leisure *from* cricket to pursue hostilities
must hearten the *aficionados* and it was further demonstrated
when the Duke of Richmond played cricket near Brussels a
few days before the battle of Waterloo in 1815.

Similarly, Montgomery's 'hitting of Rommel for six', or
the newsboards recording German air-losses in the Battle of
Britain as if they were cricket scores, had their precedents.
The cricketing metaphor had been deployed at the battle of
Alma in the Crimean War, when Sir John Astley, wicket-
keeper for the regiment he commanded, and George Duff,
his lower-born, other-ranking long stop, are said to have
exchanged pleasantries about dealing with bounding round-
shot. During the Boer War (in which, incidentally, F. Milli-
gan, the Yorkshire player, and the immensely successful
Australian bowler J. J. Ferris were killed) Baden-Powell was
asked for a truce at the siege of Mafeking. The purpose was
to arrange a cricket match between besiegers and besieged,
but Baden Powell refused, on the grounds that the British
were 200 days not out, and enjoying the game. One wonders
whether the Earl of Sandwich, Sir John Astley or the Duke
of Richmond might have been more sorely tempted, but the
point remains that cricket has both a social and a cultural
hold. Men have insisted, in the most unpropitious conditions,
on playing the game; others have exploited its vocabulary to
popular effect.

Given this degree of enthusiasm and sympathy, it is perhaps
surprising that, just as cricket's organization at home lacked
a little in cogency and thrust, there was no more co-ordinated
attempt to provide cricket in the war theatres. The army and
the RAF organized many football tours, with a representative
side playing a locally based team, usually one including
players with league experience. These were top-class morale-
boosting exercises, with the 'home' team undoubtedly keen
to humiliate the stars. Of course, the visiting tourists were
subject to considerable jesting, some of it cheerful, some of it

less so: 'D-Day dodgers' and 'PT commandos' being the choicer of the printable epithets. Compared with the abuse raining down today from the terraces, this was all innocuous enough, and one commanding officer has been quoted as remarking that, in battle-areas, one football match equalled five ENSA performances.

In May 1945 for instance, the Army dispatched an international squad, including Frank Swift, Joe Mercer, Matt Busby and Tommy Lawton, to play an exhausting five-match trip. The Wanderers, as the chief Army team came to be called, were exceedingly active in the European theatre but elsewhere the pattern was the same. Denis Compton led a team across India and it once went fifty games without defeat. Tommy Walker, the Scottish inside forward, captained a touring team in the Far East, and Harry Johnston, of Blackpool, was in charge of an RAF team which undertook a 3,000 mile tour of the Middle East.

Although football had the edge on cricket in terms of overall popularity and although cricket necessarily requires a lengthier time-span, it does remain something of a mystery why something a little more coherent was not planned for the entertainment of the troops. After all, one essence of cricket is touring. Apart from the famous nomadic teams, both professionals and amateur, in the past, all the counties were accustomed to embarking on a tiny tour or two to fulfil their season's engagements. It is not that there was no cricket, or that cricket was not encouraged. It is another example of the philosophy, swiftly developed in the first year of the war and never seriously challenged, let alone rescinded, that cricket must proceed on an *ad hoc* basis of happenstance.

Interestingly, a similar criticism was made of Australian cricket by the journalist, Ray Robinson. In the 1941–42 season a Patriotic Cup inter-state tournament had been planned, with a most intricate scoring system which allocated points by reference to wickets taken, individual run scoring, boundaries and so on. Only one match was completed, Queensland beating New South Wales by 19 runs. Apparently because of the threat posed in the Pacific by the Japs, the government abruptly cancelled the other seventeen fixtures, and substituted eleven exhibition matches which proved to be 'a financial failure'.

Ray Robinson complained that the authorities had 'departed from the logical course of carrying on until circumstances compelled cessation – shortage of players (and/or cash customers) or enemy action'. He pointed out that only half the players had been called up, that the Japanese were not all that close, that football and racing had kept going and that, now Australians were working harder than ever, they deserved cricket with 'a genuine competitive flavour'.

In the United States President Roosevelt was quick to ensure that baseball was retained and not marred by the loss of players or materials. His instincts were that relaxation was a crucial element in his nation's war effort. The resilience of football in war-torn nations was truly astonishing, and it exhibited a power that, in the post-war decades, was to prove formidable. Germany kept up its footballing interests, even playing international matches after the outbreak of war, while a fortnight after D-Day 70,000 watched the league play-off between Dresdener DC and Hamburg in Berlin. Italy, France, Holland, Belgium, Hungary, Denmark and other European countries, in spite of occupation, invasion, reconquest or liberation, contrived to sustain orderly tournaments for most of the war period. At the time of the siege of Stalingrad, that life-or-death juncture in Russian history, it is said that 300,000 footballers were engaged in various competitions in the USSR. The short and dramatic visit to Britain of Moscow Dynamo in 1945 showed how the Soviet Union had succeeded in its maintenance of sport.

By these exciting standards, cricket during the war begins to look decidedly puny.

FOUR

The Continuing Tale

So to the season of 1943. The war was now completing its fourth year and had already lasted almost as long as its bloodier – from a British standpoint – predecessor. People were inured to the habit of hostilities. From the tiny – the dried egg, the absence of bananas, the shortage of razor blades, the indoor fireworks, the National Wheatmeal Loaf – to the large – the fatigue of the ceaseless queue, the encircling gloom of the blackout – a social world had evolved which seemed ordered, self-contained and ongoing. As air raids grew less common and as the news, however bleak, was more distanced in reality for the majority, this habitual world was often grey and mundane, but not wholly uncomfortable, and most people had become accustomed to it, even though, naturally, a more comfortable existence would have been preferred.

It is, therefore, not surprising that cricket, in 1943 and in 1944, repeated wellnigh exactly what had occurred in the previous three seasons. *Wisden* records, for each summer, roughly 200 matches of all kinds, but usually of the one-day, eight-ball over variety. The pack of players, scarcely shuffled, was dealt in much the same manner, and the Lord's select programme, the fixtures of the same few enterprising counties, the steadfast endeavours of British Empire and London Counties, and the exploits of the star-filled northern and midland leagues persisted. Ernest Bevin was again 'asking that cricket should be encouraged in every way'.

There were sixteen major games at Lord's in 1943, and

eighteen in 1944, ranging from the AA Command, led by Brian Sellers, and the Balloon Command confrontation in mid-May 1943, to the high summer meet of a Lord's XI and the Buccaneers in August 1944.

There was an appetising game on 29 May 1943 when, before a 20,000 gate, an England XI defeated a West Indies XI, for whom the dashing Constantine scored 59 not out. Alec Bedser took 6 for 27, including the hat trick, while Jack Robertson and Les Ames enjoyed the batting honours. In early June, and with a goodish crowd of approaching 10,000, the Royal Australian Air Force team made its first Lord's appearance, and were soon to be perhaps the leading 'exhibition' XI in the country. On this occasion, however, they were bowled out for 100 by Alec Bedser and C. B. Clarke, with Keith Miller, on 45, contributing nearly half the score and inserting one of the first of his myriad mentions in cricketing annals. E. R. T. Holmes and the young Trevor Bailey scored most runs for Sir Pelham Warner's XI which won by 101-runs. The following week the powerful Civil Defence combine, with Gimblett on 124 and Parks 91 not out, defeated the Army, despite 93 from Maurice Leyland and a half century for Jack Robertson. Over 500 runs were scored in the day. Two days later the Army were again vanquished, this time by their air force rivals. 22,000 watched Matthews slice through the usually stalwart Army batting, taking 5 for 41, after which Les Berry and Bill Edrich saw home the RAF by nine wickets. In the final corner of that little triangle, the RAF, on 3 July, then beat the Civil Defence by 95 runs. Washbrook and Ames both scored centuries, and Berry scored 72, after which Alec Bedser took 4 for 59. Another sizeable crowd of 15,000 attended.

These services matches remained highly popular. A fortnight later 21,000 were present to enjoy a drawn match, in which the Army accumulated 284 for 6 (Compton, Leyland and Dempster achieving half-centuries) and the RAF emerged with a somewhat uneasy draw at 169 for 7, only Washbrook and Wyatt looking anything like secure. In August approaching 13,000 saw the Army thrash the Royal Navy, understandably the smallest and weakest of the services, by 176 runs.

Dempster scored a century and Ian Peebles had 5 for 31. There was a surprise in September when the Army, generally so powerful, were dismissed for 93 by the National Police, Taylor and Perks taking four wickets apiece. Laurie Fishlock scored 84 in the Police victory of 103 runs in front of 8,000 people. The Army team was not at its strongest, but the result constituted a minor shock. In the last game of the season, and with 10,000 watching, the RAAF beat the RAF by three wickets. Keith Miller's all-round performance – 3 for 23 and 91 – was carefully noted by the pundits.

In the meanwhile, and away from these uniformed gatherings, there were other combinations to enjoy. On 24 July the annual professional-amateur clash took place. The British Empire declared at 257 for 7, Fishlock and Halliday being the chief run-getters, and London Counties could manage only 201, three-quarters of the runs coming from the Compton brothers. Trevor Bailey and C. B. Clarke took three wickets each for the Empire XI. The 10,000 crowd was equalled in the Varsity game in which Oxford clung grimly on for an unlikely draw. Cambridge were still enjoying the rub of the green and playing four or five decent fixtures before meeting their old rivals, while Oxford could manage little authentic cricket. They hung on at 202 for 9, as the minutes ticked away, after Cambridge had scored a creditable 289 for 5. There was also a repeat of the combined counties fixture, but it was a disappointing affair, with fewer than 4,000 spectators, an intriguing sidelight on the public's thirst for personalities rather perhaps than for identifiable teams. D. V. P. Wright and Alec Bedser took three cheap wickets each, and Middlesex and Essex were abruptly dismissed for 75. Kent and Surrey won easily by nine wickets and, batting on, Eric Bedser and a youthful Godfrey Evans scored half-centuries.

However, the glamorous highlight of the Lord's season in 1943 was a two-day game over the August Bank Holiday, when England beat the Dominions by a whisker. An attendance of 24,000 – the highest total of the season – on the Monday, and over 14,000 on the Tuesday, demonstrated the magnetism exerted by two powerful teams. England, batting first, scored 324 for 9, with Leslie Ames making 133 and that most consistent of leg-spinners, C. B. Clarke, taking 4 for 89. Denis Compton then proceeded to demolish the Dominions with his 'chinamen'. His analysis was an incredible 6 for 5, and the Dominions were over 200 behind. England declared at 150 for 6 with R. W. V. Robins contributing a brisk 69 not out. An England victory was anticipated, but C. S. Dempster's 113, plus solid scores from Sismey, the RAAF wicket-keeper and C. B. Clarke, not usually noted for his batting, produced a most exhilarating finish. Eventually, the Dominions were all out for 351, just eight runs away from victory. Sismey and Clarke added 108 for the last wicket.

Fixtures were concocted in much the same way in 1944, although there were some rich additions to the diet. Cambridge again had the better of Oxford, winning by a comfortable six wickets, and the Empire once more defeated London Counties, who could manage only 92 against the 251 of the amateurs. Halliday (101) Crabtree (83) Appleyard (5 for 21) and, inevitably, Clarke (3 for 23) were the mainstays. The combined counties fixtures was a much closer and more exciting drawn game than in 1943. Middlesex and Essex were all out for 218, D. V. P. Wright inflicting considerable damage with his pacey leg-spinners in taking 6 for 76. There was a near classic ending with Kent and Surrey needing twenty-nine and the last man in.

There was the same round of service-focused fixtures, many of them attracting gates of 10,000 to 15,000. In May the Army lost to the Civil Defence by two wickets, and the latter, in July, then drew with the RAF for whom Hammond (returned from duties in the Middle East and providentially stationed with the Air Crew Reception Centre at Winfield House, Regent's Park, a cricket ball's throw from Lord's) charmed the spectators with 71 vintage runs, while Wyatt also obliged with 69. Later in July the RAF, in another close finish, just avoided defeat by the Army. When stumps were drawn they were 129 for 9, Dick Pollard 4 for 33 and Maurice Leyland 2 for 1, in response to a solid Army total of 211 for

8, with Wyatt, unusually, taking 5 for 81. The captains, Hammond and Sellers, agreed to move the pitch in order to complete the game, such 'enterprise', as even *Wisden* condoned this chivalrous piece of illegality, being highly commended by press and spectators. In August it rained upon the unlucky Royal Navy, just when they looked in sight of a win. Trevor Bailey was now a lieutenant in the Royal Marines and his 5 for 45 scattered the militia for only 153. The Navy were a promising 123 for 4 when the match was abandoned.

The Royal Australian Air Force were much in evidence, at Lord's and elsewhere, and their efforts contributed greatly to the variety and quality of cricket in the summer of 1944. In May they defeated the RAF by 47 runs in a low-scoring encounter at Lord's and then, in June, they beat the Army by 77 runs. Only the Civil Defence thwarted them at Lord's. Miller scored his first century at Lord's, but Fishlock's 122 enabled the Civil Defence to draw the match.

The Australian presence was influential in another mini-series of popular representative fixtures. On Whit Saturday 27 May there was a knife-edge finish which delighted a massive crowd of over 26,000. Walter Hammond, in his first appearance at Lord's for some time, scored 46 and Robins 79 in what looked like a formidable 280 for 8 on the part of the Rest. Australia, as their opponents were flatteringly designated, were well served by Workman (103) and Carmody (86) just squeezing home by one wicket in the tightest of situations. It had been an enthralling game, with 562 runs amassed. Not surprisingly, there was an even bigger attendance – 28,000 – for the return two days later on Whit Monday, and the largest crowd of the season basked in England's six wicket revenge. D. V. P. Wright's 4 for 61 held the Australians to 243, while Hutton and Ames secured the England victory with sound batting. Shortly afterwards, in June, an England XI swamped the West Indies, all out for 77, G. F. H. Heane (4 for 6) and the South Australian, C. L. Badcock (4 for 4) by 166 runs. Hammond preceded this amazing bowling with some magicianship of his own and delighted everyone with a peerless hundred. There were two similar games in August. First, England played Australia and won by 33 runs, 226 to 193, with bowlers – Ellis, the lefthander, and Roper, medium-fast, for the Australians, and Wright, with 6 for 62, for the English XI – holding a finer balance than in many games. Each innings was dominated by a master-craftsman, and a crowd of 16,000 could have asked for nothing better than the sight of the veteran genius of Hammond, who scored 105, after England had been 118 for 7, and the burgeoning talent of Keith Miller, who scored 85, in direct contrast. Second, England drew with the Dominions. England declared, assisted by a Fishlock century, at 258 for 6, and their opponents were on 225 for 6 at the close.

London Counties continued in their previous vein, playing 62 matches over the two seasons 1943 and 1944, and winning about half of them. Joe Hulme remained their strongest bat, and his oldheaded virtues permitted him to top a thousand runs in 1944. J. A. Young, the Middlesex left-hand spin bowler, was the leading wicket-taker in both seasons. The British Empire club played more matches and, on balance, maintained a rather a higher level of success. They played 87 games and won 58 in the two seasons, with H. P. Crabtree scoring over 2000 runs across the two summers, and C. B. Clarke taking a hundred wickets in each season.

The two chief touring elevens were joined in 1944 by the West of England, reminiscent perhaps of the United South of England Eleven organized, not least to his own profit, by W. G. Grace as one of the half dozen 'exhibition' teams which prospered in the mid nineteenth century.

The man whom *Wisden* called the 'zealous parent' of the West of England team was G. O. J. Elliott of Hempsted, Gloucester, a Gloucester City player and county trialist. Wounded with the Gloucester Regiment in 1940, his recovery had been slow, but, after taking up his old job in the City Treasurer's Office, Gloucester, the vision of this occidental amalgamation was vouchsafed him, and he pumped 'his tremendous transfusion of energy into the lifeblood of the game'. He had hoped to include Glamorgan among the alliance, but few Glamorgan players actually played. At first the modest administrator, he soon joined the fray with some competence. After the war he became Secretary of Leicestershire.

This new combination played a score or so of fixtures in each of the 1944 and 1945 seasons, drawing on the manifest talents of professionals in the Gloucester, Somerset and Worcester region, batsmen like F. Vigar, N. McCorkell, H. Gimblett and J. Arnold, and bowlers like R. Howorth, R. T. D. Perks, T. W. Goddard and P. F. Jackson. They won more than they lost, and, although they did not have the time or the scope to emulate the deeds of the two pioneer squads, it was an interesting little development. In one of their 1944 matches a twelve-a-side against Westland CC over two days, three bowlers contrived to take eight wickets apiece. Perks and Goddard in each of the Westland innings, with R. V. Ward grabbing eight West of England victims. The West of England, predictably, played their matches against clubs from Reading down to Bristol, with an occasional foray into higher flights, with fixtures against counties such as Glamorgan or military sides like the United Services. On 8 July they made their Lord's début and lost by five wickets to a Lord's XI. Sinfield, of Gloucester, scored 90 for the visitors and Goddard took three of the five Lord's wickets that fell.

The county circuit was much of a muchness. Derbyshire, Somerset, Surrey, Hampshire, Essex, Kent, Worcestershire, Leicestershire and Middlesex played rarely and, in some cases, not at all. That amounted to half the first-class clubs. Middlesex players, of course, were in action at Lord's and for London Counties, while Surrey organized their colts in orderly fashion, and Canterbury, Worcester and other first-class grounds continued to offer a welcome to club and service cricket. Essex Services, playing a handful of games in 1944 at Chelmsford and elsewhere, were 'officially recognized' by Essex CCC, whilst Maidstone offered a venue for two or three fine matches featuring the Royal Australian Air Force. The New Zealand Services XI figured in a couple of these matches. Gloucester staged half a dozen games in 1943, some involving the county, others being 'select' games. For instance, on 27 and 28 July 1943, the South and North drew at Gloucester in a curiously unbalanced game. Pope and Rae swept aside the South for 94 and then, despite Goddard's 6 for 64, the North scored 207, with George Pope sustaining his all-round contribution with a solid 82. Next the South declared at 327 for 3, with Wyatt and Fagg both reaching 150, in the second highest stand (285) of the war. Needing a little over 200, and with Goddard taking 4 for 25, the North subsided to 163 for 9, out of which Constantine scored 51, and almost lost. The following days almost the same cast took on new roles as Tom Goddard's XI and George Duckworth's XI. A high scoring game was drawn, with Goddard, Constantine, Pope and Wyatt once more distinguishing themselves. That little three-day festival constituted a major proportion of Gloucester's 1943 cricket and, in 1944, their efforts scarcely went beyond the West of England team.

Glamorgan, pleasantly, made something of a comeback in 1943 with fixtures against an Army XI at Cardiff, against an AA Command team at Barry, and against RAF (St Athan) on the same ground. Thus emboldened, the Welsh county embarked on a more serious list of eleven fixtures in 1944. In terms of the war, it was a conventional roster: British Empire, West of England, Western Command, an Army XI, the NFS; strangely, they never challenged a neighbouring county. They played at Cardiff, Newport, Swansea and Barry and, after so long a dormant period, it was good to notice Glamorgan easing back into action.

Yorkshire remained rather timid. In 1943 five games were staged at Sheffield, Leeds and Hull, involving services and pick-up sides. The chief match was a two-day August Bank Holiday affair at Sheffield. It was a draw, and well over 6,000 turned up on the Saturday. The scores were: RAF 192 and 144 for 4; Yorks and Lancs 310 for 2, the two Lancashire bats, Washbrook and Nutter, upstaging the local talent with a century each. The following year the Army played the Navy at Bradford, and that attracted 7,000 spectators. Bradford was also the venue for a Bradford League contest with a

Combined Counties XI. A repeat of the two-day event involving the RAF and a Yorks-Lancs XI at Abbeydale Park was utterly ruined by rain. Another two-day match at Hull brought together London Counties and a Combined Services side. The other match in 1944 was at Roundham Park, Leeds. Herbert Sutcliffe's Yorkshire XI had scored 129 for 2 (Hutton 82) against J. Appleyard's team when, yet again, rain forced the abandonment. J. Appleyard continued to be the busy organizer of these games in Yorkshire but, considering the players available in and around that huge tract of cricketing expertise, the amount of non-league but near-county cricket was small.

Northants, Sussex and, of course, Notts worked hard to maintain a decent provision of cricket in their areas. Northants, using Spinney Hill as their home ground, played British Empire (The Nelson Memorial match), London Counties, Eastern Command, Leicestershire, the Buccaneers, United Services and the West Indies in 1943. In 1944 they took on among others the RAAF and lost; Coventry and District (another loss, this game was one of the first of the war at the Northampton ground of a top-class nature); Essex Services at Chelmsford; Combined Services at Watford; as well as Leicestershire and West Indies. Northants usually seemed prepared to turn out a team to accommodate existing sides, like RAAF or London Counties.

Sussex, in 1943, planned a lively little series of fixtures, principally bringing forces' elevens together at Hove, Eastbourne, Chichester and Horsham and sometimes fielding a side under the Sussex label. The RAAF were welcome visitors at the Hove ground on 17 and 18 July. Carmody's 137 was the foundation of a ten wicket victory over the South of England, for whom Harry Parks, James Langridge and P. R. Sunnucks of Kent did well. The pattern was similar in 1944, when some seven matches were arranged, mostly for Sussex itself and Hayward's Heath and Bognor Regis were added to the venues. Northants and Essex Services were included among the visitors. The match against Northants at Horsham, ruined by rain, is said to have been the first inter-county match south of the Thames since 1939.

Nottingham remained faithful to their purpose of organizing regular cricket although, oddly, they played rather fewer games in 1943 and 1944 than in those sterner, earlier years of the war. Notts stimulated others to play. Leicester and Derby seem to have done nothing in the wartime seasons except to raise teams to play Notts. The other matches were against services teams and, on a novel note, the Notts Collieries XI. In 1943, in what was fast becoming the standard and annual two-day date, Notts played the NFS over August Bank Holiday weekend and defeated the firemen by six wickets. Heane, the Nottingham captain, turned in a good all-round performance in a low-scoring match, while James Langridge, with 60, and Achong, with 6 for 79, were the NFS stars. This was an improvement on the drawn game, against the same opposition, in that other conventional two-day date, the Whitsun weekend. Heane scored 74 in that match, and Derbyshire's Elliott scored fifty and took 4 for 61. In 1944 the pattern in style and form was very much the same. Perhaps the highlight of the season was Simpson's 133 against Leicester, who escaped, at 157 for 9, with a lucky draw.

Because of Nottinghamshire's leading role in wartime cricket and as a more detailed case-study of one county in action, it might be useful to pause briefly and scrutinize a cricket club at war. Trent Bridge was taken over by the Army, and a unit of the Second Anti-Aircraft Division was stationed there. The whole pavilion was utilized by the soldiery and, throughout the war, the press box and other rooms at the Radcliffe Road end acted as changing facilities and a temporary pavilion. The Secretary's office became the medical inspection room and the indoor cricket school – one of the country's oldest, opened in the 1920s – was the dining hall. Drill was conducted behind the Trent Bridge Hotel, where William Clarke, that doughty organizer of the All-England 'exhibition' eleven and creator of the Nottingham ground, had formerly been mine host. Later in the war women of the Auxiliary Training Service joined the unit, and tales are told of such artists as Wee Georgie Wood visiting Trent Bridge to entertain the troops.

Despite this encroachment, Notts contrived to be about the only county which managed a regular and genuine programme of matches. They arranged six games in 1940 and 1943, eleven in 1941 and 1942 and ten each in 1944 and 1945. This meant that in four of the wartime seasons Notts fielded a side, beginning usually at Whitsuntide and concentrating on public holidays, nearly every weekend. Compared with most other counties, it was a remarkable achievement and, as one inference must surely be that other counties might have improved their performance, one that demands a brief analysis.

Nottinghamshire's success was noted early in the war, *Wisden* commenting in 1942 that they were 'the only county to provide a really attractive fixture list'. The favourable factors do not seem exceptional to Nottingham. There was little enemy action and, self-evidently, Trent Bridge was nowhere near the vulnerable south-east coast but this applied to almost all the county headquarters, especially in the summer and increasingly as the war drew on. Notts were lucky with the convenient billeting of their players. J. Knowles had been a territorial, while Joe Hardstaff, Charlie Harris and Harold Butler enlisted in the Army immediately after the outbreak of war. The second eleven skipper, E. A. Marshall, and two committee men had commissions. Woodhead and Meads joined the RAF, while Bill Voce was engaged on munitions. Territorials and early enlistments often meant signing on and training at local barracks, a little like the 'pals' battalions of the first war. Nottingham's four famous soldiers were soon sergeants, and handily placed for the first two or three seasons of the war while, with a slow registration formula, the younger players awaited their calling-up papers, among them Reg Simpson and C. J. Poole. It seems that one or two players were stationed for a time at Trent Bridge itself.

Now this was not a unique circumstance. Notts developed their fixture list in the knowledge that members of the armed forces, those awaiting call-up and others in civil defence or war-work were frequently resident within reasonable distance. In a war fought primarily from, so to speak, the home ground of England this was generally true. A glance at the occasional forays made by other counties demonstrates this, for, often enough, they managed to parade something like a credible county eleven.

For instance, when Lancashire played a West Indies XI at Fazakerley, near Liverpool, in the summer of 1941, they included Hallows, Place, Washbrook, Oldfield, Iddon, Paynter, Sibbles, Duckworth and Phillipson, all capped players of Test or near-Test standard. In the same year several counties – Yorkshire, Sussex (with Capt. Maurice Tate appearing with his son, M. A. Tate), Gloucester, Kent, Leicester among them – did raise teams close to normal county standards.

Nottinghamshire did what they could to help players in the services. Soon after the onset of war, the committee 'decided to allow their respective wives fifteen shillings a week whilst they were in the Army'. Knowles, Hardstaff, Butler and Harris and 'their respective wives' benefited from these 'special payments', as they came to be labelled. The payments continued throughout the war. This additional fillip must have been welcomed by men whose wages were adversely affected by war, as opposed to the scores of thousands who did increase their income. Again, however, there were other counties who were trying to succour their serving professionals in one fashion or another, such as Kent.

As so often with human endeavour, the Notts story is primarily that of one individual, for Herbert Arthur Brown, the Nottingham Secretary, was the presiding genius, the Warner of Trent Bridge. Born at Highgate in 1890, he served with the Army in the Great War and, immediately afterwards and with no experience of playing or administering in the higher grades of cricket, he became the Nottingham Secretary. He distinguished himself by his competence and zeal, not least in his arrangements for Test Matches at Trent Bridge and, by 1939, he was a powerful figure in the club's political life. H. A. Brown announced to the Notts annual general meeting in February, 1940, that 'a skeleton staff is being maintained to preserve the playing piece, which at present is not being used by military purposes'. A memorandum on his work, published by the Notts committee in aid of his testimonial, explained why. Brown 'personally interviewed the military authorities and was successful in saving the cricket area from occupation'. H. A. Brown was variously described in wartime *Wisdens* as 'energetic' and 'enterprising', and he said himself it had been 'worthwhile' to have 'kept the game alive and provided entertainment'. It was chiefly due to H. A. Brown's detailed and capable planning that, to quote from the *Wisden* of 1943, Nottingham 'were the only county to attempt to carry through a programme during each year of the war'. H. A. Brown retired in 1959, having spent almost the whole of his career in that one post, and he was awarded the MBE. His salary by 1940 was a not uncomfortable £550 a year and he certainly earned it during the war.

At this distance it is difficult to judge why other county secretaries – for several secretaries remained at post during the war – or other stalwart officials did not emulate Herbert Arthur Brown. Obviously, demands of all kinds were being made on people during the hostilities, but it does appear that, on balance, much rested on how officials viewed the game: as something organic to keep 'alive', or something sacred to preserve for peaceful times.

It is interesting to see how a county, such as Notts, which did involve itself in a reasonable amount of cricket, fared financially, for it throws light on the economic structure of the game, both then and just after the war. Notts reported 'a slight loss' in one or two seasons, but had sensibly felt that this was more than outweighed by the benefits of providing good quality entertainment. The reason for Robertson-Glasgow's 'satire' with reference to county budgets was the reliance on membership subscriptions plus, in some cases, benevolent donations from the landed gentry or monied patrons. Arranging matches introduced an element of risk and of expenditure, over and above the safe dependence on annual subscriptions.

For instance, Nottingham's receipts in the 1939 season were about £10,000, of which £5,000 was in subscriptions. Gate money was less than £3,000, and a loss was made of £1,300. Naturally, the largest part of their costs (£5,600) was match expenses. The counties laid great store during the war on persuading their members to continue to pay subscriptions as an investment for the future, but, obviously, there was a limit to what people would pay for nothing.

Against that background, the efforts at Trent Bridge to organize a weekend programme turned out commendably well in financial as well as cricketing terms. For the first five seasons of the war, Nottinghamshire's annual accounts hovered at something in excess of £2,000, with between £1,200 and £1,500 raised in subscriptions. This dropped alarmingly to £885 in 1942, a year which also saw a recouping of back-tax on rent paid by the military for their occupation of Trent Bridge, and this led to a loss of £540 on the year's trading. There was a loss of £194 in 1941, but in 1940, 1943 and 1944 moderate profits were made. In each of those years, bare match receipts, that is, gate-money, were higher than the wages and travel expenses of players. 1945 was a difficult year for although membership netted £1,300 and match receipts again exceeded direct match expenses, there was a leap in general expenditure causing a loss of approximately £1,000 on the year. This was because of an enlarged ground staff and the purchase of seating, ready for the resumption of first-class cricket, and the loss was still less than that made in 1939, the last of the normal seasons.

It is apparent that Notts, like other clubs, was not in the healthiest of financial conditions in the late 1930s. It was reported to the 1939 AGM that 'ordinary annual income was at least £2,000 less than sufficient to meet the essential expenditure' and that only occasional Test Match disbursements – a mournful note still heard today – 'kept the club going'. At the 1940 AGM members were 'earnestly requested to pay their subscriptions forthwith', in part or whole, as, 'if the club is to be able to carry on after the war', expenditure must be met from revenue 'of which the only source is the members'.

Prices were usually a shilling for adults and sixpence or sevenpence for boys, although in 1942 the adult charge was one and threepence. This reflected the rise in entertainment tax on the gate money. It began as twopence out of the shilling, and a penny from the child's sixpenny price, but it rose to sixpence out of one and three. Like all taxes, it was much disliked, and Notts paid £700 entertainments tax over the six seasons, close on a fifth of the take. Such were the exigencies of war finance. The only escape, and it was cold comfort to an anxious treasurer, was when the proceeds were devoted entirely to charity. Exemption certificates for entertainment duty are liberally sprinkled through the accounts of county clubs, as of similar organizations. Several games at Trent Bridge, including some of the more well-attended ones, were of this type, with the NFS Benevolent Fund, the RAF Benevolent Fund and the AA Welfare Fund being the chief beneficiaries. Well over a thousand pounds was raised for charity in this manner from about ten games, and that represents a substantial slice of the revenue that otherwise might have found itself in the Nottingham coffers. Here was the bedrock of combining charity with entertainment as the dual reason for running cricket at all.

Roughly speaking, it would seem that for a home match the players' wages amounted to about £20; that is, for those unfamiliar with the financial climate of that time, £20 in total. In brief, the professionals were given a couple of pounds for a day's play. As all of them were already earning pay as soldiers or war-workers, this was by way of a bonus, well-earned in terms of the pleasure given, and welcomed by the recipients to eke out what, for some, were standards lowered by war.

The crowds drawn by Nottingham's energetic ventures are also instructive. In 1940, they ranged from 220 spectators to 885 and 1,679 spectators for the two-day Derbyshire fixture, and the season's total attendance was just short of 6,000 for seven days' play. There were 6,100 in 1941, with 200 the lowest and 1,200 for the British Empire XI and one day of the RAF match; there were eight days' play. Apart from two days lost to rain, seven days in 1942 attracted 5,000 customers, including 1,450 for the NFS game. There were eight playing days in 1943, with over 9,000 paying spectators, and including six crowds over a thousand. In 1944 there was one wet day and eight highly successful days, all drawing gates over a thousand, and including no less than 4,800 for the Whitsun RAF fixture: nearly 19,000 attended these games. Crowds topped the 27,000 mark in 1945, when eleven days cricket were on offer and when, at August Bank Holiday, there were gates of 5,000 and 7,000 for the match against the Australian services.

It is a tale of gradually expanding triumph, with the last two bringing phenomenal success. Overall, 1,500 spectators, on average, attended each day but in 1944 and 1945 the average was 2,300. All these figures, of course, do not include the county members, who must occasionally have swelled the multitude.

The figures cast an illuminating sidelight on the popularity of cricket. In 1939 Nottinghamshire's championship crowds, day by day, were as small as a hundred and generally no more than a few hundred. Only twice were the gates much above two thousand, with 3,600 for the Saturday of the Yorkshire match, and 5,200 for the Saturday of the West Indian fixture. It is a salutary fact that, in wartime circumstances, Notts often managed to exceed their usual peacetime attendances and, in 1945, had four attendances of over 3,000, including one – 7,000 on 1 September – which easily beat the best in 1939. It is further evidence that one- or two-day weekend or holiday cricket was moderately popular.

It is noteworthy that, as the war progressed, more and more good quality cricket was played in the midlands and the northwest, centring on Warwicks and Lancashire respectively. In some degree, this reflected the sheer intensity of war work concentrated in those districts, and the overriding need to proffer some sane opportunity for relaxation to a weary and stretched work-force. There were a couple of two-day matches (Coventry and District versus the RAF, and versus the British Empire) and a one-day fixture (Birmingham League versus London Counties) at Dudley. Mysteriously, after the manner of the football 'guesting' system, James Langridge and Arthur Fagg appeared in the Coventry ranks, and both scored centuries. Alec Bedser took 7 for 62 for the RAF. Holidays at Home were again a motif for many games but, as in the previous season, Birmingham adopted the idea on a grand scale. A Warwicks Festival XI was fielded to play at Edgbaston right through the August holiday week. The National Civil Defence eleven (two days), the National Police eleven, and the RAF (two days) provided doughty opposition and attracted sizeable crowds. Wyatt and Hollies were in good form for the splendidly titled Festival XI, for whom guests like Harold Gimblett, George Cox and Maurice Leyland played. Washbrook hit 107 out of the RAF's impressive score of 350 for 8 declared.

Coventry was the location for several games – West of England, Northants, London Counties, British Empire, the RAF – and a couple of fixtures were for two days. The augmented Coventry and District side acquitted itself well in a set of games almost like a microcosm of wartime cricket. The Edgbaston Festival, and probably no cricket ground could have been further than Warwickshire's home ground from the sea where most cricket festivals are sited, was repeated successfully. The West of England, the Civil Defence, the RAAF and the RAF provided the competition. Memorable moments included Simpson's run of 99, 86, 47 and 71 in consecutive knocks, and an unbroken stand by Hammond and Todd which resulted in a seven wicket victory for the RAF in a two-innings match.

Up in the north-west the combined efforts of social entrepreneurs like A. D. Procter continued to make for tidy charitable pickings and a cornucopia of cricketing delights for jaded munitions workers and listless servicemen. A score of matches, faithfully recorded in *Wisden*, were arranged over the north-western area in 1943 and the same number in 1944.

England XIs, West Indian XIs, the Lancashire XI, the Empire XI, the Dominions XI, the War Fund XI, XIs named after their captains – these and others conspired to bring always amiable and watchable and often exciting cricket to the County Palatine. Only Lord's had as ambitious a programme and none was more widely spread: Didsbury, Longsight, Bolton, Warrington, Sale, Chorlton, Blackburn, Stalybridge, Timperley, Stockport, Urmston, Bury, Dukinfield, Whitefield, Werneth, as well as Old Trafford, back into active service in 1944, and Blackpool, a compound of bustling holiday resort and busy RAF centre, and even into that other Lancastrian playground, North Wales, for games at Rhos-on-Sea and Colwyn Bay. Clubs, notable enough in local history, found themselves recorded in the pages of *Wisden*, as first-class cricketers, usually with a number of native heroes in supporting parts, were seen in more abundance on ordinary cricket grounds than for almost a century. Coupled with the mass migration of first-class players into two or three of the major leagues, it represented a disintegration of the restrictive first-class barrier, and a vivid boost for the popularity of the game.

The county 'disclaimed any connection' with these games, whether out of chagrin or diffidence is uncertain. Apart from A. D. Procter's diligence, two Lancashire committee men, J. B. Holmes and J. S. Cadman, were very actively involved in these proceedings. The match at Rhos, attended by 5,000 people, raised, with the help of a number of money spinning efforts during the game, no less than £3,664, for charity, easily a record sum for a one-day match during the war.

One could dilate on many of these friendly encounters that gave some leisure relief to often packed grounds, some of them unused to coping with such crowds. There was the two-day game at Stockport in August 1944, when an Empire XI crushed the Combined Universities by an innings and 177 runs. Fagg (137) and Emrys Davies (100) were the major contributors to a formidable total of 453, before T. B. Mitchell, 8 for 100, and Achong, 6 for 34, wrecked the University XI's two innings. One might nostalgically reminisce about the players, among them the Lancashire lads, old and new, Eddie Paynter and Charlie Hallows, Winston Place and Cyril Washbrook, and the mix headily strengthened by the brio of the West Indians, chief among them Learie Constantine, but with Martindale, Achong, St Hill and others also in the van.

Learie Constantine was definitely the draw card. In seasons 1943 and 1944 he scored 51 in 22 minutes for North versus South, 60 in 32 minutes for George Duckworth's XI versus Tom Goddard's XI, and 63 in 38 minutes for British Empire versus Coventry District. In 1944 he scored 42 in 10 minutes for West Indies versus an England XI, and 61 in 23 minutes for the North of England versus London Counties. All but a few sparse singles and twos were grandiose sixes and shattering fours.

In the leagues, forsaken by Constantine, professional cricketers very much ruled the roost. West Bromwich Dartmouth pursued their monopoly of the Birmingham League, of which they were champions in all but the first year of the war, losing only seven times throughout the six seasons. Eric Hollies remained their prime executioner. He took 74 wickets in 1943 and 81 in 1944 and, all told, he captured 499 wickets during the war in the Birmingham League. The Bradford League was more open, with Saltaire winning in 1943 and Spen Victoria in 1944. Eddie Paynter eventually scored 4426 runs and Wilf Barber 3746 runs in wartime Bradford League cricket, while the Derbyshire trio of G. H. Pope, A. V. Pope and W. Copson were the most successful bowlers. In addition to taking 445 wickets, George Pope also scored 2236 runs. D. Smith, another Derbyshire player, scored 2731 runs in Bradford League cricket. A record number of 70 first-class cricketers were engaged in the Bradford League in 1943, among them eleven English and three West Indian internationals.

The two seasons brought the usual crop of collector's items. Nineteen-year-old Trevor Bailey, then an officer cadet, made 106 for a Royal Navy XI against Sussex in 1943, while Joe Hulme aged thirty-nine made 119 for London Counties against British Oxygen. A week later he scored another hundred, his third in his last seven innings, against Handley Page. This luckless works team was summarily dismissed for only 15, the lowest recorded wartime total. Frank Woolley, now aged 57, made his second appearance in a major match and scored 16 for the Festival XI versus the Civil Defence at Birmingham. The youthful J. R. Bridger scored 204 not out for the Trundlers against his old university, Cambridge, in May 1944, and thus became, with J. O'Connor, one of only two batsmen to score a double century in the war. Finally, on 21 August 1943, Molly McLagan, one of the rare number of familiar female names in cricket, scored 148 for the ATS against the WRNS. She had almost reached a century against the WAAF a fortnight earlier. The three women's services provided much of the senior cricket played by women during the war.

Great courage and enthusiasm went into the organization and playing of all these games and of the hundreds of fixtures played at club level. E. W. Swanton has praised members of the MCC and others for their fortitude, and he wrote of how the heroic veterans, returning to London after a long day in the field, would, in the absence of taxis, shoulder their crickets bags for the pavement trudge home.

In 1944 there was more than fatigue to try them. After the relative calm of 1942 and 1943, the placid skies of 1944 were filled with that unpredictable scourge, the flying bomb. The first fell on 13 June and by the end of July a million and a half had left London in an unexpected and unwanted re-run of evacuation. The flying bombs, basically pilotless planes loaded with explosives, did extensive damage and 6,000 people were killed. By August the prospects of destroying them in mid-air before they reached London had been substantially improved, and eventually about four-fifths could be disposed of in this way. In September, just as the season ended, the even more menacing curse of the flying rocket, the V2s as opposed to the V1s, were launched, and there was little opportunity of shooting them down. It was the primitive beginning of ballistic rocketry, and some 1,100 rockets slaughtered nearly 3,000 Londoners. Plans were laid to abandon

London entirely, as the invading armies attempted to overrun the rocket pads continued.

Conventional bombing had been mainly confined to the dark wintry nights, leaving the lighter days of summer much more untrammelled. The 'doodle-bugs' took no account of light or weather, and made their malign appearance at random. The Lord's programme was severely disrupted. The 1943 attendances at Lord's had been over 230,000, nearly double the figures for 1942. In 1944 they fell back to 168,000, and the flying bombs were blamed, although it is fair to recall that the price had also been doubled from sixpence to a shilling. A further explanation may have been the departure of many likely customers to the Continent, as the massive flow of troops began to support the invasion of Europe. Just four days before Hammond's century had laid the foundation for England's 166 run defeat by the West Indies at Lord's, 6 June had witnessed the Allied landings in France.

In 1814, just before the new Lord's ground was opened, there had been a small explosion caused, mysteriously, by gunpowder, and six people had been burned and injured. That was perhaps an evil omen for, throughout the war, Lord's seemed to attract all manner of explosions. Now it was flying bombs. On 29 July, as the Army were batting against the RAF, a flying bomb approached and seemed likely to hit the practice ground at the nursery end. The players lay down in what Sir Pelham Warner described as 'curious postures', in this the first Lord's match actually to be interrupted with play in progress. Fortunately for the cricketers and spectators, the warhead drifted on a couple of hundred yards and crashed near the Albert Road, north of Regent's Park. R. E. S. Wyatt, the bowler, had lain down clutching the ball in the middle of his run-up. He coolly rose, continued his run and bowled to Jack Robertson who, 'amid tremendous cheers', dispatched it for six in a widely appreciated and defiant gesture.

On 11 and 12 August there was a match at Lord's, featuring a Lord's XI and the Public Schools XI. A flying bomb fell very close to the ground. Shrapnel and debris were flung on to the playing surface, but no one was injured and, to the pleasure of the small crowd, the public schoolboys were soon ready for play again, in the best traditions of 'Vitaï Lampada'. Incidentally, of rather more immediate consequence for their peace of mind, R. W. V. Robins provided his own personal aerial attack by scoring 127 and 43 in this two-innings match, as well as taking 9 for 58 and 8 for 73.

Earlier in the year, on 18 June, Capt. G. D. Kemp-Welch, a former Warwickshire bat, was killed when a flying bomb hit the Guard's Chapel, during a service at Wellington Barracks. This last Nazi fling was costly in life and property and the flying bombs, particularly the rocket variety, were a fundamental threat to the age-old security of Britain's island home.

Inevitably, 1943 and 1944 brought other deaths in action. Flt Lt F. G. H. Chalk, who had captained Oxford University and in the last two pre-war seasons, Kent, was killed in February 1943, and no less than six other Oxford players perished that same year. They were T. G. L. Ballance, F. C. Boult, K. B. Scott, P. M. Whitehouse, M. H. Matthews and P. H. Blagg. The Cambridge 'blue' and Hampshire player, J. P. Blake, also died. Apart from Kemp-Welch, two other 'blues' died in 1944, J. W. T. Grimshaw of Cambridge and W. J. Pershke of Oxford. Surg. Lt F. M. McRae, who had played three seasons for Somerset, was killed in action with the Royal Naval Volunteer Reserve, and Jack Lee, brother of Frank Lee, was killed in the Normandy campaign. He had played for Middlesex as well as Somerset, and was also a noted professional footballer. He played regularly and effectively during the war for London Counties. The Royal Australian Air Force were doomed to lose one or two players. Flt Sgt W. A. Roach, of West Australia, and Flt Sgt C. P. Calvert of New South Wales, were both killed in aerial combat in 1944, after playing in several RAAF matches with distinction. D. K. Carmody, later to give his name to the celebrated Carmody 'umbrella' field, and another member of the RAAF side, was shot down and imprisoned in Germany. He later returned to take up his place again.

In August 1944 Maurice Turnbull, the Glamorgan and England player, was reported killed. A product of Downside and Cambridge, and a high-class hockey and rugby player to boot, he played nine times for England at cricket. His most sterling achievement was as secretary and captain of Glamorgan, putting – in E. W. Swanton's words – 'that somewhat rickety institution on a firm basis'. He transformed a large financial debt into a credit, and did as much for the playing side. Aged thirty-eight at his death, he was one of several county captains (P. T. Eckersley, G. B. Legge and F. G. H. Chalk being others) and one of eight varsity skippers killed in the war.

On 31 July 1943, Hedley Verity died from wounds received while fighting with the Green Howards during the Italian campaign. He was shot in the chest near Cantania in Sicily, leading an attack through cornfields. 'Keep going' was his final command, and he was last seen by his men lying hurt, his head cradled by his batman, Thomas Reynoldson of Bridlington. He died later in an enemy military hospital, and the news reached England on 1 September, exactly five years after his last and devastating first-class cricket appearance. He was thirty-eight, and had played forty times for England in a relatively short career of ten seasons. He was buried in the military cemetery at Caserta, in Italy, and his grave became something of a shrine for cricketers passing through Italy.

He had fought as he bowled, thoughtfully and bravely, and it is superfluous to claim that this was England's harshest cricketing loss of the war. He had taken 1956 wickets for an average of just over 18, and was a left-hand spin bowler to be bracketed with Wilfred Rhodes and certainly no more than two or three more of that rare pedigree. It was said of him that he relished the struggle on a perfect pitch against master batsmen more than the demolition of poorer talents on a helpful wicket. That he was as chivalrous a cricketer as he was an impeccable bowler must be his dual and lasting epitaph. Robertson-Glasgow wrote of him that 'he was the ever-learning professor, justly proud, yet utterly humble'.

Every death on active service was, of course, a sorrowful bereavement for someone, and it may seem churlish, even offensive, to select one fatality or other for specific mention, because of his sporting prowess. None the less, men like Ken Farnes and Hedley Verity were household names, and the nation, as well as their families, mourned. It may also seem chilling to draw attention to that malignant providential streak in sporting disasters which seems deliberately dissonant. In Manchester United's Munich air crash, two international goalkeepers survived, but four half-backs perished or never played again. Colin Blythe, killed in the 1914–18 conflict, was, like Verity, a phenomenally successful left-hand spin bowler, while the 1939–45 war robbed England of its only two bowlers of world class with years to spare, whereas all her gifted batsmen remained unscathed.

Len Hutton, however, had severely damaged his arm. Attempting a fly spring in March 1941, as a part of his army physical training duties, the mat had slipped and he broke his left arm and dislocated a bone in his wrist. After an operation and a hospital stay of eight weeks, he had played some cricket in that summer, not without success, but with resultant pain. For two and a half years he underwent bone grafts and substantial orthopaedic care, chiefly in Leeds, which left his arm two inches shorter than its companion. It would often swell and the grafts made him susceptible to sore shins but, along with the other leading batsmen, he was to enjoy a most distinguished post-war career and, by 1944, was playing again. He scored 84, for instance, during England's six wicket defeat of Australia on 19 May at Lord's. He was discharged from the army, which Yorkshire at first found 'disturbing', and became civilian inspector of works and buildings for the Royal Engineers. Herbert Sutcliffe was also invalided out with nose and shoulder problems and obtained employment with a paper manufacturing firm.

By the end of that 1944 cricket season and with the news from Europe optimistic enough, hopes were rising, despite the flying bomb menace. There were even thoughts that the 1945 season might be the first post-war season.

FIVE

The Victory Parade

Although the Wehrmacht, under von Rundstedt, counter-attacked in the Ardennes, giving rise to anxious concern, the Triple Alliance of Russia, the United States and Britain survived long enough to defeat Germany. VE day was Tuesday, 8 May, practically marking the start of the 1945 cricket season: indeed, I was sitting in the local cricket pavilion when the ageing club secretary arrived with news of the preliminary announcement of peace in Europe. The following Saturday, 12 May, saw the beginning of the Lord's programme of major matches, and the RAAF easily accounted for the British Empire XI by seven wickets. Keith Miller and R. G. Williams, the latter but recently repatriated from a POW camp, scored half-centuries, while Ellis, a small left-hander with a short right-angled run, had the impressive analysis of 8 for 21.

Virtually the whole 1945 season was played with the country in an unreal condition, for a part of the war was not yet over. It is true that, despite the heavy losses and the cruel treatment of British prisoners, the Japanese aspect of the war had never attracted quite the attention given to the German dimension, predictably so, given the latter's proximity and emphasis. There were matches in progress at Nottingham, Hove, Edgbaston, Swansea, Canterbury and Northampton on 6 August, when the atomic bomb was dropped on Hiroshima, and on 9 August, when Nagasaki was similarly devastated, Sussex were busy defeating the Warwicks Festival XI at Birmingham, despite Learie Constantine's haul of 6 Sussex victims for 60.

There were just a few weeks of the 1945 season left when, on Wednesday, 15 August, VJ day was declared in Europe and, after practically six years, Britain was once more fully at peace.

The indeterminate political state was further illustrated by the dramatic shift from Winston Churchill's wartime coalition government to a Labour administration under Clement Attlee, who is said to have consented to the installation of a ticker-tape machine at 10 Downing Street only when informed that it provided county cricket scores every hour. To complete the political and sporting analogues, it was on 26 July, as the Australian Services drew with Sussex at Chichester, that the results of the General Election (held on 5 July but with counting delayed to allow for the collation of servicemen's votes) were being announced, with a huge Labour majority as the outcome.

There was, then, a curious air of near-normality about the summer of 1945. It was a neo-Tolstoyan phase of neither war nor peace. People were anxious to return to normal, putting the hostilities behind them, and yet doing so in the knowledge that the war still continued elsewhere, that Europe was devastated, and that Britain was exhausted. It must not be forgotten that few foresaw so rapid an end to the fighting with Japan, which looked, in that summer, as if it might grimly continue for some considerable time. Its awesome finale, in the fatal mushrooms of Hiroshima and Nagasaki, was both sudden and shocking.

There was plenty of cricket and, as the public tried both to lead ordinary lives and to seek diversion when life insisted on being extraordinary, plenty of people to watch cricket. *Wisden* records almost 270 games, an increase of a third on the previous two seasons, and the crowds flocked to them. Of these games, eleven were three-day and twenty-four two-day, a great increase in the amount and type of cricket. There were a score of major matches at Lord's, slightly more than in the previous seasons, but, in addition, eight were three- or two-day fixtures, so that there were over thirty days of major cricket at St John's Wood. The year's attendance was a remarkable 414,000 an average of over 12,000 a day, and the gates were locked four times, allowing for smaller attendances at minor matches. This made the 1939 total of 330,000 look a trifle puny, and convincingly demonstrated the popularity of wartime cricket. The 1945 figures were boosted by three Victory Tests and an extremely attractive fixture, England and the Dominions, but, even so, it was a cheering position.

Counties began to emerge, sometimes with delicate care, from their wartime cocoons. County grounds were used and county elevens officially fielded for the first time since 1939. With the lifting of the coastal ban, Hampshire played their first game since the end of the 1939 season, beating Southampton Police by six wickets. They played four other matches, with convincing wins over Sussex, Northants and the RAF. Herman and McCorkell were in especially fine form, and Hants fielded a large proportion of their pre-war side.

Derbyshire, who had done little of note during the war, played at Chesterfield for the first time since 1939. They lost their annual battle with Notts, Jepson and Woodhead dismissing them for 78. They played four other games, a distinct advance on earlier wartime seasons, losing twice to Lancashire in low-scoring contests, drawing with Yorkshire, and then thrashing Leicester by an innings in one day, the only occasion this happened during the war. Leicester were out for paltry scores of 58 (Pope 6 for 12) and 68 (Truswell 3 for 14). Leicester also lost to Notts and beat the RAF Regiment in another poorish season.

Kent played only three times, at Beckenham, when they defeated Northants, with H. Taylor 101 and Murray-Wood 6 for 51; at Canterbury, where, before a gate of 7,000, they beat the Rest by a large margin; and at Ramsgate, where they drew with the British Empire. Middlesex were still in purdah, although Uxbridge, the county's second home, enjoyed three pleasing matches involving service sides. Bill Edrich scored 90 and took 5 for 45 for RAF (Uxbridge) against the Metropolitan Police in one of these encounters, while the Desert Air Force figured in the other two, one of these being a two-day drawn match with the RAAF. Surrey were not much better. They played twice, very late in the season. They beat Sussex at New Malden, and then enjoyed a three wicket victory over the Australian Services in a two-day fixture at Kingston. Somerset and Worcester continued to disappoint. Harold Gimblett's blustery 65 and Andrews' 7 for 31 made for a comfortable win over the West of England XI at Bristol, another ground in use for the first time since the onset of war and then, at Glastonbury, in a high scoring drawn game over two days with the same opponents, Vickery scored a century and Notley took 6 for 95. Arnold (157) and Meyer (6 for 137) did well for the visitors. Glastonbury was the scene of another high-scoring draw between the West of England and New Zealand. Worcestershire beat the RAF in an exciting game on 4 August. They passed the RAF's 239 for 7 with two wickets to spare. The West of England played another game against New Zealand at Worcester, but these two matches were the only major cricket in the county.

Essex saw very little main-line cricket. Tremlett's XI beat Cambridge University at Colchester; the East of England drew with the New Zealand Services at the same venue; and then drew again in a two-day game with the same opponents at Clacton. The East only just avoided defeat replying with a beggarly 76 and 166 for 8 to the New Zealander's formidable 354 for 6, James scoring 129. And that was that. Gloucester, after a slight flurry in 1944, fell back and played no one. Gloucester was the location for a close win by the RAF over the RAAF, but the county itself did not field a side although, of course, the West of England XI, which played eighteen matches in 1945, fielded Gloucester, Worcester and Somerset players.

All this was rather disappointing, given the optimistic mood of 1945. It was left to the other seven counties to continue or even improve on their wartime practice of organizing a rational little series of fixtures. Of course, several of the counties which seemed to figure less prominently were active in encouraging junior and club cricket: we are concerned here mainly with describing wartime cricket intended as a spectator sport.

Glamorgan furthered their renaissance of 1944 with half a dozen games against the RAF, Western Command (a towering win for Glamorgan at Briton Ferry), Learie Constantine's XI at Barry, the Army, and the RAAF, the last two being two-day games. The name of Gilbert Parkhouse was beginning to be remarked, especially for his 45 and 71 in the Army fixture. On 18 August, at Cardiff, Glamorgan lost to the West of England XI, for whom Barling scored 99 and Hammond 51. This was sadly, the Maurice Turnbull Memorial Match. More cheerfully, there was a Glamorgan fixture with a Future of Glamorgan XI.

Northants followed their sensible practice of former seasons in fulfilling about nine fixtures, several of them at the Northampton ground, with two at Kettering and one at Spinney Hill. These included a drawn two-day game with Buckinghamshire and one-day matches with the RAF, War-wicks, Coventry and District, Leicestershire, New Zealand services and the West Indies. Notts completed the wartime seasons as they had begun them, with a sane round of pleasant fixtures, against much the same sort of opposition, Leicester, the RAF, Northern Command, Notts Collieries and the National Fire Service. There were two attractive two-day matches. Notts lost to Derbyshire by eight wickets after a kindly, some might say foolhardy, declaration, leaving Derby needing a mere 73 to win; and then they were defeated heavily by the Australian Services, for whom Keith Miller scored 81 not out, and Pepper and Christofani, respectively in each innings, proved wellnigh unplayable as bowlers. The game was also distinguished by Bill Voce's performance: he took 11 for 113 in the match.

Lancashire played relatively few matches in 1945, compared with the heady days of 1943 and 1944, when Lancashire professionals were out and about all over the north-west in a plethora of charity games. In this the last summer of the war they settled down to play a smaller number of higher quality games, several of them at Old Trafford. Their programme embraced such opposition as an England XI, the RAF, and Warwickshire (a ten wicket victory for the red rose, Paynter on 82 and Nigel Howard, a future Lancashire and England captain, on 43). Northern Counties beat London Counties at Old Trafford which was also the venue for a clash between the RAF and the RAAF. Washbrook, 66, and W. J. Edrich, 55, paved the way for an RAF win. There was a two-day game of stern tradition at Old Trafford when Yorkshire were the visitors. It was more enthralling than many 'roses' conflicts. It was a game of low scores and Yorkshire were 82 for 5 at the close, requiring another 20. Booth took 8 for 54 in the Lancashire second innings, an encouragement to the left hander expected to replace Verity. Pollard bowled consistently for Lancashire throughout. Another two-day game was arranged at Stanley Park, Blackpool. The North of England ran up a massive 438, with Norman Oldfield on 171 and D. Smith 109. Despite a Hassett century for the Australian Services XI, the bowling of George Pope and Eric Hollies saw home the Northern Counties by an innings and 89 runs. As the war drew to its welcome end, the money-making aspect of war charities was less pronounced, and there were many fewer such games throughout the country. It was particularly noticeable in the north-west where this had been an enduring and strong motif.

Across the Pennines, Yorkshire, which had remained stubbornly quiet for much of the war, remembered its heritage. Although matches had been organized across the broad acres of the ridings, it was July 1945 before the white rose county actually staged a county fixture, that is, after peace in Europe had been declared. It was a two-day match at Bradford, with Hutton scoring 82 out of 156 in a slow-scoring draw with the Australian Services. A reprise of this fixture, later in the month at Sheffield, provided better entertainment, although the two-day match was again drawn. Crowds totalling over 15,000 watched first Miller and then Hutton score centuries, cameos in the varied manifestations of the batting science. Hutton also scored 76 and the young Willie Watson 63 in another two-day draw at Sheffield, this time against Derby-shire, for whom George Pope (invalided out of the Royal Corps of Signals with a knee injury) contributed a fine all round display with 113 and 5 for 62 in the Yorkshire first innings. Thus did Yorkshire take a firm step from a negligible effort throughout most of the war, via a small sequence of tough two-day games, to the rigours of full-scale champion-ship cricket in 1946.

Two counties really strove to provide genuinely top-class cricket by way of entertainment. These were Sussex and Warwickshire who, directly or indirectly, as was the way in wartime cricket, deployed teams and players to an extent not conceived of by most of the other first-class counties. Both played in or helped substantially with the arrangement of more than a dozen fixtures apiece. Sussex played Hants, Northants, the Australian Services, the New Zealand XI, the West Indies, the Club Cricket Conference, the Forty Club and Eastern Command. They fared well in these hard-fought games, with old favourites like the Langridge brothers distinguishing themselves. Against the West Indies at Chichester, for example, James took 6 for 46 and John scored 107 in the county's resounding win. Leveson-Gower's XI drew with the Australian Services at Eastbourne, and, unusually, Hastings was the ground on which Northants played and beat Surrey, in mid-September. Bognor Regis was the setting for a drawn match between the New Zealan-ders and, a most avant-garde team-tag, the Commandos. A. W. H. Mallett proved himself an all-round commando, scoring 57 and taking 4 for 16 including the hat-trick.

Warwickshire was by now the most ambitious of the counties. After an uneasy start to the war and with much war damage with which to contend, the midland county, by 1945, had a programme which was second only to Lord's. Edgbaston's first and most important game of the season was on 8 July. A large crowd of over 14,000 watched an exciting exhibition of batting. Donnelly's 100 for New Zealand was well-matched by 132 from Bill Edrich for Wally Hammond's XI, for whom J. G. Dewes also scored a useful 54. There were games at Dudley, Coventry, and Birmingham involving local league sides, the RAAF, the NFS and other teams.

The grand focus of Warwickshire's wartime cricket was the Edgbaston festival week, the fourth and last of its kind. R. I. Storer, first Councillor and then Colonel, had organized the four festivals with immense skill and ingenuity. Approaching 150,000 people had attended this series of wartime festivals, and some £10,000 had been raised for local charity. The use of loudspeaker commentary and highly informative programmes were also widely praised. The first match, on 7 August, against the RAAF, was ruined by rain; on the following day, Sussex beat Leatherbarrow's XI by seven wickets, despite Hollies' 5 for 48; on the next day, Sussex scuttled out the Festival XI for 107 and won by 92 runs; the day afterwards, the Festival XI scored heavily enough to defeat Northants decisively. On the next day, 11 August, the RAF were victorious on a day when near to 500 runs were scored. Half-centuries from Halliday and Hammond, left the Festival XI in a comfortable position, but Edrich, enjoying a bountiful season and ably abetted on this occasion by Washbrook, scored 165. The RAF won by six wickets.

It was a well-earned and colourful end to a week of non-stop, interesting sport. The following week three more games were played. This time the RAF lost by seven wickets. Wyatt with 58 and Edrich with 40 were the only two airmen to withstand the probing complexities of Eric Hollies, who ended with 6 for 55. Halliday and Hammond obliged with repeat half centuries and the Festival XI enjoyed a swift revenge. On the following two days R. I. Storer's XI easily overwhelmed a weakened New Zealand team, once by eight wickets and once by 97 runs. Warwickshire certainly ended the war on a high note, offering the Birmingham public a rich programme of good cricket.

Other vehicles for cricket continued to prosper. In 1945 the Lancashire League forwent its not very satisfactory act of self-abnegation and allowed clubs to pay a professional for the first time since 1939. T. Lowe obtained 85 wickets at a cost of 5.6 runs each for Church, who won the last championship of the war as they had won the first two. Among the new professionals were G. H. Pope at Colne, for whom he took 87 wickets, J. H. Parks at Accrington, L. J. Todd, with 512 runs, at Rawtenstall, Jim Smith at East Lancs., the 1945 runners-up, A. E. Nutter at Nelson, F. R. Santall at Ramsbottom, and E. Achong at Burnley. It surely revitalized the Lancashire League, which won back some of its lost preeminence.

West Bromwich Dartmouth, for whom Eric Hollies took 90 wickets, carried off the Birmingham League for the fifth consecutive time. Charlie Elliott was the chief run-maker, with a total of 513, average 57, for Stourbridge. Undercliffe were top of the Bradford League, Section A, and Bingley of Section B. Charlie Harris, playing for Yeadon, averaged over 50, with a total of 478 runs, and was the league's main scorer. Johnnie Lawrence took 69 wickets for Bingley. All in all, first-class cricketers made a major contribution to the upkeep and, indeed, strengthening of league cricket for the duration of the war.

London Counties completed their wartime mission with a fixture list of 33 matches in 1945, 16 of which were won. Joe Hulme and Frank Lee batted steadily as ever and both scored over 4,000 runs in the six seasons of London Counties' activity. Jack Young took close on 300 wickets for them over that same phase. It has to be said that in its last year the London Counties XI, which had stuck so carefully to its stern principles, was somewhat on the decline, owing to the widening of professional opportunities in the leagues. No attempt was made to keep London Counties going beyond 1945.

The British Empire team played as many as 45 matches in 1945, winning 28. C. B. Clarke surpassed his previous magical bowling exploits, obtaining 135 wickets which gave him a British Empire total of 665 for an average just less than ten. Ray Smith reached the commendable half-double of over 500 runs and 50 wickets. H. P. Crabtree, with 602 in 1945, made over 4000 runs during the six seasons, and Westcliff was

obviously a favourite ground for him. He scored 116 not out
against the Army there in June, and then proceeded, in July,
to score 90 against the RAF. C. J. Andrews scored 125 in the
latter game while, in the former, Crabtree and Hunt, who
scored 103, made 213 together, one of the highest stands of
the war.

During 1944 the British Empire club had 'decided to
disband when hostilities cease'. At a valedictory dinner at the
Lord's Hotel on 28 September 1945, it was announced that
£15,000 had been raised from 238 games played. The innocent
hopes for a future for both British Empire and London
Counties ran vainly into the sands of conservatism, like so
much else.

Services cricket was still significant with the RAAF becoming increasingly prominent. Australian soldiers were less
numerous in England than in World War I, for many of
them were required elsewhere, but this was more than compensated for by the presence of so many young airmen.
During 1945 Australian and New Zealand service men's teams
took part in roughly forty of the hundred or so major matches
played. That is a proud record, and many young Antipodeans
gained telling experience of English conditions. Perhaps the
most interesting individual performance of the year was on 1
August, when Lindsay Hassett scored 189 for the Australian
Services against the Royal Navy, at Portsmouth, in a two-day
match. The Australian Services scored 331 and the match
was drawn with the Navy on 204 (Ken Cranston 78) and 139
for 7. Hassett's 189 was the highest individual score of 1945
and, apart from the two double-centuries of J. O'Connor and
J. R. Bridger against much inferior opposition, the highest of
the war.

A sign of approaching normality was, paradoxically, the
report of much cricketing action in Italy, while the troops
continued to find plenty of cricket in India, South Africa and
the Middle East. Even Scotland warrants a mention for, in
July 1945, a large crowd watched Scotland play their first
official match since before the war. It was at Hamilton
Crescent, Glasgow, and there was no happy ending for the

Scots. They were, like many another team, outclassed by the RAAF.

The Lord's programme for 1945 illustrated both the little traditions and the innovative novelties of wartime fixture-making. At the end of June Sir Pelham Warner's XI took on General Dempsey's Second Army or, at least, their cricketing representatives, in the presence, for part of the game, of that famous military leader, together with the then CIGS, Lord Alanbrooke. Rain was a nuisance and the teams contrived to play two one-day matches over three days, both of them drawn. In the first, Warner's batsmen reached 327 for 8, while the Second Army managed only 105 for 4 in reply. The second meeting was more engrossing. White (132 not out) and Allen (93) allowed Pelham Warner's XI to declare at 270 for 3, with substantial time available. P. G. T. Kingsley, with a century, led a spirited response, and, at the end, the Second Army were 23 behind with only two wickets in hand. The Army team was captained by the Revd. J. W. J. Steele, chaplain to the Brigade of Guards and a Hampshire amateur.

Field Marshal Alexander, who thirty-five years earlier had played for Harrow against Eton in a match that earned a place in cricket history, heard of these happenings and arranged for the Central Mediterranean Forces XI to play a similar fixture at Lord's. A two-day match, late in August, proved to be that classic thriller, a win by one wicket. It was a game of low scores. The CMF made 167 and 163, F. R. Brown taking nine wickets in the match. The Lord's XI could make only 138 at their first try, but then scraped together the necessary 193 for 9, G. A. Wheatley, the Oxford wicket-keeper, scoring 36 and most of the others contributing something. The run tallies were disappointing, given the galaxy of stars. Apart from Freddie Brown, the Lord's XI had Donnelly, Meyer, Mallett, Bailey, Eagar and Carr, while the CMF witnessed the return to their native shores of Smailes, McIntyre, Merritt, Wellard and Dollery. They were captained by the Hon. A. G. Hazlerigg.

Otherwise matches at Lord's followed the wartime pattern. The RAAF beat the British Empire XI; an England XI easily defeated the West Indies; a Lord's XI drew with New Zealand; the RAF drew with the British Empire and then with the RAAF, Wyatt scoring heavily in both matches; and the RAAF humiliated the Army, before a large crowd of 14,000, by no less than 183 runs. The game on 30 June between the RAAF and the South of England excited the *aficionados*, because, for the first time since 1857 when Grundy, playing for the MCC, had been similarly dismissed, a batsman was out 'handled the ball'. G. O. Allen played a ball from Roper, which rolled on to the stumps. He picked it up and Roper, either involuntarily or because he mistakenly thought the bails were dislodged, appealed. Although Carmody, the Australian skipper, asked G. O. Allen to resume his innings, he 'rightly declined', according to Pelham Warner's judgement. There was some barracking directed at Roper who may, of course, have actually felt it was injudicious to retrieve a ball in that fashion. It was a neat example of cricket's ambiguity over the letter and spirit of the law, for a rule which it is unsporting to invoke must be pretty pointless.

The rest of the season offered few other legal conundrums of this kind. J. R. Bridger, quite a wartime success, scored 136 not out as Pelham Warner's XI defeated the New Zealanders, for whom Donnelly scored 82, while the Buccaneers took part in a merry thrash with the West of England. The Buccaneers raced to 304 for 4, with Fishlock compiling a powerful 143. Gimblett hit back with a characteristically beefy 104, but the West of England were left clinging to their last wicket as Wellings took 5 for 58. So it continued. The RAF, helped by a Parker century, drew with the New Zealand XI and there was a hard-fought draw between the RAF and the Army, in the last of their memorable wartime clashes. Happily, the Royal Navy had a rare win. Dewes scored 90 for the Navy and the Army, weakened these last two seasons by portentous events in Europe, fell apart miserably. Finally, there was the usual university one day match – and with the usual result. Cambridge continued to fit in more cricket and to find more players than Oxford, who could score only 137 runs in the face of Eckersley's bowling.

Bishop, who went on to make a century, and Dewes passed that tiny total undisturbed.

So much for a summary of the last season of non-first-class, but good quality English cricket. In terms of *Wisden*-recorded cricket, the famous had more than held their own throughout the war, with Hammond, Compton, Fishlock, Hardstaff and others leading in the batting stakes and Young, Goddard and Hollies taking the bowling honours. In all cricket, C. B. Clarke took nearly 750 wickets, an amazing record, for Young and R. Smith were the only other bowlers to reach 300 victims. J. G. Dewes and J. R. Bridger, both of Cambridge University, looked and were admirably productive while, of course, R. T. Simpson, Keith Miller, Alec Bedser and Trevor Bailey were, in effect, wartime 'discoveries'. In all cricket, however, it was veterans like Joe Hulme and H. P. Crabtree, both of whom scored over 4000 runs during the war, and R. E. S. Wyatt, Arthur Fagg and L. J. Todd, with over 3000 runs, who eventually were most effective overall, though falling short of the remarkable 5000 runs compiled by F. S. Lee, of Somerset.

With so many types of matches of widely varying quality, it is no simple task to rank achievements, but an impressionistic decision would suggest that much weight should be placed on runs scored and wickets taken in wartime cricket, and in this respect such players as Clarke, Hollies, Lee, Hulme and Crabtree cannot be faulted.

Thankfully, the list of deaths in 1945 was mercifully brief, especially after the heavy toll of the preceding two years. J. G. Halliday, the Oxford blue, was killed, and the Dominions lost a number of players. A. W. Briscoe and A. B. C. Langton, of South Africa; D. A. R. Moloney and W. N. Carson, of New Zealand, were numbered among these. Ross Gregory, of Victoria and Australia, and Charlie Walker, the Australian reserve wicket-keeper on a couple of tours of England, were also killed. According to E. W. Swanton, about sixty first class cricketers from England and the Dominions died on or as a result of active service during the war. It was a heavy price, but mercifully could not compare with the slaughter of the Great War.

Stock might now be taken of cricket's direct contribution to the war effort. In preparing the *Wisden* of 1945, counties had been requested to list those of their playing staff who had been or who were in the armed forces. Although the compilers used slightly differing criteria, the picture is fairly comprehensive and suggests that just under 300 county cricketers had been or were engaged. Middlesex had sent forth a veritable platoon and the overall average of eighteen a county was a gallant showing. Various mentions of other players' activities suggest that perhaps another 150 were in the civil defence or on essential war work so that, in total, county cricketers made an impressive contribution to the war effort.

The *Wisden* roll of honour was just touching 200 by the end of the war, but this followed the precedent of World War I in recording the untimely deaths, not only of first-class cricketers, but also of minor county, noted schoolboy and other players. Kent seemed to be the worst hit of the counties, losing eleven men associated in some way with the club. Some sixty cricketers were made prisoners of war, and about seventy were decorated, although that figure includes one or two who received honours such as the MBE or CBE. For example, S. C. Griffith and Hugh Bartlett, both of Sussex, won the DFC with airborne forces over Holland; B. H. Valentine, of Kent, the South African and Oxford blue, P. G. Van der Bijl, and D. J. C. Ward, of Derbyshire, were awarded MCs; and Sqn Ldr P. A. McKenzie, of Hampshire, won both a DSO and a DFC.

Of course, not all the deaths recorded in *Wisden* in the war years were the result of enemy action and many older players died comparatively unnoticed by the cricketing public and so without receiving the tributes that peaceful times would have evoked. Among the most notable of these were Bobby Peel, Cecil Parkin, A. J. Webbe, C. T. B. Turner, Fred Tate, Richard Tyldesley, J. T. Hearne and the superb Archie Maclaren.

However, the salient feature of 1945 was the MCC's

decision to give a number of games first-class status. In that oddly two-tone summer, this accreditation of eleven three-day matches, in practice, all the three-day matches played, was at once on indication of returning normality and a question mark over unfulfilled potential. For, if those eleven games were of that standard, could dozens of other two- and one-day matches have been so inferior? The dogma of first-class validation still mars the face of cricket. A century taken off the callow innocents of Oxbridge at Fenners or the Parks is somehow valued more than one in a critical World Cup one-day game.

One would not, obviously, have expected anything different in 1945: one could not have hoped for a valuation to have been placed on a one-day game between, say, the RAF and the Army, even with every manjack a first-class cricketer and the majority of Test standard. But, given the happy thought of restoring some first-class matches to the schedule, it seems a pity that imagination did not soar sufficiently to permit of something a little more invigorating by way of competition. This is no more than a re-emphasis of the point urged earlier that, had the authorities had the temerity to eschew the three-day, two-innings county convention, then some national scheme, however rough and ready, might have quickly been arranged. In 1945 an enormous amount of cricket was played and watched avidly. Things were on the road back to normal although, pre-season, one could not have foretold how long the European, let alone the Far Eastern, aspect of the war would endure. That in itself could have been an extra fillip, for surely, had the war, however unthinkable this now is, persisted over another one or two summers, some framework would have had to have been introduced, lest cricket became slothful and sketchy beyond redemption.

With the West of England going strong, alongside the British Empire and London Counties combines, with the RAAF an athletically potent brew, with the Army, the RAF, the Civil Defence Services and, improving yearly, the Royal Navy in decent trim, with the New Zealanders and the West Indians no easy mark, and now with seven or eight counties with solid enough fixture lists, it is reasonable enough to muse retrospectively over the entertaining tourney, league, knock-out or both, that could have been devised for sixteen or so talented sides.

The argument may be pressed again, specifically in the context of 1945, even if for the superficially unjust reason that the authorities then demonstrated speed and ingenuity in fabricating a set of majestic first-class games. Encouraged, and rightly so, by the exploits of Australian servicemen in 1944, readjustments were summarily made to fixture lists and, in 1945, five non-official Tests, three of them at Lord's, were planned. Six other matches, including three for a revitalized Scarborough Festival, were likewise programmed and granted first-class status. All of this was right and proper. It just seems as if the obsession with first-class play blinded the establishment to the broader requirement.

In spite of these criticisms, there is no gainsaying the delight which attended the resumption of first-class cricket in England. In mid-August Yorkshire played Lancashire at Bradford in the first three-day county match since the former had destroyed Sussex and the latter had been left, along with Surrey, in limbo, on that Friday before the outbreak of hostilities. Cyril Washbrook, who had scored runs steadily throughout the war, made 97 out of Lancashire's 239, and Wilf Barber's 88 enabled Yorkshire to lead slightly on the first innings. Eddie Paynter, in just about his last innings for Lancashire, was 47 not out and his team were 107 for 3 when, not untypically, the resumed war of the roses petered out in a draw. On 1, 3 and 4 of September, six years to the days after the Polish invasion and the declaration of war, the Over Thirty-threes played the Under Thirty-threes, a first-class fixture more redolent of Victorian fixture-lists than those of the modern era. George Pope, Palmer and Davies scored freely for the seniors, who made 335, but Fagg, with yet another century, Watson, Mallett, Bridger and Brookes all batted comfortably and the junior eleven declared at 421 for 7. The older players had just edged into the lead, at 100 for 5, when play ended in a draw.

In late August and early September the decorous spectacle of the Scarborough Festival was renewed, albeit with warlike overtones. First the Yorkshire XI played the RAF in a drawn match. It was a close finish. The RAF, with only three wickets down and with Edrich 50 not out, needed only ten to win when stumps were drawn. Hutton had scores of 55 and 73, Wyatt made a half century for the RAF; and Edrich also scored 45 in the RAF's first innings, Matthews took 5 for 66 as Yorkshire collapsed rather in their first attempt. Secondly, the Australian Services thrashed Leveson-Gower's XI by an innings and 108 runs. Fishlock apart, the English team batted abjectly. Ellis took ten wickets in the match but their fate had been laid by a mammoth total of 506. Sismey, Miller and Whittington helped themselves to seventies, while Cec Pepper crashed his dynamic way to 168, including a six that flew over five-storied boarding houses into an adjacent square, one of the biggest hits ever. Thirdly, Leveson-Gower's XI made amends by defeating the New Zealanders, for whom Donnelly made 100 and 86. Hutton, 188, and Washbrook, 83, gave their team a solid start but the New Zealanders made a typically sporting declaration, leaving Leveson-Gower's XI requiring only 60-odd, although in short time. Badcock took 6 for 166 for New Zealand.

The other six first-class matches were the famous Victory Tests and a prestigious clash between England and the Dominions. What E. W. Swanton has called 'the long hiatus' was reaching its conclusion, and cricket was returning to normal consciousness. It meant that the Victory Tests have been faithfully and fully described and analysed elsewhere so only a précis of those happenings will be given in the present account.

The Australian premier, John Curtin, then very ill and near to death, bravely cabled Lord's with his 'sincere good wishes for the reopening of a series which I hope will never again be interrupted', and thus it was, on 19 May, that the first English first-class match since September 1939 got under way.

Hammond, of course, captained England for the series. He

had been discharged from the RAF in the previous winter, because of fibrositis, but was to play an important part in the rubber. Lindsay Hassett captained Australia. He was one of but a handful of soldiers in the Australian squad, Cheetham, Pepper and Whittington being other members of the AIF. The curious thing was that Hassett was a warrant-officer, while almost all his colleagues were commissioned officers, principally in the RAAF. Thus a civilian and an NCO captained two international sides bristling with commissioned officers.

Batting first, Leslie Ames (57) Jack Robertson (53 and 84) and Bill Edrich (45 and 50) allowed England to make respectable totals, in spite of Pepper's attacking bowling. The Australians, however, twice demonstrated what was to be the sharp lesson of the next seven or eight years, namely, the brittle quality of English bowling. Miller (105) and Hassett (77) first helped Australia amass 455 and then, with but 70 minutes remaining, Hassett and Pepper created a whirlwind of run-making. The necessary 107 were scored for the loss of only four wickets, the last forty runs arriving in twenty minutes, and the winning run was scored with only a couple of minutes remaining. E. W. Swanton has spoken of the 'violence' of Pepper's assault as he clubbed his way to a savage 54 not out. It was a tremendous match, and nearly 70,000 people watched it. Even that old chestnut about record sales of throat-pastilles in London was trotted out to illustrate the fervour of those crowds. On the Whit Monday the gates had to be closed.

A month later 50,000 gathered over three days at Sheffield for the Second Test and enjoyed what E. W. Swanton called 'a see-saw match of sustained interest'. Hammond's century and Washbrook's 63 gave England the purchase for victory. George Pope then took 5 for 58 as Australia collapsed for 147 but, apart from Hutton with 46, England batted dismally themselves. This left the Australians wanting about 330 for victory and they batted very steadily, chiefly through the competent dedication of Workman and Whittington. Just when it seemed that they would achieve this tall order, important wickets fell. Dick Pollard ended with 5 for 76 and England won by 41 runs.

Back, then, to Lord's in mid-July for the third game of this unofficial rubber. The selectors, in Australian fashion, gambled on youth, and, in English fashion, they lost. The Etonian, the Hon. L. R. White, the Reptonian, D. B. Carr, and the successful Cambridge and Royal Navy bat, J. G. Dewes were invited to play but, in Pelham Warner's charitable phrase, they 'did not quite realize expectations'. E. W. Swanton's simpler assessment – they were 'outclassed' – is probably a more realistic one, for they scratched together only 47 runs in their six innings combined. An old man's complaint, lumbago, led to Hammond's disappearance from the game after one day, so that the mix of ancient and modern failed disastrously. Washbrook also suffered a nasty hand injury, Phillipson was left out because of a strain, and George Pope was contracted to play league cricket. It was left to the maestro, Len Hutton, with a chanceless 104 out of 254 and a valuable 69 out of 164, to restore some rationality to the proceedings. He was helped by Pollard's fiery swing bowling in the Australian first innings (6 for 75) and a fifty from Bill Edrich in the English second innings, but Australia now needed only two hundred or so to win. Keith Miller's rapid-fire 71 not out and a Sismey half-century paved the road to a four wicket win. Miller was badly dropped, however, at square leg when 38. Christofani, a quickish spin bowler in the O'Reilly mould, took nine wickets in the match.

Early in August the England line-up at Lord's for the Fourth Test had a more familiar aspect and a record crowd awaited them. The figures quoted range from 85,000 to 93,000. Whatever the true attendance, it was, and remains, a three-day record for Lord's, and the gates had to be closed at or before noon. Montgomery paid a visit and responded affably to a warm reception. Less welcome was the rain and bad light of the second day which made a result, never likely in a high-scoring match, impossible. The first-day crowd marvelled at the debonair batting of Keith Miller, who scored 118 out of 388, with those consistent performers, Sismey and

Pepper, contributing half-centuries. Hutton and Washbrook, who compiled a careful century, gave England a most solid start, upon which Fishlock (69), Hammond (83) and Edrich (73 not out) built with equal professionalism. England were 80 ahead but they had little hope of dismissing the Australians in time, and the teams moved north to Manchester with Australia ahead in the series.

German POWs had been paid three-farthings an hour to prepare, repair and redecorate the ground and its surrounds but, in another ironic wartime twist, Old Trafford's heavy roller was on active service overseas, constructing air strips in the Western Desert. Possibly in consequence, the wicket was a natural one, balancing advantage to batsmen and bowlers in a fashion many thought admirable. It certainly led to what E. W. Swanton described as 'sustained and taut excitement', despite a long stoppage for rain on the second day. Pollard took 4 for 78 as Australia sank to 173, Keith Miller yet again, with 77 not out, being far and away their mainstay. Cristofani took another five wickets, but excellent batting by Hammond (59) and Hutton (64) permitted England a 70-run lead. It looked plenty, as Phillipson, Pollard's Lancashire partner, garnered wickets early and cheaply. Then Christofani revealed his all-round capacity. Aided by the patient Williams, his four-year sojourn as a POW behind him, he drove and pulled his way to a defiant and undefeated 110 out of 210. This meant that England had to graft urgently through the late afternoon to make the 141 runs they needed, but Edrich and Robertson guided them home to draw a fascinating rubber. Old Trafford was packed each day and, in total, over 72,000 watched a thrilling game.

Finally, there was the Dominions game, with the visitors fielding eight Australians, a South African (Fell), a New Zealander, and a West Indian. The match was prefaced by a slight contretemps because Lindsay Hassett was ill and, racial prejudice not being unknown among cricketers, there was some hesitation over the choice of captain. However it was amicably agreed that the self-evident choice – Learie Constantine – was the proper choice and his strategy and fielding were to have a profound impact on a sterling game: 'many thought it to be', according to Pelham Warner, 'one of the finest matches played at Lord's'. *Wisden* concurred: it was 'one of the finest games ever produced'.

It was surely an epic demonstration of the batting arts in all their finesse and power, and a fitting triumph of cricketing talent to celebrate the much-sought victory over the German enemy. 1241 runs were scored, an average of 400 a day, and the sixteen sixes struck (including one from Miller off Hollies that rattled the guttering of the main stand by the press box, and one from Hammond that bounced through the Long Room door and clattered a display case) remains a record for a three-day match at Lord's.

The Dominions scored 307 in their first innings, thanks largely to a graceful 133 from New Zealand's M. P. Donnelly, then perhaps the prince of the world's left-handers. England nearly closed the gap with 287, Wally Hammond's 121 and Edrich's 78 being the chief contributions. When the Dominions batted again, Keith Miller treated his opponents disdainfully and the spectators enchantingly. With, in Swanton's phrase, 'devastating power', he completely dominated the game and, in less than three hours, scored 185, including seven sixes and thirteen fours. Pelham Warner judged it to be 'perhaps his best innings at Lord's'. Constantine added a brisk forty and England required over 350 to win.

Walter Hammond was at his imperious best. His 102 meant that he overtook Hobbs' record as he had now scored two centuries in a match for the seventh time. Emrys Davies grafted over 56, and an England win seemed possible. It was then that Constantine, with a prehensile bound and lethal throw, ran out Phillipson, just as he seemed to be settled, and the Dominions won by 45 runs. The batting had reigned supreme, but the fielding had never fallen below the highest class, and there had been commendably steady bowling. Doug Wright had actually kept England in contention. With his whiplash leg spin he could be wellnigh unplayable just as, like other bowlers of his type, he could be embarrassingly extravagant. Over these three days he sustained marvellous form, taking five wickets in each innings, for a total of 195. This was, quite simply, one of cricket's outstanding games and Sir Pelham Warner heaped praise upon it. It was, he wrote, 'a feast of brilliant stroke-play. It was cricket *in excelsis*. A *joie de vivre* in the batting sparkled through a game which fulfilled any known axiom as to how cricket should be played.'

In the relaxed and celebratory mood of 1945, both players and spectators appeared to sense something of the brio which, in its late Victorian and Edwardian era, gave cricket its golden reputation. The exchanges were amicable but determined; the spirit was cheerful and the approach indubitably positive; the crowds were huge, friendly and appreciative. Of itself, even that would have been insufficient without the surfeit of gifted players, like Hammond, Hutton, Donnelly and Miller.

It was almost too exhilarating. The heady and luxuriant pleasures of those half a dozen games made men's hearts beat quicker, but may have restricted the use of their minds. What were the benefits and drawbacks?

On the one hand, the Victory Tests and that renowned Dominions contest preserved the interest of the older generation and established the enthusiasm of the newer cohort. They gave deep-rooted hope to the many who yearned to see cricket restored in something like its prime, but they also enlisted the lifelong support of the next echelon of followers. For the generation now in their fifties, the Victory Tests formed the function of baptism. Speak to any cricket-lover in that age-range, and he will inevitably recall the Victory Tests as his rite of passage into the mysteries and rituals of first-class cricket. It all augured well.

On the other hand, some wrong lessons were learned. The wartime boom for cricket, exploding so vitally in 1945, left the authorities complacently believing that the style of the 1930s would endure for ever. What the establishment missed was the essential ingredients that guaranteed the kind of support they needed for the upkeep of the game. Thrilling finishes created, in carnival style, by exuberant artists: that was the recipe and, as the 1940s became the 1950s, and cricket grew ever more humdrum and dour, it was evident that something was dreadfully awry.

In a minor key, there was another disadvantage. The shrewder critics noted with alarm that, through the inspirational haze of 1945's magicianship, young Australians were infinitely mightier than young Englishmen. While Dewes and White and Carr failed abysmally, a bunch of Australian soldiers and airmen, only one of whom – Hassett – was capped, could challenge and successfully vie with pretty near the select of England. Denis Compton and Joe Hardstaff were in India but otherwise England fielded very strong teams. Miller, of course, was to come to fruition as one of the great all-rounders and Hassett was to continue his neat and consistent world-class career.

These two apart, what is frightening about the 1945 Australians is how many were not to be judged, by the exacting standards of post-war Australia, to warrant later selection. Sound batsmen like Carmody (a Beaufort pilot with Coastal Command), Workman and Whittington; a highly accomplished stumper such as Sismey; the all-round ferocity of Pepper; the quicker bowling of Roper and Williams; the cunning spin of Ellis and Pettiford; the impish presence, with bat or ball, of Christofani; all of these remained at competent state level, or joined English teams, or dropped out of the top class game altogether.

What this group of fine young athletes exposed was the frailty of English bowling, now miserably shorn of Ken Farnes and the irreplaceable Verity. As long as Hammond, Hutton, Washbrook, Compton and Edrich could defy most attacks, England might flatter to deceive. In the field, they were, for nearly a decade, to look feeble and toothless. Somehow Australia's young cricketers, at home or abroad in England, had contrived to negotiate an efficacious apprenticeship, whereas England's young cricketers had not matured in the same manner.

That was for the short-term future. In 1945, there was entrancing cricket and it bred an optimism at once understandable and fragile. It was in tone with the general mood.

There was no Mafeking in the May of 1945. It was not like the hysterical rapture that welcomed Boer War incidents like the relief of Ladysmith, or occurred, most noisily and furiously, at the 1918 Armistice. The celebrations of 1945 were more moderate and a little watchful. They were genuine enough and men and women dared to hope. They were, however, once bitten . . . Cricket lovers, too, might have been well advised to be temperate in their anticipations, for there were to be disappointments in peacetime for cricket, as for many other features of civilized life.

The Bishop of Leicester, on being made Patron of the Leicestershire club, is quoted in the 1944 *Wisden* as saying that 'cricket will always have a stable place in the nation'. That was and is true, but it was in danger of becoming static rather than stable. In 1946, *Wisden* was to conclude that there had been 'enormous value in keeping the game going during the uphill years of strife', but that again sounded a slightly lame note. It was all about hanging on, and nothing about progressive advance. By dismissing these very wartime endeavours as 'impromptu cricket', the cricketer's bible was at the same time refusing to read the signs and assess what might be learned.

SIX

The Way Ahead

Reconstruction was a word which appeared early. The war seemed to be no sooner under way than thoughts turned to the aftermath. Some of this was whistling in the dark but, on the whole, it betokened a commendably positive attitude to the likelihood of victory. It also indicated a sense of need for reform. The war brought problems that required forward planning. Housing was the most pressing of these for the material damage, caused by German bombing, was very extensive. Strangely, although much thought had rightly been given to the issue of personal safety, few plans for overcoming the effect of shattered accommodation were in evidence. In illustration, one in six Londoners had been made homeless for some period as early as May 1940.

Social reform was in the air, however, not because of the war *per se*, but because of the opportunity it offered. There was a feeling that the 1930s had been a period of stalemate and that a political dead-hand had lain upon the nation. The post-war promises of 1918 and 1919 had not been kept – the homes fit for heroes had not been built, and the Blitz had only emphasized the impoverishment of Britain's housing stock. It was as if an unwritten and unspoken contract had been agreed, with the people willing to withstand the suffering of total war in return for civilized treatment afterwards. The Butler Education Act of 1944, although perhaps not so radical in practice as in precept, is a case in point, whereby, at the height of the war and with middle-class consciences touched by the social plight of evacuees from deprived districts, officials and politicians had sat down to reform the schooling system. A famous illustration is the Beveridge Report of 1942, one of the seminal points in the evolution of the welfare state. Again, this was discussed initially when the course of the war was very much in doubt and, while, as with the Education Act, the consequences were not quite so fundamental as some have imagined, it assuredly caught the mood of the hour.

There was a general willingness to consider change. The co-ordination of theatrical activity for the war effort was, from its inauguration, viewed by its creators as the likely base for a national theatre or scheme of national sponsorship. It was not just a matter of ensuring that the railways would survive the war, or that improved wage structures would be maintained, or that some form of uniform health protection might emerge. It touched every aspect of British life. War has, of course, that catalytic effect. By dint of shaking people from their mundane ruts and confronting them with startling new horizons and situations, it breeds some degree of dissatisfaction, an often unconscious or ill-defined sense of disappointment, about one's past lot, and an ambition, equally indeterminate, for betterment.

Cricket was no stranger to this mental state. Sir Home Gordon was musing about the future in *The Cricketer Spring Annual* of 1940. His predictions were to prove amazingly accurate. Lord Northcliffe had told him in 1918 that the Great War had 'completely killed' cricket, and Lord Northcliffe had been absolutely wrong. Home Gordon felt that those now prophesying a similar catastrophe would be proved equally false. That was a reasonable guess, for cricket, like other traditions, such as pantomime or seaside resorts, appears to attract the Cassandras. Sir Home Gordon waxed, nevertheless, a trifle pessimistic. There would be 'a boom at the outset', reflecting revitalized economic life, and then a slump, as 'the practical support of so many thousands' would not be forthcoming for the counties. The years lost in development would sap the playing-power of the county elevens. Colts 'will not have concentrated on acquiring skill', it will be difficult 'to revive the habit', of first-class play, for the necessary 'assiduous nicety cannot be cultivated' except in the esoteric conditions of county cricket.

Much of this came to pass, as did the forewarning that, as after the 1914–18 war, the Australians would be all-conquering. Home Gordon dilated on the finances of the game, which had shown signs of shakiness in the 1930s. He forecast that wages would be £2 or £2.10 a week, plus match play, and that the scandalous business of cricketers earning £400 a year or drawing basic summer wages of £5 and £6 must be stopped. It now cost, he estimated, £10,000 to run a county and that, in his view, was too much. To the extent that many counties were in trouble trying to raise that kind of money, he was perfectly correct, although his estimates of what, with inflation and changes in social values, would be acceptable in the post-war years were unrealistic. He did, however, whisper aloud the vague possibility of Sunday play.

The Cricketer Annual examined the subject thoroughly in 1941, a touching instance of optimistic thinking, as the invasion scare was hardly past and the Blitz continued nightly. It placed its suggestions for cricket among the 'plans for the betterment of the world', but called severely for 'a true perspective'. Although the county championship was 'not an ideal competition', three-day matches were essential, and proposals to the contrary were frowned upon. As with so many topics, the experience of the previous war was close – maybe too close – at hand and lessons were drawn from the apparent errors of 1919.

The first war, like the second, produced a pother of suggested alterations, many of which *Wisden*, predictably, found 'too preposterous'. The banishment of left-hand batting, being declared 'out' for slow scoring, batting penalties for maiden overs: the 'evil chance' of war had, among other wickednesses, brought forth 'faddists' with such bizarre ideas. The shortening of boundaries – 'this most mischievous proposition' – was one additional fad which, many years later, was to be accepted. One fundamental change was agreed and that was, experimentally, a two-day county championship in the summer of 1919. It was Lancashire who made the proposal, and, in February 1919, this – according to *Wisden* – 'unhappy' decision was taken. It was heralded as 'a sad blunder', and *Wisden* wished that Surrey, Kent, Middlesex and Yorkshire might have 'stood firmly together' and flung out the heresy. *Wisden* would have preferred a blank season but, after the four years famine, the counties wanted 'a systematic competition'. Counties had to play at least a dozen matches, six at home and six away, to qualify. This 'great mistake', as Warner called it, was not endorsed by the MCC, and the University match and the Gentlemen and Players match were three-day events.

The arguments in favour of two-day cricket were partially sporting, for it was felt that a gloss on Parkinson's Law was obeyed, with cricket expanding to fill the time made available for it. It was hoped that two-day matches would encourage bolder and brisker exploits and that cricket would lose some of its somnolence and atrophy. Supporters of the status quo were convinced that the first-class game had evolved slowly and naturally so that three days had become the optimum time required by rational trial and error.

The cricketing argument tumbled over into the economic one. Much was made of the meagre takings on the third day. Several county secretaries and treasurers calculated that, in relation to the expense of opening and managing the ground, the gate-money taken then failed to cover costs, whereas the first two days tended to be quite popular. Admittedly, members, paying an annual subscription, would lose a third of their cricket, but they, too, it was said, were not regular visitors on that depressing third day. Statistics were bandied. In response to the gloomy financial prognostications came evidence that only 41 (some 16 per cent) of the 261 first-class games played in 1939 had been completed in two days although, of course, it had to be recognized that they were not designed to be.

Major testimony was culled from what many regarded as the fiasco of 1919. Even Lancashire, the 'prime movers' of the pilot scheme, confessed it had not been effective. The main difficulty had been time. Hours were extended until late in the evening and several counties had very packed fixture lists, although one or two, like Somerset and Northants, played only the minimum of twelve. It led to frustration and tension as players tried to finish matches and catch trains, often arriving at the oddest hours at their next venue. It was also noted that spectators left the grounds well before the advertised time for drawing stumps of 7.30 p.m., lest, as Robertson-Glasgow recalled in 1942, 'their wives, cooks and servants' be kept waiting.

However, it was what Robertson-Glasgow also termed 'the scrambling inconvenience' of the 1919 system which was its drawback and he, among others, was ready to reconsider a two-day scheme after the war. Indeed, both *Wisden* and *The Cricketer* were prepared to argue the merits of two-day cricket as early as 1942, although it was conceded that minor county matches, normally of two days' duration, were too frequently drawn. One proposition in *The Cricketer* was for two-day county matches and three-day major matches such as Test Trials, fixtures for the tourists, Gents and Players and so forth. As an extra flavouring, a regional competition, in four groups, was advocated within the ordinary championship; that is, the same game played against a local rival would count toward two competitions, the national and the regional. Robertson-Glasgow felt that a pattern of thirty-two two-day matches, of fourteen hours each, had 'much to commend it'. He expected, however, that there would be a return to the three-day set-up, but he pointed out, with eminently good sense, that 'tradition so easily degenerates into inertia and habit into self-satisfaction'. It was a warning that was not altogether heeded.

It has to be said that admiration for the two-day game was, in part, dictated by horror of the one-day game, and had more to do with the lesser of two evils than genuine affection. Robertson-Glasgow blisteringly pooh-poohed the idea of 'a regular process' of one-day matches. There were those who, because wartime one-day matches 'have given such good entertainment, strongly recommended their utilization in peace-time'. Robertson-Glasgow was scathing. 'The new clockwork monkey in the nursery . . . delights for a few hours,' he claimed. 'The dubious highbrow and the benighted philistine' would raise 'a little clatter against cricket', but it was in fact, 'a subtle as well as a strenuous game'. First-class cricket was 'a three act play, not a slapstick turn' and, as for the ignorant who thought otherwise, 'such spectators are, frankly, not wanted at county cricket'. The weather and the sheer lack of time would make a shambles of any one-day competition.

A year earlier, also in *Wisden*, the same commentator had drawn the same distinction between one-day cricket, as played in the leagues, and the first-class game. 'It must sparkle', he wrote, 'if it is to rival the horses and the dogs.' The 'showmanship' and 'flamboyant manner' of league cricket, with a hefty responsibility on the shoulders of the star professional, was 'foreign to the temperament and the habit of the average county cricketer'. There was some exaggeration here, both social and sporting. It was a mild calumny to regard league cricket so pompously and it showed scant understanding of the values of the northern culture in which it was based. The comparison with dogs and horses was a snobbish and silly one. Moreover, the distinction between the types of cricket was overdrawn. Admittedly, first-class cricket, as one would expect, was of a loftier standard, but there were bridges. League cricket was a useful preparation for the first-class game and a decent resting-place for those leaving first-class cricket. It was shortsighted to criticize one-day cricket so blatantly.

On 8 December 1942 the Advisory County Cricket Committee met at Lord's, for a preliminary discussion about the game's future, prior to a decisive meeting in the spring of 1943. 'Haste,' said *Wisden*, 'so ardently urged from some quarters, was not necessary or helpful.' All the counties except Derbyshire managed to send a representative, and there was some talk yet again of a two-day competition. This time Sussex were the proposers and Lancashire, unperturbed by the seeming fiasco of the 1919 experiment, the seconders.

The new model was for a Saturday and Monday, followed by a Wednesday and Thursday game, the latter hopeful of coinciding with half-day closing in practially all towns. All counties would play each other home and away. Norman Preston reviewed the debate in *Wisden*. By 1943 the counties were 'far healthier financially' than in 1939 but they must, he warned, 'plan carefully' to avoid a recurrence of the lean times. During the ninety-five minute meeting, the monetary losses that occurred on a lean third day, the greater likelihood of amateurs finding the time for two- rather than three-day contests and the stronger incentive to provide entertaining cricket were stressed. There would not be so much fatigue and, as for cricket weeks and festivals, an extra day would be available to play a local XI and thereby encourage budding talent. The Australian example was cited. Ordinary grade matches were played on two consecutive afternoons, with a modicum of state matches to offer the necessary representative experience.

The cricketing knights, Pelham Warner and Stanley Jackson, were stoutly opposed to these proposals and spoke severely of 'the danger of tinkering with the game'. They introduced in evidence the 1937 Findlay Commission, which had condemned the idea of two-day matches and claimed that expenses could not be saved by an abandonment of the third day. The Findlay Commission solution had been to reduce the number of counties to fifteen, and provide a goodly selection of representative matches. These were influential contributions: 'I can see nothing wrong', said Sir Pelham, 'with modern cricket'.

There were other proposals, such as ten points for a win, and four points for a first innings lead, plus the application of one-day match rules where rain had curtailed games to that limited period. Surrey put forward views on the follow-on and about first-day declarations, and there was weighty, if short-lived, support for the 'welcome total deletion of all distinction' between professional and amateur. It was 'surely humbug' to persist with the Players and Gentlemen categories – but persist they did for nearly twenty more years.

The discussions continued at the county meetings, with Sussex opining that 'the crux of the problem' was the captains, for an eleven 'is a reflex on its leader'. On 13 July 1943 thirty-seven delegates attended the subsequent Advisory County Cricket Committee meeting, and made two far-reaching decisions. One was to plump decisively for the retention of three-day play, and the other was to ask the MCC to create a Select Committee to facilitate 'a speedy resumption' of first-class cricket when peace was achieved.

The request was granted, and the Select Committee met first in the winter of 1943, and published its 6,000 word report on 20 March 1944. It was an enclave of cricket's notables, presided over by Sir Stanley Jackson, and with Sir Pelham Warner and Colonel R. S. Rait Kerr in attendance from the MCC as joint secretaries. There were sixteen other members, either famous county captains like G. O. Allen and R. W. V. Robins of Middlesex, A. B. Sellers of Yorkshire, R. E. S. Wyatt of Warwickshire, A. J. Holmes of Sussex, Maurice Turnbull of Glamorgan, or much-respected county officials and secretaries, like H. A. Brown of Notts, Major Howard of Lancashire, W. Findlay of Derbyshire, H. A. Henson of Gloucester. Walter Hammond was added to the committee later, and evidence was heard from five other county officers. Cricketers themselves were represented by Leslie Ames, Frank Chester, Maurice Leyland, Bertie Strudwick and Ernest Tyldesley. It was a glittering gathering of cricket's immediate past but one fancies there were few there with the intellectual courage to be sceptical and unsentimental about bygone seasons and to envision the summers of the 1960s and 1970s.

The Latin tag *status quo ante bellum* summarizes the report succinctly. There was no reconstruction. A 'dynamic attitude' was called for, to make full use of the time available and to avoid delays, as cricket looked forward to the first peacetime season. It was in 'every way desirable' to resume smartly and ensure that cricket became 'an essential feature of the post-war social structure of the nation'. It was recognized that, as troops were demobilized, cricket must make its mark. There was a call for fast and natural wickets, quick-moving sight-screens and fewer appeals against the light. The emphasis was upon adding zip to the conventional formula.

All else was negative. There should be 'no compulsory elimination' or amalgamation of counties nor the deployment of two divisions. There should be no Sunday cricket and no eight-ball overs. There should be no Central Fund or 'pooling' of receipts. Time-limit cricket was rejected; whether by time in itself, overs per innings or rate of scoring. It would be 'detrimental' to the 'art and character' of captaincy and toll the knell of the all-rounder. Incidentally, this was to be proved false, for all-rounders have been dominant in limited-overs cricket, to the point where the reverse criticism is made – that there are over many 'bits and pieces' players! It was calculated that any form of restriction would have affected only 5 per cent of games during the 1938 and 1939 seasons. Obviously, no thought was given to the application of restricted play to one-day cricket.

In the first 'normal' season it was proposed that each county would play exactly twenty-six matches in the championship, thus avoiding the complication of percentage or average points which had been needed when counties played unequal fixtures. This was to include no fewer than thirteen home games, but every county had to be played once. 'Traditional matches' were to be preserved. Each county would maintain four permanent double fixtures, and an attempt would be made to find a 'fair balance' of weak doubles and singles. The concept was of ten home and away doubles, plus six single fixtures, giving twenty-six matches in all. As a further protection of the status quo, a 'priority list' of the 1939 umpires was proposed, with those over sixty standing at the MCC's discretion. Saturday and Wednesday starts should be retained along with the 1939 scoring system of twelve points for a win and four points for a first innings lead. A 'points only for a win' recommendation was voted down. After fifty-five overs a new ball or – sign of hard times – 'a used one in better condition' might be taken. As for qualification, players would remain under original contract but might leave 'with their county's consent', if they were not wanted.

Sensibly, the Select Committee invented an emergency scheme, should the war end suddenly and cricket have to resume abruptly, or if transport created an overall difficulty. It consisted of two regional groups, each subdivided into two smaller sets. The northern section was Derbyshire, Lancashire, Yorkshire and Notts (the North subgroup) and Leicester, Northants, Warwicks and Worcester (Midland). The southern section was Glamorgan, Gloucester, Hants and Somerset (South-West) and Essex, Kent, Surrey, Sussex and Middlesex (South-East). There would be three phases: the first of ten weeks with home and away fixtures, within the groups; the second of six weeks in which any matches might be arranged; and the third of three weeks, with games between the various leading teams and some first-class and minor counties cricket. Although, of course, this was never utilized, it is important to recall that regional cricket was contemplated.

The report was 'accepted without amendment' by the full Advisory Committee in October, 1944. Three points only caused any debate. The suggestion that it was 'illegal' to cover wickets at any time during a match was rejected, and the 1939 ruling whereby counties made their 'own arrangements' stood. Those in favour of granting points solely for a win were denied, and the notion of first innings points was retained.

The final point at issue was the promise of a knock-out competition. It is a curiosity of cricket history that, in the wake of the establishment of the FA Cup in 1872, a similar scheme was planned for cricket. C. W. Alcock, the Secretary of the Football Association, based the knock-out competition on the cock house contest of his old school, Harrow, and he was also Secretary of Surrey County Cricket Club where, indeed, the early soccer finals were played. Only a handful of counties accepted an invitation to compete and the proposition was to play the matches at Lord's. Kent played Surrey there on a fearsome wicket, and the hazardous pitches at Lord's were one of the reasons why, after that one game, the Challenge Cup was shelved. It was postponed for a conservative ninety years until, in 1963, the Gillette Cup was inaugurated.

The Select Committee examined the idea of a knock-out competition but they rigidly stuck to their view that 'any departure from the existing method' of three-day cricket would be disadvantageous. Strangely, they never considered a limited time or overs contest, settled over a day. 'For many reasons', the Committee reported, 'we do not consider it satisfactory.' They mentioned the 'many practical difficulties' and thought it would take time for a 'satisfactory scheme' of three-day matches to 'be evolved'. When the Advisory Committee met to endorse the report, its members recorded their opinion that there were 'big problems' of developing a 'suitable plan' for a knock-out cup in the short English summer and with 'the greatest obstacle' of the weather contributing to unresolved draws and perhaps the tossing of a coin to decide the victors.

Col Rait Kerr and four county secretaries (Howard of Lancashire, Brown of Notts, Henson of Gloucester and Davey of Surrey) were given the task of looking further into this live issue and they reported the following year. They proposed a bye-round, with a replay if necessary, followed by eight first-round matches, leading to a four-day final, with even a fifth day built in to help guarantee a result. In the case of a draw, the Cricket Cup, as it would be labelled, would be shared. In earlier rounds, draws would lead to replays. 'Even with imperfections', opined this highly experienced quintet of administrators, the competition had 'potential long term value' and they opted for a two-season trial. The draw was a complex device, based on the team's place in the championship table seven days before the next round, or, where places were equal, the placements in the preceding season's league. The final would begin on the first Friday after the championship finished, even if it took place during the football season.

The five admitted that they were 'very conscious of the shortcomings of the scheme' and, in June 1945, just after the war in Europe had ended, the Advisory Committee 'decided to leave any experiments in regard to a knock-out competition until county cricket was re-established'. A crucial difficulty was the drawn game. The consequence of replays was potentially alarming and they might create havoc among the fixture lists. The Test Match bogey was raised. In a season with five Tests, counties would be unfairly disadvantaged through the loss of key players. Many were opposed to the sudden introduction of a new competition in the first peacetime season which now looked like being 1946.

Nearly eighteen months later, in November 1946, and after that first season of post-war cricket, the Advisory County Cricket Committee 'decided to defer further consideration' of a knock-out competition for the kinds of reasons already advanced. The issue was shelved indefinitely. It was not formally abandoned until the Advisory Committee meeting of November 1957 but, three years later, the agitation for a cup competition stirred fervently, and, on 20 December 1961, the decision to establish the Gillette Cup was taken by a small margin.

The innate conservatism of the cricket authorities is lucidly demonstrated by this episode. The insistence on considering only full three-day matches for knock-out purposes is evidence enough of what, to modern eyes, might seem shortsightedness, while the general unease about cup contests is plain to behold. Indeed, only the *cognoscenti* of cricket history will recall this vain flurry of interest in cricket's equivalent of the FA Cup which took place as the war neared its end. It is a characteristic episode. The doldrums of war were an occasion and the mood of victory a motive for reconstruction. In cricket, as in other affairs, there was rejoicing and valiant rhetoric but, as frequently, a retreat from the brink.

At the heart of the debate lay a much-used text from *The Times*, quoted in *The Cricketer Annual* as early as 1941: 'first-class fun but not first-class cricket'. There was the dread that, if the first-class guard was dropped, the arcane mysteries would be undermined and there are plenty arguing currently that this has been the price of an excess of one-day and limited-over cricket. *The Cricketer Annual*, having rung the changes a little on its views, became, by 1944, a stout antagonist of knock-out cricket and called for more representative games. Where tradition offered its precept, the *Annual* weakened. Having urged, in 1941, that there should be no tours for two years after the war, it agreed, in 1945, that, however unready, England should be prepared to visit Australia and, by taking up the challenge, demonstrate that we had fought for 'freedom from fear'. Tours to Australia were part of the accepted pattern. A rather more trivial, if picturesque, instance of obedience to tradition was A. J. Holmes's apologia for Sunday cricket. Accepting the rightful correlation between Christianity and the sacred game, and noting that non-professional cricket did take place on a Sunday, he suggested Sunday cricket, inclusive of an open-air service, characterized by what he called 'hearty worship'. This eccentic scheme fell on deaf ears and, perhaps sadly, the world of cricket was denied, for example, the Right Reverend David Sheppard, Bishop of Liverpool, leading the players and crowd at a John Player Special League match in a powerful chorus, directed at the Great Umpire in the Sky, of 'Lord, dismiss us with thy blessing.'

How right was the cricket establishment to stonewall on the question of change and stick inflexibility to the set pattern? It was said that 'the main object is the revival of public interest and not the winning of matches' and that very statement contained something of an ambivalence. Perhaps it was the exciting results of World War II cricket which attracted so much popularity. A critical verdict, ensconced in the introduction to the 1944 Select Committee report, was that 'cricket was increasing in its appeal' and that 'no radical changes' were called for. Pelham Warner predicted in the 1944 *Cricketer Annual* that, on peace, 'the game will be more popular than ever'. Later Sir Pelham Warner was to write of how 'cricket enjoyed a boom' in the war years and that, in the splendid programme of one-day matches at Lord's, 'time after time a thrilling finish was seen'. Sir Home Gordon, always troubled by the apparent unpopularity of three-day cricket, noted that 'the public went to see stars not results' and commented that 'one wartime development is that spectators have become thrilled over close finishes'. One conclusion to be drawn from those two premises might have been that crowds hunger for stars fighting out finely balanced combats.

Possibly in a desire to re-create the past ritual, the authorities misread the lessons of the thousands who trooped to Lord's and other grounds to enjoy wartime cricket. The emergence of the game 'stronger than ever' led, in the opinion of the cricket historian Rowland Bowen, to 'a period of delusion'. Crowds continued to flock to see the old heroes of the 1930s, parading their virtues for a final summer or two, and hundreds more, demobilized and returning from abroad, shed their uniforms and relaxed easily in the pastoral atmosphere of cricket. The astounding success of the Victory Tests contributed to the mood.

In Rowland Bowen's words, this 'apparent popularity blinded far too many' to the signs of likely decay. Other factors apart, there was not much else to occupy the sporting-minded leisure-seeker in the late 1940s. It was not foreseen that, as newer pastimes attracted support, as petrol rationing was jettisoned and the motor car became ubiquitous, as family outings grew more prominent, as television gradually exerted its comprehensive and baleful influence, cricket audiences would dwindle alarmingly. There was – another of Rowland Bowen's words – 'a bonanza', with excellent crowds and, very important to the county clubs, no shortage of members. Everything remained as it was. Subscriptions were not raised; wages were not increased; inflation, at first gradually, crept insidiously high, and the trend had not been appreciated by cricket's administrators.

The economy had an adverse effect on the discovery of players. On top of the difficulties caused by the war itself, the wartime and post-war labour market did not assist cricket. In the years before the war and, in fact, for most of the history of the first-class game, paid cricketers had earned considerably more than the wages of the ordinary working man. Now incomes were higher and more consistently so, and job opportunities in that era abounded. Alternatively, the so-called 'true amateur' was passing with changes in the social and economic fabric, and traditionalists mourned the departure of the aesthetic glories brought to the game by Ranji, Jessop, Maclaren and others. The universities, once the nursery of such blossoming amateurs, turned, quite rightly, to educational matters. Many schools, again rightly, widened the appeal of their sporting facilities and stopped concentrating on the magnificent First Eleven, at the expense of hundreds of neglected children. The famous touring clubs and the gracious country house matches of the preceding era began to vanish. 'The inevitable result', in one verdict, 'was mediocre recruits'. Professional captains, once *de trop*, were now *de rigueur*.

Some commentators have pointed also to the peculiarly hybrid features of the immediate post-war game. On the one hand, there was uniform and centralized coaching of a type guaranteed to create dreary and defensive play. It was certainly said critically of several first-class coaches that they taught the bowlers to bowl off the wickets and the batsmen to leave the ball alone! Moreover, there were perhaps too many fidgety alterations to rulings about taking the new ball, or the points system, or declarations; none of them really approaching the root of the negative play that often ensued. It soon became noticeable that both runs scored and wickets taken were down in number. After 1949 batsmen scored 3000 in a season on only two or three occasions: between the wars it happened sixteen times. Bowlers taking a hundred wickets were fewer and further between, and this was still before one-day cricket was introduced.

On the other hand, the old structure of the MCC governing seventeen first-class counties, a system which had prided itself on maintaining the zest and grace of the sport, continued to dominate. Harsh critics, such as Rowland Bowen, claimed the MCC 'refused to study any remedy' in the light of over-professionalism of the 1950s and that, although cricket's 'mystical aura no longer exists', the pretence of the 'holy game' was sustained. For instance, the Eton and Harrow game, once attracting 20,000 spectators a day, collapsed as an event for socialites, although Ascot, Henley and Buckingham Palace garden parties still remain as upper-class junkets. Probably the most significant part of this refusal to look realistically at the future was the continuing mystique of the seventeen first-class counties, only one of them (Glamorgan) being of post-1918 vintage, only one other (Northants in 1905) having joined the élite in the twentieth century.

This odd combination of professional dourness and backward looking rigidity brought English cricket fairly low by the late fifties. Some counties were struggling to avoid bankruptcy and were manifestly ill-managed. It was absurd to accept that all the championship geese were swans and that no new counties might have been promoted to, or, more realistically, some counties combined or demoted from first-class status.

The wartime West of England XI was a working model for county combination, drawing, as it did, on Somerset, Gloucester and Worcester players. Northants and Leicester was another practical possibility, where a strengthened side might have provided pleasant fare for more people by a strategic selection of several venues. Minor county combinations – Northumberland, Cumberland, Durham, for instance – were another possibility. Even Sir Pelham Warner had conceded that there might be too many counties. He did so, however, in the context of a speech in 1942 where he stressed 'I can see nothing wrong with modern cricket'. Just because 'we live in an age of speed', it did not follow that cricket needed to be acceleterated for 'it is not necessary to have fast scoring to have interesting cricket'.

A central problem was the two-innings convention, not much practised outside the first class and minor county games for, since the rising mastery of batsmen many years before, the attractive feature of the second chance had become virtually impractical in ordinary club games. The notion of, for example, a one innings game over, say, a day and a half, with noon or early afternoon starts, was never canvassed. As for the one-day game, that remained anathema. Elton Ede, the cricket writer, said condescendingly that it was 'just a jolly wartime expedient for the full rigour of the game'. As practised by several captains in the war, it had been rather more than that and, without the time or overs restriction, it left the added option of a hard fought draw and, more especially, the cleverness of the artfully timed declaration. County members might not have liked to see games senselessly thrown away for the delectation of the *hoi polloi*, any more than football supporters prefer an exciting drubbing to a boring, scoreless draw. Members, however, ran the risk of losing all, as counties like Warwickshire, Lancashire and Surrey had to make urgent appeals for large sums of money for ground and pavilion renovations and, in smaller counties, benevolent patrons were cajoled into bailing out all-but bankrupt clubs. It was not edifying, and the financial situation was to grow ever more critical. In any event, a balance of one-day knock-out matches with one-day league matches, allowing for the honourable draw, might have proved satisfactory.

Eventually, the one-day treatment had to be applied to restore some vestige of economic stability and, equally important, social credibility, for it had become bizarre for twenty-two men to earn their living, day in, day out, by playing cricket in the hushed silence of eerily empty grounds. The treatment, applied late, had to be applied liberally, with three one-day competitions taking over a sizeable proportion of the season.

Soon the old arguments were rehearsed again. One-day cricket, especially in an epoch which tolerated a great phalanx of overseas stars, did not give youngsters a rational chance. One-day cricket spoilt the sane and careful development of batsmen, particularly those not batting in the first three, and it destroyed spin bowling, particularly leg-spin bowling. Its proponents, apart from pointing to the crowds that assembled and the black figures on the bank accounts, claimed that many West Indian players somehow managed to succeed both in restricted and unrestricted play. They might have added

W. G. Grace to the list, for he and his contemporaries were as adept at the one- as at the three-day game. They also pointed out that skilled spinners, when utilized, were often successful, and that it was a grave misconception that military medium in-swing was the sole fashion for limited over defence. They could emphasize too, the immense improvement in running between the wickets and, above all, in fielding. In the years before and just after the war, most counties carried a portly passenger or two in the field. Nowadays a county eleven hardly dare risk one second-rate fieldsman.

Interestingly, the international match retained its popularity and, as the new cricketing nations rose to fame and fortune, most Test Matches and, eventually, one-day internationals attracted massive support. A curious cycle was evolved. Funds from Test Matches became the life-blood of county clubs, together with several forms of sponsorship. First-class cricket was necessary as a training-ground for Test Matches, even though few, if anybody, watched it. County cricket and Test cricket became mutually supportive.

There does seem some absurdity, none the less, in preserving a complex and, in itself, economically unsound construction in order to equip an international side whose financial aim is to save its practice haunts from ruin. Armed with a little more prescience and fortitude, maybe the Select Committees and the Advisory Committees of the early 1940s might have been a little cleverer and actually undertaken some genuine reconstruction.

They might, for example, have seized one proposed initiative and instituted a more open 'county' system, perhaps with a small first division of seven or eight leading clubs of reasonable economic stability and competence, and a larger second division, possibly regionally grouped, of another score of counties, that is, inclusive of successful minor counties, Scotland, Ireland, the combined (that is, *all*) universities, and so forth. One lesson of wartime cricket, exhibited by the RAF, the Army, the NFS, the London Counties and the

British Empire XI, was that there are several foci, apart from the county, for recruiting teams.

These teams might have played, along the lines suggested during the war, two-day games, preferably at weekends, and including Sundays, for, of course, the Sabbath soon had to be deployed as a cricketers' day. The mode might have been, in a heightened version of the wartime league device, to retain three, four or five excellent professionals, so that aspirants from club cricket could train and play with the counties without fear of being trapped by poor form into unemployment. In other words, it would have allowed many to enjoy the challenge of professional cricket and ultimately take it up full-time without at first risking some other career.

Relegation and promotion is not entirely foreign to cricket. In 1890, two years after the formation of the Football League, cricket toyed with the concept of three divisions, with teams promoted and relegated. As with the notion of a cricket cup, this scheme was indefinitely shelved. What might be argued is that both might have been introduced in the post-war years, with one or two ups and downs between these two divisions. A single one-day tournament, incorporating the richer sixty-over formula of the Gillette, then NatWest, trophy might have been sufficient for the time, thereby avoiding the immoderation of the current three essays into one-day activity.

But there would still have needed to be an intermediate level, a truly first-class plateau, between this broadly based endeavour, and the Test scene. It is axiomatic that the gap between first-class play and second-class play is, not surprisingly, wide, as seventeen groups of professionals sedulously corner its opportunities for themselves. Predictably, when the miserly annual chance comes the way of a minor county, in one or another of the one-day tournaments, giant-killing is a rarity.

What could have been tried was a larger programme of mid-week representative matches, another proposal pooh-poohed by the wartime authorities. These might have been played over four days, if it were felt the rigours of Test cricket required that degree of commitment and preparation. Groupings of counties, north versus south, England against the rest – a whole series was possible. In older times, such matches had figured prominently and, whatever its social drawbacks, the Gentlemen and Players fixture had served well as a bridge to international cricket. It was, incidentally, not until 1963 that the amateur-professional distinction was abolished, despite its having been declared so much snobbish humbug in the stirring days toward the end of the war. The divisive business of separate travel, dressing rooms, scorecard labelling and the like continued for a distressing seventeen years after the war – a gross illustration of the crass anxiety about change.

The need for a secondary level of first-class play could have been met with, say, three or four counties, regionally grouped, fielding a side, and this compromise suggestion would have allowed it to happen less painfully and more naturally. Wartime crowds responded to interesting cricket, finely played, as present day crowds do, judiciously, by attendance at Test matches. Somewhere there must be an optimum number of first-class matches that need to be played to sustain the national squad. Certainly most other countries survive on many fewer than the English, with their interminable dozens of vacuous county matches. Had the required number been estimated in 1945, had they been devised imaginatively and located strategically in time and place, the outcomes might have been an all-round improvement in the standard of play and a definite increase in the audience for non-Test cricket.

In summary, there would thus have been *three* levels of good-class cricket: the expanded two-tier county league, played over two days (perhaps three in the first division) and a one-day knock-out cup; a solid programme of first-class representative or regional matches, played over four days; and the international tier.

So much for might-have-beens, albeit all of them logical extensions of propositions urged by hardy or eccentric souls as cricket's future was debated in the last years of the war. This is but one scenario, conjured up with the solid benefit of hindsight, but there could have been other modes adopted, equally in tune with the times, both then present and coming. As it was, and for reasons good, honourable and well-intentioned as well as bad, vacillating and self-interested, cricket's rulers set their minds against revision. Their uncompromising tone was authentically caught in E. W. Swanton's forthright description of how the powers-that-were 'condemned without hesitation all proposals to tamper with the fundamentals of the game, and pronounced decisively in favour of three-day matches', placing their faith irrevocably in 'a sound psychological approach to the game' led by captains willing to 'animate their sides into enterprise'.

SEVEN

The Final Account

The most glaring depredation of the war for cricket lay in the six seasons stolen from great cricketers in their prime. This is the most overt cause for mourning. The war robbed established cricketers of a quarter at least and sometimes a third of their first-class careers, including the opportunity of winter tours throughout the cricket-playing Commonwealth. Cricket is so arithmetically oriented that it is more possible than in some other games to estimate, with the primitive aid of a pocket calculator, what the achievements of eminent English cricketers could have been, had the turmoil of the war somehow been avoided.

These, then, are fictitious might-have-beens. They are based on the career figures of men in the immediate pre-war seasons, for the most part well-established and successful – cricketers, that is, who might confidently have anticipated six substantial seasons from 1940 to 1945.

Len Hutton, for example, could have been one of the main losers in terms of total runs scored. He would probably have scored another 13,000 runs and thus found himself, rightly, among the select handful of batsmen with over 50,000 runs in all. Denis Compton, too, might have topped that rare 50,000 mark, with another 11,000 runs. Leslie Ames and R. E. S. Wyatt, both of whom enjoyed long careers, are two others who would have approached that same standard, had they had the chance to score another 10–11,000 runs during the war. One should not, however, wax too complacently about English players. Don Bradman was also denied the opportunity of scoring many more runs. Both Bradman and Hutton might have scored 3,000 or so of these imaginary runs in imaginary Test matches – and this would have given them the exceptional record of some 10,000 runs in international cricket.

Bowling offers equal chance for this nostalgic form of retrospective mathematics. Hedley Verity was to prove the most savage loss. So precipitately was his career ended that he does not appear in the list of thirty or so bowlers with 2,000 wickets. The log of his brief career shows, however, that he only just missed the 2,000 cut, with as many as 1,956 wickets in a mere ten seasons. It is almost certain that he would have taken 3,300 wickets in a full career – and only four bowlers (Wilfred Rhodes, Verity's distinguished predecessor in the Yorkshire and England elevens, Tich Freeman, Charlie Parker and J. T. Hearne) have, in fact, achieved more than 3,000 wickets. Given his solid striking rate of 144 victims in forty international appearances, it is arguable that, had he lived and had cricket prospered, Verity might have become the first bowler to have captured 300 Test wickets.

Eric Hollies, Tom Goddard and, possibly, Reg Perks might have edged towards that coveted mark of 3,000 wickets, such was their consistency over many seasons. Ken Farnes and Doug Wright, Billy Bowes and Bill Voce are four Test-class bowlers whose records would obviously have been further enhanced by six more seasons of international and county cricket. Of those just starting their bowling careers in the last pre-war season, Alec Bedser and Cliff Gladwin were to be the chief losers. Alec Bedser might well have added 600 or more wickets to his tally of 1,924 in all matches and, had he obtained an England place a little earlier, he would naturally have ended with more than the 236 Test victims that stand to his credit.

Such a reverie about what affectionately recalled cricketers might have achieved is, thus far, like *Hamlet* without the Prince of Denmark. For it is entirely reasonable to suppose that had that prince of cricketers, Walter Hammond, pursued his path of excellence for six more seasons, his place in the pantheon of champion cricketers would be doubly assured.

Hammond amassed 50,493 runs in a career lasting from 1920 to 1951, and this places him high in the list of batsmen. If one concentrates on the central thirteen seasons (from 1925 to 1939) of this period it may be calculated that, including overseas tours, he had a yearly average of well over 3,000 runs. Had he continued in this vein for another six seasons (and it should be remembered that he scored 1,783 runs in the first post-war summer) he might have scored another 17,000 or 18,000 runs. This would have given him a career sum of approximately 68,000 runs, far and away ahead of anyone else.

Like all diversions into make-believe statistics, there is a tiny catch. The leading quartet of run-makers – Jack Hobbs, Frank Woolley, Patsy Hendren and C. P. Mead – were also losers by dint of war. According to his record, and including the rarer overseas tours of that era, Hobbs might have scored another 10,000 runs in those earlier lost seasons of 1914 to 1918. This would have given him over 70,000 runs, leaving Hammond, fortified by his imaginary exploits of 1939 to 1945, a creditable second in the ranking.

In the halcyon years of the late 1920s and the 1930s Hammond averaged nine hundreds a summer, apart from winter centuries abroad. He is currently third, with 167, in the roster of century-makers, and of course the two ahead, Hobbs and Hendren, would have scored more hundreds without a First World War. However, Hammond would have scored another fifty or more centuries, and ended with well over two hundred centuries to his name. He would certainly have increased the number of seasons in which he scored a thousand runs to twenty-eight and joined Grace and Woolley, the only two on that particular pedestal.

On the basis of the cancelled tours and the normal pattern of such events, England would have played over thirty Test matches. Hammond would have played in the vast majority of these, and this would have given him the England record of Test appearances. With any fortune at all, he would have scored an additional 3,000 and more Test runs, and might have become the chief run-maker in all Test cricket, with a Test tally of well over 10,000 runs.

So the statistics may be unrolled. Wally Hammond was a highly capable all-rounder. On average, he would have taken close on 300 wickets between 1939 and 1945, which, added to his factual 732, would have given him over a thousand victims all told and, with thirty or forty more test victims, he might have taken over a hundred wickets for his country. Finally, Walter Hammond was a supremely effective slip fielder, with 819 catches to his credit. Given another 190 or so catches during the six vanished seasons, he would have passed the thousand mark, challenging Frank Woolley, the only man with a thousand catches, as the world's best-ever catcher.

Many sound judges are ready to proclaim Walter Hammond's pre-eminence, and several would rate him the greatest of all cricketers. The record demonstrates how much easier that case would be to urge had Hammond been permitted those extra six years. Numbers do not begin to tell the tale of the game's glories. Nevertheless, what W. S. Gilbert in *Princess Ida* called 'the mighty "if"', is a fascinating device, and it does help to show how grievously the war played havoc with the careers of great cricketers.

The abiding losses, however, were not the great cricketers but those who never played and cannot be named. They are the unknown warriors of the lost seasons. At its simplest, a generation of cricketers disappeared almost completely. In effect, for six years there were no apprenticeship schemes. Coaching, training, nurture in the lower echelons for the big-time, the gentle initiation into the county championship – none of this was available, and what little high-class cricket existed was played by established stars.

The public schools grappled with the problem and, as in the First World War, the MCC encouraged this spirit, sending forth elevens as of yore to oppose major school teams. Come eighteen, the schoolboys became soldiers and airmen. There were opportunities to play cricket, but the key chances for regular competitive cricket had been seized by recognised players. It was difficult to break into the select and comparatively tiny number required for top-class play.

It is true that, with clubs denuded of players because of war service, youngsters were often thrown prematurely into the fray, but it was usually a stop-gap measure, lacking any sense of design. School teachers and club officials struggled heroically to keep teams going, but they usually also had civil defence, home guard or fire watch duties, and this left neither the time nor the energy for the assiduous and patient development of young players. For example, Arthur Fagg, by the end of the war, combined cricketing duties with being coach at Cheltenham, an air-raid warden and a market gardener.

With the post-war emphasis, understandably and rightly, on giving pre-war participants a fair run, the cards were then stacked further against youngsters, and few young players emerged in the immediate post-war years. The impact of this was quite staggering, though its negative character makes it difficult to express. Plainly, there are no star names to be sighed over: there are no names at all. It is a black hole in cricketing annals.

It can probably be best represented by birthdays. According to *Wisden*, and using some elementary arithmetic, it would seem that a thousand or so first-class cricketers were born between 1905 and 1935, that is, aged as old as 45 or as young as 15 in 1950, very clearly the extremes for playing cricket in the opening post-war seasons.

From 1905 to 1915 – even ignoring *Wisden*'s progressive removal of the more ancient names for space reasons – the yearly average of births of English first-class players is a little over 30. From 1930 to 1935 the average is again over 30. The crisis years are 1915 to 1930, for they give rise to the cricketers who, in 1950, had an age-range of 20 to 35, the prime for a cricketer. The average births for these years are little more than 20, and, indeed, for the central years, 1921–5, the figure falls below 20.

For instance, Len Hutton, born in 1916, played his first

game for Yorkshire in 1934, aged 18, and made his England début against New Zealand in 1937 at the age of 21. Players born during or just after the Great War might have hoped to become established by the outbreak of the Second World War. Born a few years later, say in 1923, the would-be cricketer might have found himself on his twenty-first birthday not making his first Test appearance, but engaged in the D-Day landings.

The war cropped away, then, a generation of potential players. Some were killed or seriously wounded, but most vanished because there was no learner-cum-journeyman stage for them – no precious hours of net and match practice under the watchful eye of seasoned coaches.

Emergency training schemes, particularly for teachers, were cobbled together to resettle demobilised soldiers, many of whom had scarcely embarked on a career before their call to the colours. Many trades refilled their ranks through short-term contingency training programmes, but first-class cricket was – or so it seemed – too arcane and solemn an art-form for such improvised measures. A. B. Sellers, the Yorkshire captain, was horrified by the raw habits of young players joining his post-war team. He found himself forced to inculcate into them what he regarded as the most elementary skills.

The worst quinquennium was undoubtedly 1924 to 1928, when scarcely more than 65 English first-class cricketers were born, hardly 13 a year, compared with an overall par of 27 a year for the entire 1905–35 era. These would have been young men of 18 to 22 in the first post-war season of 1946.

Sixteen of these played for England but they shared only 151 caps, a woeful record compared with earlier or later periods. Moreover, the genius of Tom Graveney towers over the others. Born in 1927, he was 19 in the first post-war season; he gained 79 caps, one of the best hauls in cricket's history, leaving his comrades born in the mid-twenties with a beggarly 88 Test appearances between them. No one else made double figures. They were, on the whole, hard-working cricketers forced into late development by the exigencies of the war, earning the meagre reward of a cap or two, frequently when almost veterans.

The early twenties yielded a finer harvest. Godfrey Evans (1920), Jim Laker (1922) and Trevor Bailey (1923) made, of course, the most prominent of marks, with nearly 200 Test appearances between them; significantly, each was in his mid-twenties before his Test début. The decade from 1919 to 1928 produced only a few more internationals of note, with Reg Simpson, Willie Watson and Johnny Wardle the pick of these. It was altogether a lean time.

There are two comparisons to be drawn. The first is with the periods just before and just after this in terms of English cricket. Birth-rates were on average down during the years of World War I, with fathers and putative fathers away in the trenches and with domestic life overshadowed by the uncertainties of war. Even so, they were vintage years. Cyril Washbrook, that defiantly jaunty opening batsman and incomparable cover point, Harold Gimblett, a Somerset batting force in the Jessop style, and Doug Wright, Kent's leg-spinner of the kangaroo-like run-up and giddy sharpness of pace, and S. C. Griffith, of Sussex and England, were all children of 1914. 1915 witnessed the arrival of Norman Yardley into the world. Len Hutton and Bill Edrich were born in 1916. 1917 did not produce such a pair of glittering stars, but F. G. Mann, the Middlesex and England captain, Cliff Gladwin, the Derbyshire medium-pace bowler, Ken Cranston, the mercurial Lancashire all-rounder who made such a startling impact for a couple of seasons, before retiring to the relative obscurity of dentistry, and the urbane Middlesex opener, Jack Robertson, were all born in that year and mustered 34 caps among them. In 1918, and apart from two such reliable and courageous performers as Johnny Ikin and Roly Jenkins, Alec Bedser and Denis Compton were born.

Imagine an eleven selected from World War I babies. For good measure, add to the reckoning Joe Hardstaff and Ken Farnes, both born in 1911; Eric Hollies, the diminutive Warwicks leg-spinner, Dick Pollard, the Lancashire outswing bowler, and Jack Crapp, the Gloucester bat, born in 1912;

and H. J. Butler, the Notts opening bowler, and Paul Gibb, the Yorkshire and Essex wicket-keeper, both born in 1913. What a formidable combination might have taken and, on one or two occasions, almost did take the field.

Much the same might be argued for the years following the fallow period. English cricketers born in the four-year period 1929 to 1932 collected the staggering sum of 687 caps. Peter May (66 Tests) and David Sheppard (22) were 1929 babies. So were Tony Lock (49 Tests) and his Surrey team-mate, Peter Loader. The latter won 13 caps, but his vigorous pace was widely respected on the county circuit, and he was also unfortunate in his choice of contemporaries. With the exception of John Warr, who had 2 caps and was born in 1927, Loader was the first genuinely fast English bowler to be born this side of the first war. It had been in vain that *The Cricketer* of 1945 had assumed that 'there must surely be some potential English bowlers in our forces and mines'.

Then, in 1930, both Brian Statham, with 70 Test appearances and Frank Tyson, whose meteoric rise and fall brought him 17 caps, were born. Fred Trueman arrived in 1931. It was corn in Egypt. Four penetratingly quick bowlers after years of dearth: of course, much could be due to accident and fortuitous circumstance. None the less, it is hard to ignore the thought that there could have been half a dozen possible Loaders or Tysons, born five years earlier in 1925 or 1926, and who missed their chance of glory because of the war.

It was not all fast bowlers. The dourly combative Barrington won 82 caps and was born in 1930. The following year Brian Close (19 Tests) and Basil d'Oliveira (29 Tests) were born. 1932 was a proud year. First, there were Fred Titmus and Ray Illingworth to parallel the Laker/Tattersall twinning of exactly ten years before. Then there were two fine Surrey opening bats in Micky Stewart and Raman Subba Row. Finally, as lord of them all, was Colin Cowdrey, with his record haul of 108 Test Matches, and over 7,000 Test runs.

Once more let fantasy hold sway, and visualize an eleven drawn from the births during those three or four years of the depression. These were thirteen to sixteen year-olds when the war finished. They were to have the opportunity to develop into highly effective first-class cricketers.

Apart from indigenous comparisons, a second form of contrast may be drawn with overseas players; for cricket in South Africa, the West Indies, India and Australia did not suffer structurally quite so much as in the United Kingdom. That is not to say these countries managed to sustain major systems of first-class cricket, but they were less incommoded and cramped by the dislocations of war than was Britain.

So it was that, while the 1920s witnessed what was to become a drought in English cricket circles, a flood of players were born abroad. The average number of overseas players listed in *Wisden*, normally by the stricter touchstone of having represented their country, varies much less than with the English players. Apart from a mild slump in the First World War, a steady par of nine a year was maintained over the thirty-year period, 1905 to 1935.

Some of the great names that spring from the 1920s list make for thrilling reading. Many of the all-conquering 1948 Australian tourists were born in the post-World War I phase. Beginning with Keith Miller and Ian Johnston in 1918, there followed Ray Lindwall in 1921, W. A. Johnson and Arthur Morris in 1922, and so on, until the birth of that sweetest of left-hand batsmen, Neil Harvey, in 1928. Bert Sutcliffe, the New Zealand star, was born in 1923.

Most momentous of all, the three 'W's of the West Indies were born in consecutive years: Frank Worrell in 1924, Everton Weekes in 1925 and Clyde Walcott in 1926. The great spin duo of Sonny Ramadhin and Alf Valentine, each a child of 1930, and a team, as jubilantly successful as any ever recruited, was in the making, exactly at a time when few English cricketers were being born.

What it amounted to was that the Great War breed of cricketers – Hutton, Compton, Edrich, Washbrook and Bedser – were obliged to hold the fort of English cricket, well into the 1950s, when one or two of them, talented as they were, had grown a little old for international honours. It was the early 1950s before, in Graveney, a regular batsman of substantial stature emerged. Bowling was the greater problem. Alec Bedser, a member of the Surrey staff before the war, carried the burden of the fast-medium bowling with enormous application, while pre-war stalwarts like Bill Bowes (born in 1908) and Bill Voce (born in 1909) tried and failed to rediscover their fire of the 1930s, not surprisingly in the former's case, for he lost three stone as a prisoner of war, having been captured at Tobruk. It was not until the babes of the early 1930s – Statham, Trueman and Tyson – burst on a surprised cricket world in the 1950s, that any kind of high pace was available to England. The distinguished exceptions born in the 1920s, like Evans and Laker, Simpson and Bailey, were gradually more and more in evidence, but it was really not until the mid-fifties that a relief column of cricketers born around 1930 emerged to reinforce and indeed save English Test cricket.

The typical England eleven in the immediate post-war seasons might have read: Hutton, Washbrook, Edrich, Compton, Hammond or Hardstaff, Yardley, Evans, Bedser, two of Voce, Bowes or Pollard, and Wright or possibly Hollies. The batting was very sound: even against the high pace and consistent support bowling of the superb 1948 Australians, it really only foundered once or twice. The first four batsmen enjoyed proud records against the Australians, as against the then frailer countries. Three were well-established stars before the war, and Washbrook had had a brief taste of international cricket. Hammond and Hardstaff dropped out fairly quickly but Norman Yardley picked up the reins of the captaincy sensibly and batted and bowled rationally. Evans, of course, was a godsend, the perfect successor to his county colleague, that immaculate wicket-keeper, Leslie Ames, of whom it is said he missed only four chances in 47 Tests. He had just make his mark pre-war, and was to become an institution, albeit lacking the solemn dullness associated therewith.

The solid advance of Alec Bedser, another who had just touched the first-class fringes of 1939, was a decided bonus, while D. V. P. Wright and Eric Hollies, each in their quite distinctive styles, contributed the leg-spin variation. Jim Laker made his début in 1947. The opening attack was left to the exhausted hulks of once fast men, like Bill Voce or Bill Bowes, or to the journeyman honesty of Dick Pollard, 't'owd chain-horse', as he was affectionately known on his native Lancastrian heaths. In each war a macabre providence removed England's leading exponent of left-hand spin, Colin Blythe and Hedley Verity. Verity, needless to say, must be numbered among the finest three or four left-handers of all time and the loss was to be devastating. Since then no left-hand spin bowler, apart perhaps from Tony Lock, has secured the kind of regular situation in the England team enjoyed by Verity, and by Rhodes or Peel before him. A series of pretenders, from J. A. Young of Middlesex through to Phil Edmonds of the same county, have played, passed some sort of muster but failed to become automatic choices. Partly because of changes in the fabric of the sport, but partly because there was no Verity or his equivalent, the classic idea has died that – in any type of cricket – left hand spin must inevitably contribute.

The death of Ken Farnes, denying England her single hope of a fastish counterpart to Lindwall and Miller, was also a vicious blow, and one made sorer by the natural earlier decline of fast bowlers as opposed to batsmen: a still commanding Hammond, for instance, was 43 in 1946 and Voce, just about finished, was 37. It was in attack that England did badly, as the two Australian onslaughts – in Australia over the 1946–47 winter, and on tour in England in 1948 – demonstrated. In the ten Tests of those two series, England scored at about 30 per wicket lost, not a desperately poor return against Lindwall, Miller, Johnston and Toshack. The Australians scored at roughly 49 for every wicket, a formidable average. In intervening series, against India at home in 1946, then in the West Indies in the 1947–8 winter and, in particular, against the visiting South Africans in 1947, the batting was most assured. The Compton and Edrich partnership blazed away throughout that heady summer, as South Africa's by no means incompetent bowlers wilted.

One might pursue the matter of the Australians, said by many commentators to be the strongest and most balanced eleven ever fielded. During those two crushing series, the Australians scored over 300 in eleven of their fifteen substantive innings, four times surpassing 500. They were only once all out for less than 250, and that was for 221 at Old Trafford. In ten Tests they never collapsed once. England did collapse, on occasion humiliatingly: seven times out of twenty they were dismissed for under 200. But they did bat successfully as well, and in nine of those twenty innings they scored over 300 runs, often enough to save a match, given adequate bowling.

It was a team of mature batsmen and mature bowlers. The average age of the team that had shared the series in 1938 was about 28. The average age of the England eleven vanquished by the Australians ten years later was nearer 32. It was a matter sometimes of only two or three over-thirties in 1938 and as many as nine in 1948. Maturity tends to benefit batsmen but handicap bowlers, and this was the key. The non-emergence of young batsmen because of the war scarcely mattered at first, but the similar absence of young bowlers was crucial. It is a curious fact that no leading English opening bowler, with the arguable exception of Bailey, was born between 1918 and 1929.

A study of the county sides in the first full post-war season confirms the diagnosis. A collection of dad's armies took the field, and the reasons are straightforward enough. In the first place in so far as the public yearned for yesteryear, it was imperative to parade the heroes of the 1930s. Like finding a faded collection of cigarette cards, cricket lovers seized on the chance to enjoy, nostalgically, a last glimpse of R. E. S. Wyatt, Harold Gimblett, Laurie Fishlock, Alf Gover, Joe Hardstaff, Maurice Leyland and other celebrities of the passing generation. That attempt to mark victory over the Nazi threat by a restoration of bygone joys was understandable, amiable, within its own terms successful, and akin to what happened in other parts of the entertainment world.

In the second place, the counties must be given due and

appreciative credit for giving their established players an opportunity to pursue their careers. There was concern about the resettlement of returning servicemen or of civil defence and war-workers no longer needed for what had been exacting and necessary tasks. Natural justice rightly demanded that men and women should have first call on their original positions. Counties kept their professionals under contract, and many paid retainers or special grants to those on war service.

In the third place, there was literally no one else. The dislocation of cricket's nursery system, with young players gradually being weaned into the first-class game, had been pronounced. Few counties appeared to have budding young players waiting and avid for chances in the championship. Particularly noticeable was the glaring absence of quick bowlers.

Thus a Rip van Winkle of the 1940s, having avoided military service with the assistance of a six-year doze, might have been forgiven for not realizing that time had slipped away over English cricket fields. Had he fallen asleep as the 1939 season drew to a close on one or another of the county grounds and awoken as play began in 1946, he would have found himself watching many of the same players.

In practically every case a hard core of survivors formed the backbone of each county side in 1946, just as they had done in the last pre-war seasons. A glance down those parallel scorecards testifies to this truth. Some with but a little pre-war first-class experience who came to the fore during the war have been included.

Derbyshire: D. Smith, A. F. Townsend, A. E. Alderman, T. S. Worthington, A. E. G. Rhodes, H. Elliott, W. H. Copson

Essex: T. P. B. Smith, F. H. Vigar, T. H. Wade, T. N. Pearce, R. M. Taylor, R. Smith.

Glamorgan: A. H. Dyson, E. Davies, W. Wooller, E. C. Jones, A. D. G. Matthews, J. C. Clay, P. F. Judge, C. Smart.

Gloucestershire: C. J. Barnett, G. M. Emmett, B. O. Allen, J. F. Crapp, W. R. Hammond, W. L. Neale, T. W. Goddard, C. J. Scott, G. E. Lambert, A. E. Wilson.

Hampshire: N. McCorkell, J. Arnold, J. Bailey, E. D. R. Eagar, G. E. M. Heath, G. Hill, O. W. Herman, A. G. Holt, T. A. Dean.

Kent: A. E. Fagg, L. J. Todd, L. E. G. Ames, B. H. Valentine, T. W. Spencer, D. V. P. Wright, N. W. Harding, J. W. Martin, T. G. Evans.

Lancashire: C. Washbrook, W. Place, W. E. Phillipson, R. Pollard, W. B. Roberts, J. T. Ikin, L. L. Wilkinson.

Leicestershire: L. G. Berry, G. S. Watson, M. Tompkin, F. T. Prentice, J. Sperry, V. E. Jackson, G. Dawkes.

Middlesex: S. M. Brown, J. D. Robertson, W. J. Edrich, D. C. S. Compton, L. H. Gray, J. M. Sims, R. W. V. Robins, L. H. Compton, W. F. F. Price, F. G. Mann.

Northants: D. Brookes, J. E. Timms, H. W. Greenwood, P. C. Davis, R. J. Partridge.

Nottinghamshire: W. W. Keeton, G. F. H, Heane, J. Hardstaff, C. B. Harris, H. J. Butler, A. Jepson, W. Voce, F. G. Woodhead.

Somerset: H. Gimblett, F. S. Lee, H. T. F. Buse, A. W. Wellard, E. F. Longrigg, W. T. Luckes, W. H. R. Andrews, H. L. Hazell.

Surrey: R. J. Gregory, L. B. Fishlock, J. F. Parker, H. S. Squires, A. R. Gover, T. H. Barling, E. A. Watts, G. S. Mobey, B. Constable, and the Bedser twins.

Sussex: James and John Langridge, G. Cox, H. W. Parks, J. H. Cornford, S. C. Griffith, J. K. Nye.

Warwickshire: H. E. Dollery, R. E. S. Wyatt, J. S. Old, P. Cranmer, W. E. Hollies.

Worcestershire: E. Cooper, R. Howorth, R. O. Jenkins, R. T. D. Perks, A. F. T. White, P. F. Jackson, J. S. Buller, H. Yarnold, H. H. T. Gibbons.

Yorkshire: L. Hutton, P. A Gibb, W. Barber, M. Leyland, A. B. Sellers, N. W. D. Yardley, T. F. Smailes, W. E. Bowes, A. Coxon, C. Turner, E. P. Robinson.

Some counties contributed more than others to this cricketing air of *déjà vu*. With the sad exception of Hedley Verity, Yorkshire reported almost to a man their fine championship winning side of 1939 – and Arthur Booth, who replaced Verity, was older than his predecessor, having reached his forty-third birthday in 1946. Herbert Sutcliffe and Arthur Wood, the wicket-keeper, had retired, and five of their old team-mates left the first-class game within a season or two, but, in 1946, there was scarcely a change. Gloucestershire, Nottinghamshire, Worcestershire, Surrey, Somerset, and Glamorgan all fielded eight or nine 1939 players in their usual eleven early in 1946. Equally, the lesser-known performers who completed the team-sheets were often enough players with a little first-class experience in the pre-war seasons. Alec Bedser and Godfrey Evans are illustrious examples of this. Players such as Reg Simpson and Trevor Bailey, who emerged in the war and immediately found a regular county place are the exceptions.

Some counties were not quite so well-served by their pre-war stalwarts. Derbyshire lost some players to the leagues, among them George Pope and T. B. Mitchell. Others were to follow. Leicester, Essex, Warwicks and Northants seemed to be the strangest sounding teams, with no more than half the pre-war names remaining, but these were perhaps counties which, at this time as well as before the war, had not enjoyed the consistency of personnel of a Surrey or a Yorkshire. M. S. Nichols, J. O'Connor and others had left Essex, for example. Kent had perhaps suffered most grievously from war casualties, but six or seven 'golden oldies' remained intact.

Where gaps existed, counties turned, like Yorkshire with Booth, to hoary age rather than green youth. Lancashire, for instance, had lost Eddie Paynter and their wicket-keeper, Bill Farrimond, to league cricket, while their two likely candidates for the captaincy, W. H. L. Lister and T. A. Higson, Jr, did not make themselves available. Moreover, Norman Oldfield and A. E. Nutter secured contracts with Northants. Finally, the stylish all-rounder, Jack Iddon, who had intended to play as an amateur, was killed on 17 April 1946 in a motor accident near Newcastle under Lyme, a fate which had earlier befallen the famous Australian and Lancashire fast bowler, E. A. McDonald in 1937. Not without some local criticism, the Lancashire committee turned its back on youthful native talent, and hired T. L. Brierley, Lancashire-born but an ex-Glamorgan player, B. P. King from Worcestershire, and two of Bill Edrich's brothers, Geoffrey and Eric.

It was hardheaded, if a trifle short-sighted. The lack of schooling of young players was apparent, and A. B. Sellers is only one of several county captains who bemoaned the absence of rudimentary techniques among the fledglings. At Middlesex C. R. N. Maxwell was introduced as wicket-keeper, but he was not quite up to par, and Fred Price, aged forty-four, was redrafted.

There was, then, a fairly undramatic return to the past, eked out with a marginal game of general post as a few players changed counties under the provisions allowed at the end of the war by the authorities. Some older players had, of course, volunteered for one or perhaps two more seasons, to help their county resolve its problems before retirement. Others, understandably, were keen to retain employment. Few youngsters took a bow.

The all-round effect was startling in its familiarity. The county championship was more or less unchanged in 1946, and it was served, not without some cheerful and solid success, it must be said, by the same old faces.

EIGHT

The Unsought Opportunity

A study such as this must inevitably have a comparative aspect, with side-glances at how theatre, cinema, radio, football and other forms of public entertainment carried on in war conditions. Cricket emerges badly from the comparisons. This could have been expected. To begin with, cricket was less popular and ubiquitous than such rivals. Its pre-eminence as England's chief spectator sport between 1880 and 1914 had long been eroded. In the first Cup Final at the Oval in 1872 there had been a gate of only 2000, whereas the same ground might have attracted 10,000 for an ordinary county game. In 1890 about two millions watched the hundred first-class matches during the shorter summer season, while but a million attended the Football League's hundred fixtures of 1889/90. By the onset of the last war, the tables had been for some time turned, with 330,000 attending all matches in 1939 at Lord's, an average of 4000 a day, while the successful Arsenal team had attracted an average of 40,000 a home match in the previous football season. As for the other leisure pursuits, most households had wireless licences by 1939, and cinema-goers bought 20 million tickets a week in the same year. The variety and legitimate theatres were also still going strong, despite the mechanized counter-attractions of sound and screen.

Cricket also suffered from the disadvantage of its complicated and relaxed formula. Apart from the logistics of the personnel and the equipment required for a watchable cricket match, it is difficult to offer a worthwhile and skilled exposition of cricket in less than five or six hours. Today's John Player Special League, with its forty-over thrash for each side, occupies at least four and a half hours, and this would seem to many to be the irreducible minimum for any possibility of top-class cricket; indeed, there would be no shortage of commentators to aver that, in fact, it already falls well short of the time needed for legitimate cricket to be at all feasible. The ninety-minute soccer match, the race meeting, horse or dog; the conventional two hours in the theatre or the cinema – all these are relatively brief and were, in consequence, perhaps easier to organize in terms of assembling participants and audiences, less exposed to enemy attack, and less wasteful of valuable time that might otherwise be expended on the war effort.

These two points – the lesser popularity and the greater complexity of cricket – are valid enough but cannot absolve cricket from further criticism. Other entertainments were infinitely more effectively co-ordinated than cricket and made a more praiseworthy contribution to the war effort.

It is true that some other sports did not fare too well in the war. The Home Guard trampled over the Wimbledon tennis courts and Twickenham rugby ground was shared between the civil defence and allotment holders – yet, by 1943, 20,000 enthusiastic Welshmen gathered at Swansea to watch an England and Wales rugby international. In any event, both tennis and rugby union remained amateur although, in an inspired but soon forgotten concession, rugby union and professional rugby league players were permitted to play together for the duration of the war.

Horse racing was a prime sufferer. It wasted too much petrol and other resources in transporting race-goers, horses, jockeys and trainers to its far flung venues. It was stopped altogether for three months after the fall of France and, in the February of 1942, it was acidly condemned by the puritanical Sir Stafford Cripps, then Lord Privy Seal. Land and food were short, and the number of foals fell by a third. It was, however, the gambling aspect which evoked what has been called the 'moralistic ire' of the British, half of whom, according to a wartime poll, wished to see racing abandoned completely. In 1943 there was no flat racing at all in Scotland, while English racing was regionalized, with locally-trained horses competing at six central courses. The exceptions were a makeshift Derby and St Leger, both run at the Gosforth course, Newcastle, instead of at Epsom (commandeered by the military) and Doncaster. Gambling continued unabated, the crowds gradually returned and, in the last couple of years of the war, the BBC broadcast commentaries on the races.

With a mixture of shrewdness and patriotism, the football pools operators merged and, to save the post office extra work, had the 'Unity' pools published in the press. These were under way by November 1939 and a penny invested could result in an £11,000 prize. Neither the Football League nor the Football Association was sympathetic towards the pools, perhaps because they received no revenue from them, perhaps because of football's long-standing mission to provide virtuous and athletic fun for the working classes. There were, then, some moral voices raised about the distastefulness of the pools but compared with the outcry against gambling on the races, it was negligible. Most people felt that the workers' and housewives' pennies, dispatched with a newspaper coupon, were escapist rather than satanic.

Football itself went from strength to strength. After a sluggish beginning, the regional league and war cup competitions worked with increasing success. As the risks from air raids decreased or as the authorities balanced the need of entertainment against safety more realistically, crowds grew in numbers. Crowds at the League South Cup Finals at Wembley increased from 75,000 in 1943, to 85,000 in 1944, to 90,000 in 1945. Some forty unofficial international and Victory international matches were played, some of them before enormous gates, including two full houses of 133,000 for Scotland-England games at Hampden Park, Glasgow.

The style of soccer's triumph was just as significant. It is true that performances were often unpredictable and patchy, because of the difficulty of finding players or because the 'guest player' system was frequently abused. To some degree, this added to the excitement and good cheer and, throughout the war, goals were certainly more plentiful than they have been since. The pleasant absence of too neurotic a competitive edge and the security that came with no fear of being dropped liberated many players and much of the football was skilful and imaginative. Some critics still consider the Arsenal and Preston 1941 Cup Final – a one-all draw, with Preston winning the replay – Wembley's best-ever final. George Allison, the highly successful Arsenal manager, assuredly preferred wartime to pre-war football apropos quality. Many players were in the forces and involved with physical training and this meant they kept sufficiently fit. Denis Compton reckoned that he was at his most athletic during the war.

Representative and international games abounded, with Stanley Rous, the FA secretary, acting as all-round administrator in constant touch with the services chiefs. It worked pragmatically and effectively, and there was a bonus. Top-class players played much more together than before or since the war and international teams developed uncanny understanding. For instance, the England team was composed in part of the RAF XI and in part of the Army XI, the result being that England, in the last two years of the war, had possibly its finest ever side. England's 8-0 defeat of a strong Scottish team at Maine Road, Manchester, in 1943 has received scores of accolades, with some commentators regarding it as the most co-ordinated exhibition of team-work in the history of football.

The reputation of football grew. By paying relatively tiny match-fees – no more than £2, even in the later wartime seasons – and through necessarily reduced overheads, the football industry operated zealously and carefully. The establishment smiled kindly on association football, at one time regarded as somewhat outré. Apart from its sparkling appeal to jaded war workers and servicemen, it raised many thousands of pounds for charity and provided substantial government revenue through the swingeing entertainment tax. Co-operation with the armed forces and with the police was also officially appreciated. In return, the dozens of international and representative matches were patronized by royalty and other dignitaries in abundance. Winston Churchill, accompanied by no fewer than seven cabinet ministers, attended the England and Scotland game at Wembley in the autumn of 1941, and celebrities galore contributed to these public relations exercises. As a final gesture, and as the war approached its end, trips abroad were arranged, including a five-match tour of Italy by the all-international army squad.

It cannot be denied that association football was more actively organized than cricket during the war and that the public and football were the mutual beneficiaries. Soccer emerged from the war in excellent shape and with its stature much enhanced in governmental and other élitist circles.

Much the same is true of other media of entertainment. The theatre built on its solid start to the war, already described. It has been calculated that ENSA arranged over two and a half million shows during the war and that they were watched by over three hundred million war workers and service personnel, at home and in every possible overseas theatre. At its peak, ENSA gave 8,400 shows a week, a little less than half 'live', the rest on film. ENSA has suffered harsh criticism, and it was indeed sporadic and piecemeal in terms of quality: its reminted acronym – Every Night Something Awful – was not entirely affectionate, as many mediocre artistes sheltered behind its massive organization and standard rates of pay. Nevertheless, a considerable amount of its activity was extremely popular, and many anecdotes demonstrate ENSA's vitality. There was George Formby, leading the variety charge after D-day: on one afternoon in Normandy he cheekily strummed his insouciant ukelele through six shows all within 300 yards of the German lines, and one no more than 80 yards from the enemy. There was the Hallé Orchestra, conducted by John Barbirolli, caught up in von Rundstedt's push in the winter of early 1945, but remaining to play concerts, wearing mittens and balaclava helmets because of the freezing cold.

Eighty per cent of show business people had some involvement with ENSA and it is an interesting sidelight on a more modern interpretation of morale that, when ENSA was 1500 artistes short for its broadly developed programme in 1944, labour exchanges were instructed that girls on the stage summoned to register for national service might opt for six months overseas with ENSA, who had fourteen days to decide whether it wished to accept such an option.

Although a trifle tawdry at the edges, ENSA not only did a superb and complex task well, it occasionally – as the presence of the Hallé reveals – pushed forward the cultural frontiers. Its rival in the classical field was CEMA, yet another wartime abbreviation, standing for the Council for the Encouragement of Music and the Arts. In factories and in barracks, an interest in the arts, especially in serious music, was very apparent and, here again, the dramatic and musical theatre would benefit. Basil Dean has written of ENSA that 'in audience-making alone, as distinct from its work for national morale, it was in some part both the cause and effect of changes that are still going on.'

The British cinema matured during the war, its impetus principally created by the wealthy corn merchant, J. Arthur Rank, who, when the cinema business seemed slack and unattractive, moved in to occupy half the studio space and own two of the three major circuits. A third of the public went at least once a week to the cinema in wartime while many, particularly adolescents, visited the local Odeons and Gaumonts two, three, four and even five times a week. All in all, 25 to 30 million tickets were sold a week, a decisive upward move on the already busy figures of the 1930s.

Apart from the Hollywood imports, there was some emphasis on providing a decent British product, as films like *In which we serve, Millions like us, The way ahead* and *Henry V* illustrate. Newsreels and documentaries flourished, especially the 'information' films under the aegis of the governmental Crown Film Unit, with such classics as *Fires were started*. Sunday cinema spread, although local referendums had to be arranged to sanction such cultural blasphemy, and, in a typically British sop to the nonconformist conscience, a percentage of the take had to be given to local charities.

The very triumph of the cinema was, in part, its own downfall, for, in post-war years, the industry took its audience rather too much for granted, did not always treat it – artistically or socially – generously, and found itself highly vulnerable to the television attack. However, for the late 1940s and early 1950s, the British cinema was set fair to do reasonably well in terms of clientele and critical acclaim, not least in the field of light comedy.

The cinema and the theatre, along with spectator sports, benefited from the wartime boom in expenditure on entertainment. Wages were higher and better regulated. Through the adept negotiation of Ernest Bevin of the Ministry of Labour income levels were improved substantially for many classes of worker and, in any event, there was work for all. It is often forgotten, especially in the south-eastern region of Britain, that the unemployment associated with the Great Depression had by no means been solved. In 1940 unemployment still stood at about a million, a grave indictment of the peacetime economy and the wartime government. Soon the benevolently despotic mobilization and direction of labour changed the scene completely. With a thoroughness never emulated by our foes or our allies, the British tolerantly accepted this vast piece of bureaucratic engineering which, along with evacuation, contributed to the registration of a phenomenal 34 million changes of address during the war.

By the middle of 1941 half the economically active population were on some form of government work, military or civil, and Sir John Anderson (then Lord President of the Council) produced a manpower budget, every whit as significant as the conventional fiscal version. Food was rationed and, just as important, heavily subsidized, and that in itself led to a rise in living standards, up to 30 per cent more than the 1939 average; indeed, by D-Day in 1944, the cost of living was 50 per cent more than in 1939, but incomes were 90 per cent higher.

The war produced the curious paradox of people with more

money but less to spend it on. During the war expenditure on food fell by an eighth, compared with 1938–39 figures; on clothing, which was also scarce and eventually subject to rationing, by a third; on household goods which, again, were extremely difficult to obtain, by two-thirds. With severe petrol rationing there was little leisure motoring, and holidays, with the consequent pressure on an overworked railway system, were discouraged. Thus there was a disproportionate amount of money available for local entertainments, like the cinema or sport. During the 1939–45 war the money expended on entertainment rose by a colossal 120 per cent. However, the crushing entertainment tax meant that, in net terms, the increase was much less. Even so, with incomes soaring, with the scope of domestic purchases clearly restricted, this huge increase in leisure expenditure was a striking wartime phenomenon. It was also welcomed by the government because the tax revenue helped finance this most expensive of wars.

Pub-going was boosted into a much more regular and widespread habit, with three-quarters of male and a half of female adults indulging, a switch in social values on some scale. Drink, also heavily taxed, was more expensive and spirits were largely unobtainable, but beer consumption rose by a quarter during the war, even if this was diluted with water and based often enough on somewhat mundane vegetables.

At the other end of the spectrum from the conviviality of the local hostelry was the sobriety of the wireless. The BBC really seized its chance in 1939. It became the premier medium of information, news overseas propaganda and entertainment, for broadcasting was a crucial aspect of World War II. The BBC had prepared carefully for the contingency and was quickly able to decentralize and regroup. After an uneasy week or two, with news bulletins eked out by Sandy Macpherson on the organ and Christopher Stone's record programmes, the BBC constructed a mighty network. Before the war the BBC had broadcast in only eight languages: by 1943 it was consistently offering programmes in 47 tongues. At home, the BBC was enlarged severalfold. In 1939 four thousand

employees, with 23 transmitters, broadcast 50 hours of programmes daily. In 1945 the BBC employed 115,000 staff,
with 138 transmitters, broadcasting 150 hours a day. By any
measure, it was a gigantic achievement. In every way the
BBC confirmed its institutional setting in the British way of
life, built grandly on that platform and, in the post-war years,
was able to make the major and initial running in the
deployment of television.

It is essential to examine the wartime successes of cricket's
competitors in the world of entertainment. By such severe
and by no means exactly parallel standards, the endeavours
of cricket look tame. By the side of such giants as soccer, the
cinema or the radio, cricket must be found wanting in two
principal respects: it did relatively less than the others *vis à
vis* the war effort; and, chiefly in consequence, it was much
less well prepared for the postwar years.

The totality of war for the British had the effect of
producing something like an integrated culture, in which
cricket had its part. W. J. Edrich has written of how 'many
of the men I met in uniform, who had never handled a bat in
their lives, seemed to feel that one of the essential roots of
England was intact so long as Lord's did not entirely close
down' and, sentimentality apart, there is truth in this assertion
of a nebulously outlined set of institutions and values worthy
of sturdy defence. Whether 'it would have been tremendous
propaganda for Goebbels if we had stopped' cricket has
already been questioned and, in a vital sense, was irrelevant.
What was relevant was that the British believed it to be
meaningful enough to wonder about Goebbels' reaction. It
was akin to the utilization of St Paul's Cathedral during the
Blitz, when firemen and other civil defence workers, many of
them not ardent church-goers, responded courageously to the
protection of that awesome symbol as it was enveloped by
surrounding blazes.

The mood was earnest and tempered. The cheap hatred of
the first war, as manifested by the shrill tones of journals like
John Bull had vanished and patriotism was a saner and more
mannered commodity. A. J. P. Taylor has written that 'this

was a people's war in the most literal sense', in so far as most citizens felt it was a war worth fighting and that it was winnable. 'The British people', he averred, 'came of age' and, throughout this 'noble crusade' they remained 'tolerant, patient and generous'. That is a kindly verdict, but a considered and wholly accurate one.

This climate of communal purpose, this democratic sense of commonwealth, was reflected culturally: 'the English people at last found their voice'. That voice was dramatically different from that of the 1914–18 war. There were really no war poets after the style of Wilfred Owen or Siegfried Sassoon and, with exceptions like Evelyn Waugh, there were no actual war novelists of much account. Where the newspapers in the first war had whipped up a frenzy of shallow nationalism, the premier organ in the second war was the *Daily Mirror*, very much the soldier's friend, ready to criticize the establishment and put the ordinary person's viewpoint articulately and forcefully. Its leading columnist, Cassandra (the pseudonym of William Connor), became an influential figure, but the paper had other attributes, such as Barbara Castle dealing with social welfare queries or the 'Old Codgers' letters and complaints feature. Its popular spread of cartoons was, of course, highlighted by the saucy, but never reprehensible, exploits of Jane, the consistently underclad pin-up and chosen belle of many a tank or bomber crew. The *Daily Mirror* was a unique expression of the worries and hopes of everyone.

Again, the compression of the wartime experience into everyone's hearth made a salutary difference, for soldiers were 'much less a race apart' and the divisiveness of the First World War was less corrosive. Not only were civilians under aerial threat, but alterations in the way that war was waged meant that the ratio of supportive to active participants increased, and many more of the latter were engaged on less dangerous duties than between 1914 and 1918. The mechanics of air warfare added a dimension to this. Whereas the sailor at sea or the soldier committed to battle was continually in danger, the airman was often faced with a peculiarly intermittent life, hurtling riskily into fierce combat one hour, nestling cosily back in the quietude of the countryside the next.

W. J. Edrich wrote movingly of this experience. He had volunteered for air crew duties in October 1939 and, after waiting impatiently for some months, he joined the physical training branch at Uxbridge, where his old skipper, R. W. V. Robins, was an official instructor, and found a back way to air crew instruction at Hastings. After spells at Torquay (in the company of Hammond, Ames and George Macaulay) and Derby, he was stationed in Norfolk, involved in low level bombing of shipping on the Dutch and German coastlines. Whenever possible, he played cricket in between times, hacking up to Hendon in a borrowed plane for the one-day games at Lord's.

One Saturday the squadron team were due to play the local village eleven, Massingham, at Massingham Hall but, on the morning, the squadron undertook a raid, sinking German vessels but, inevitably, losing some planes themselves, including members of the squadron eleven. Reserves were hurriedly recruited and the game went ahead. 'I shall always remember that match,' wrote Bill Edrich. 'It seemed like a strange dream. There were the big elms throwing grave shadows on the English grass, the wild roses in the hedges, the lazy caw of a rook passing overhead, the old village in the distance, and the quiet sound of bat and ball; then came a sudden vision, as real as the other, of a 5000-ton ship heeling over with pathetic little black figures scrambling up her tilting deck. . . . Every now and then would come the old, accustomed cry – "Owzatt?" – and then one's mind would flicker off to the briefing and to joking with a pal whose broken body was now washing in the long, cold tides. . . .'

With more or less emphasis, many millions of service personnel and civilians shared this joint experience, these ambivalent shades of commitment and release. Comedy, as always, was a shrewd mirror of cultural mores. In the 1914–18 war, comedy had remained essentially true to the music hall tradition of character-players, associated with individual songs; for example, Harry Champion and 'Any old iron' or Vesta Tilley and 'Burlington Bertie'. In general, these comic performers sustained their familiar content and imagery, and paid strangely little heed to the war as a subject. Their task was to amuse *in vacuo* and, for instance, George Robey continued his mirthful roles as cod-vicar and the like. War was too gruesomely solemn for humour and, with one or two exceptions, such as the stoic resignation of Old Bill in the Bruce Bairnsfather cartoons, was eschewed. When the boys returned home for a spot of desperately needed leave, it was the chance of joining in the old-time choruses that awaited them.

Not so in World War II. The war experience was both ubiquitous and, in relative terms, less harrowing. It was unavoidable and, for most people for most of the time, it was an inconvenient nuisance, not the unrelenting nightmare that the trenches had been. Comedy took to the war like a wisecracking duck to water. A counterpoint to George Robey might be Robb Wilton who, in the Robeyesque wake, had lugubriously mocked the dilatory confusions of magistrates and fire and police chiefs in the mid-war years. Now he offered wry consideration, from 'the day war broke out', of the foibles of minor officialdom on a war-footing, the ARP warden, the special constable and, most memorably, the home guardsmen. Much revolved around the steely demands of his unseen wife, the dominant Rita. A still figure, with just the fingers of the right hand tapping with hesitant edginess at the pallid face, he told of his domestic miseries. On the outbreak of war, she had commanded him to find work. There would be a deathless pause and then he would remark mournfully, 'ee, she's a cruel tongue, that woman'. Contemptuously, she had pointed to the unlikelihood of the home guard recognizing Hitler were he to land on English shores: 'doesn't she know I've got a tongue in me head?' he would splutter in exasperation.

Everything was up for comic grabs. The anomalies of rationing, the rigours of squarebashing or factory discipline, the horrors of travel, the unintelligibility of regulations, the turpitude of officials: many of the topics which, needless to say, were the subject of informal and ribald comment in the first war, were shouted from the roof tops and laughed at formally in the second. Over against the petty bourgeois clerkliness of Robb Wilton's uniformed postures was, for instance, Billy Russell, 'on behalf of the working classes', and a whingeing victim of the abnormalities of the black-out – 'I ended up in my own house three times last week', he would angrily confess. Arraigned by an upstart warden for the chink of light beneath his door, he astutely retorted that he didn't expect the Germans to be coming on their hands and knees.

The authorities had learned, or had had forced upon them, the medieval lesson that a jester diverts, but never destroys. He exposes the humour in the serious situation in order to make it more tolerable. The Germans and Italians, their leaders especially, were guyed unmercifully but it was the banter of ridicule, not the howls of detestation of the 1914 to 1918 years. Hitler, Mussolini, Goering and their colleagues were rendered pitiable figures of fun, in the manner of Charlie Chaplin's 'the Great Dictator'. The domestic régime was satirized mildly, in that fashion which conveys affection, and perhaps there were those in authority wise enough to recognize that, by being seen to be able to play a joke, respect was increased. Did not Harold Macmillan pay more than one visit to watch Peter Cook lampoon him brilliantly in the 1960s revue, *Beyond the Fringe*? We always laugh, perhaps, at those we love and, as for those that might cause irritation, laughter is a safety-valve.

The focus for this psychology, consciously or unconsciously, was, without doubt, ITMA, most famous of radio programmes and a veritable war-winner. Oddly enough, Tommy Handley's 1921 music hall sketch 'the Disorderly Room' was one of the very few war-orientated cameos to emerge from that struggle, but, come World War II, the comic assault was almost entirely civil. It is not always remembered now how reluctant were the BBC to experiment initially with the magazine comedy programme, of which 'Bandwaggon', starring Arthur Askey and Richard Murdoch, was about the only forerunner to ITMA, which itself suffered several vacillations before establishing itself as the keystone of the integrated culture of the war years.

The scriptwriter, Ted Kavanagh, aimed at a hundred laughs, one every eleven seconds, in the eighteen or nineteen minutes of dialogue, the half hour being completed by two musical interludes. These laughs were puns and digs at the expense of wartime bureaucracy, and there swirled about the salient figure of Tommy Handley, reputedly the finest ever reader of a radio script, a colourful troupe of bizarre characters, like painted savages around a totem pole. Each had his or her own incantation, the ritual intonement of the catchphrase, each of which was soon incessantly on every lip and several of which persist today. No cultural device – not a Dickens' family novel nor a television soap opera – has quite so comprehensively captured and imbued the psyche of the nation. It was a magnificent and inventive *tour de force*.

The wireless came of age alongside the people and World War II was and will be the only war where radio was sovereign. It is instructive to note that the BBC manufactured a comedy show for each of the services: Charlie Chester's 'Stand Easy' for the Army, with its celebration of that elusive figure, Whippit Quick; 'Merry-go-round' for the Navy, with Eric Barker and Pearl Hackney; and, most famously, the RAF's 'Much Binding in the Marsh', a vehicle for the cabaret-style sophistications of Richard Murdoch and Kenneth Horne. Just as the services had their very own cricket teams, they had their very own comedy shows.

The radio, naturally, was also the prime medium for that other important yardstick of public taste, popular music. In the 1914–18 war the output had been strident and irredeemably martial. There were the marching songs, like 'Pack up your Troubles' and 'Tipperary' (sold for five shillings by its composer, a denizen of Ashton-under-Lyne), and a whole series of what can only be described as recruiting songs, such as 'Goodbye-ee'. At their most emollient, the lyrics never aspired to be less exhortatory than 'we don't want to lose you, but we feel you ought to go'.

Possibly the British were rightfully humbled by the inanity

of 'We're gonna hang out the washing on the Siegfried Line', and carefully forswore songs that might trip lyricists as disastrous history unfolded. There were songs of defiance, like 'There'll always be an England', 'The King is still in London', and 'Some chicken, some neck', one of the few songs to be based on a politician's – Churchill's – phraseology. It is often said that the British never composed a war song and had to commandeer the haunting German melody, 'Lili Marlene', sung by Lale Anderson, for this purpose. Firmly rendered by the buxom Anne Shelton and parodied a hundred times, it certainly filled the bill.

The crucial British contribution, however, was from Vera Lynn, who, if the analogy is not too strained and it is intended as a compliment to both, was to popular music what Pelham Warner was to cricket. Both of them drew off the sentiments of the few World War I songs which yearned for happier times. 'Keep the homes fires burning' and 'There's a long, long trail a-winding' were two such, and it was indeed the task of some to keep alive hopes and personal goals through 'the anxious night of waiting' until 'the time when I'll be going down the long, long trail with you'.

Heartfelt numbers, 'Yours', 'We'll meet again', 'There'll be bluebirds over the White Cliffs of Dover', were Vera Lynn's *métier* as she strove, with great courage and stamina, to entertain troops abroad and their loved ones at home. The message of 'Forces Favourites' was a plaintive one, of separation and its anguish, mingled with the genuine tone of steadfastness in personal relationships as a succour to both. It was about the effects not, as in World War I, about the cause of war. Few recall now that the vestigial blimpishness of the War Office, underpinned with some narrow snobbery at the BBC, led to a constant alternative war for Vera Lynn who, whatever else, was perfectly sincere in her portrayal of herself as 'the Sweetheart of the Forces', the non-threatening, sisterly friend or go-between of separated men and women.

Her unceasing emphasis on the personal, rather than the national, repercussions of war, with its stress on the pain and unease of enforced estrangement, was believed by some to be, not only puerile in its syrupy sentiment but likely to dilute the rich blood of fighting men. They would, it was urged, be suborned by the private thoughts and weakened in their military resolve. This was, at once, a calumny on most servicemen and their unspoken sense of decent purpose, and an exaggeration of the appeal hitherto of trumpeting, martial airs. None the less, that conception of Vera Lynn as no more than a differently garbed Tokyo Rose was a nasty problem for her throughout that part of her career. And, in its melodic way, this bristling disapproval corresponded to the frowns over the players and spectators who enjoyed their cricket and other sports.

The wireless, which brought Robb Wilton, Tommy Handley, Vera Lynn and their confrères to a vast public, was also, in the Reithian tradition, in the van of another significant wartime development. It is a singular characteristic of wartime Britain that there was a definite increase in cultural and intellectual interests. It was, squarely, a middle-brow attitude, in the best sense of avoiding the fidgety élitism of the hoity-toity highbrow. In broadcasting, the phenomenal success of the 'Brains Trust' took even its proudest advocates by surprise. The balance given by Professor Joad, the loquacious personification of everybody's idea of an academic, Julian Huxley, kindly, objective and humanist, and Commander Campbell, with his plain man's tales from Patagonia, made for an eminent and irresistible blend and listening figures of 12 millions. Little recollected now are the amusing illustrated lecturettes, often broadcast, by Dobson and Young on the delights of music while, from the Radio Doctor on bowels to C. H. Middleton on compost heaps, the BBC, for a good proportion of its time, offered what now would be called a college of the air.

CEMA (Council for the Encouragement of Music and the Arts) had its squabbles with ENSA but there is no denying its attractions, nor indeed those of ENSA when it offered talented actors in well-crafted plays. It is also clear that the post-war popularity of ballet owed much to increased interest in it during the war.

J. B. Priestley, another influential wartime broadcaster and booster of morale, proclaimed the slogan 'Let the People Sing', and that was the title of a popular song, ENSA's signature tune. At a popular level, 'Music While you Work', a BBC attempt to encourage factory girls with what now would be termed a singalong, 'Workers' Playtime', a rejig of ENSA for industry and 'Works Wonders', a chance for work-based amateur talent, accomplished this, but there were higher values. Classical music was well-established in the forces: Southern Command, for instance, had no less than thirty chamber groups in rehearsal at one time, as well as a full-strength symphony orchestra. When the BBC Symphony Orchestra visited Aldershot for a Saturday evening concert, Gracie Fields' record audience was surpassed. Sybil Thorndike led an Old Vic company on a successful tour through the Welsh mining villages. Even the tube stations-turned-shelters (at the peak of the Blitz 79 stations housed 177,000 people) had concerts, films, libraries and current affairs discussions.

Throughout the country, in evening classes, in factories and in ARP posts, there was this same accent on adult education, primarily, as one might have expected, in current affairs and social issues.

The education of the services was another notable feature as the Army Bureau of Current Affairs manfully did its stuff, with *British Way and Purpose* its standard text. With the exception of Cromwell's New Model Army, the 1940s army had the opportunity to be more politically aware than any other British militia. As with the Central Office of Information films, the general thrust was unequivocal: if, the argument ran, it had needed unprecedented central planning and mobilization to win the war, then a similar approach, a substitute for the haphazard and ramshackle economic mêlée of the 1920s and 1930s, would be required to win the peace. It is a moot point whether Jane and the *Daily Mirror* or ABCA won more votes for Labour in 1945, as the forces lurched overwhelmingly to the left.

One needs to maintain the perspective. Not everyone

flocked to the National Gallery to hear Dame Myra Hess play classical piano, or tuned into Donald McCullough, introducing the Brains Trust. Many a weekly ABCA session was an excuse for a rest and a smoke. Winston Churchill's broadcast oratory, admired in awed silence in four million households was, predictably, greeted with gleeful barracking and salted wit in many a barrack-room and on many an industrial shop-floor. The British cinema may have matured into *One of our aircraft is missing*, but the exorbitant tushery of *Gone with the wind* made it the greater money-spinner.

It would also be as wrong to delineate British domestic life exclusively in Vera Lynn's terms of devoted and unbroken romance as it would be to characterize such feelings as completely banal and unrealistic. War is an undeniably ugly business and, as George Trevelyan said, one cannot humanize the inhuman. At a psychological level it magnifies and distorts emotions. That warping and inflaming had led Sigmund Freud, in 1917, to write of 'war aphrodisia', of a reckless throwing aside of repression and a libidinous overexcitement. For those sceptical of psychoanalytical exposition, the sheer disruption of war was sufficient explanation for what some anxiously saw as 'a breakdown of morals'. The massive movement of people hither and thither, often in circumstances of emotional upset, both threatened and encouraged relationships. For instance, three out of five women had near relatives in the armed forces, half a million of whom were either killed or maimed, physically or mentally. Traditional patterns were dislocated; divorce, illegitimacy and venereal disease, sad indicators of social turmoil, were high. There was what Barbara Cartland called 'the quick, rush wedding of wartime' and its 'problematical future'. Apart from the GI Brides in their thousands, there were romantic affiliations of all kinds. When the *Stirling Castle* a 'dry' and government-chartered ship carried the MCC tourists to Austrialia in 1946, there were also aboard some 200 war-brides *en route* to join their Australian husbands, much to the delight, according to his affectionate obituarist, of Bill Edrich's amorous nature.

There was, of course, liberation in all of these experiences,

as well as what moralists felt to be excess. Women were freer
to choose work, leisure and degrees of social relationship,
although they were doomed to some disappointment post-
war, especially with regard to keeping jobs and obtaining
equal pay. Sexual mores were relaxed and, for example,
broadcasting censorship was less stiff-necked. Lady Astor,
who had banned the almost faultless George Robey from her
World War I concerts for troops because of his supposed
suggestiveness, must have been disconcerted by the raunchier
tones of the BBC in World War II.

With morals, as with all facets of wartime life, there were
no exclusive extremes. The United Kingdom was not a
democratic and egalitarian society. Ex-public schoolboys had
a fourteen-to-one advantage over state schoolboys when it
came to commissions; in 1938 one per cent of the population
owned 14 per cent of the wealth and in 1947 that had only
drifted to eleven per cent; those with money could eat out
and then blew their rations extravagantly on just a few meals
at home. An epoch which coined words like 'bull', 'browned
off' and 'had it', and ensured they were permanent fixtures in
the patois, was never convincingly united in an obsessively
democratic way.

None the less, the United Kingdom was *more* equal,
democratic, culturally cogent and all-round purposeful than
before. The cricket authorities never quite understood this
sea-change in British life and never quite came to terms with
it.

Cricket was an accepted part of 'British Way and Purpose'
and was seen as an aspect of that 'better Britain after the war'
which the public demanded. Cricket was an item in the argot.
Chalked placards (paper rationing meant an absence of the
real thing) proclaimed: 'Biggest raid ever – score 78 to 26 –
England still batting' while, in 1940, Tom Webster's cartoon
of a cricketing lion was enlarged and posted on the Gaiety
Theatre, with the caption, 'help to keep his end up by war
savings'. So far, so good, but it never did go much beyond
that hitting-them-for-six sort of metaphor.

There was, for example, no building on either the spirit or, through opportunities afforded by the county organization of sports equipment rationing, the letter of this newer democracy. Even in the obvious case of the sterile dichotomy of amateur and professional, reform was too long a-coming, particularly when one recalls how diligently professionals like Verity, Robertson and Edrich performed their duties as commissioned officers. There has been righteous lament about how public school cricketing standards 'fell seriously away'. The preparatory entry was less well trained, the cadet corps made excessive demands, agriculture sometimes, and aged equipment often, spoilt the splendour of the playing fields, coaching was reduced and less competent, schools were evacuated and understaffed, competition with other schools was slacker – it is an elongated litany of complaints. It is a sorrowful fact that the majority of the score or so dead 'blues' were schoolmasters, an indication of the loss of effective teaching in cricket at the public schools. E. W. Swanton ruefully concluded that the youngsters were 'never trained on into anything good'. J. R. Bridger of Rugby did play a little for Hampshire, and H. A. Pawson had a few seasons with Kent. Along with D. B. Carr (Repton), Bailey and Mallett (Dulwich) and J. G. Dewes (Aldenham) they were the main entrants, of any standard, into the first class game from wartime public schooling. Stories about P. B. H. May, at the Charterhouse, were beginning to be told by 1945, but there was little else.

Admittedly, it would have taken prescient vision to embark on a remedy. Few would have believed in 1945 that the state schools would, in years to come, feel emboldened to offer a breadth of leisure provision to children, with some detriment to cricket. The schools were well-advised to do so, for their task is the recreational development of all, not a restrictive concentration on the odd one who might make the grade as a cricketer. Nevertheless, in that more open and mixed society, there was a chance to create an interest in cricket for all youngsters from an early age. It needed (perhaps it still does) the equivalent of short tennis or mini-rugby, some novel blending of the required skills that, under cover or on artificial pitches, might have touched the responses of many school children. The MCC devoted much energy to ensuring that cricket was kept alive at the public schools during World War II, as it had done in World War I. Possibly some more thought should have been given to keeping it alive among the evacuees and among youngsters robbed of many aspects of peacetime leisure.

Cricket, unlike football, is not street-wise. It is not, and this was already happening soon after the war, as much a commonplace of the child's own culture as perhaps it once was. The modern model is the West Indies where, we are told, cricket engages the happy attention of thousands who are only too eager to associate the sport with their own indigenous culture. In England, cricket became too far removed from the ordinary ken of children and, once it was identified with none too popular institutions, like school, a tap-root was endangered. In consequence, many of today's cricketers are, in fact, ex-public schoolboys of major and minor brands. Many of them, set against the touchstone of their predecessors, are unprepossessing. The cricket establishment blames the anti-sports ethic of the comprehensive school but, equally, the cricket establishment must be held culpable for not itself working to maintain the heartfelt allegiance and participation of boys who could genuinely believe in cricket as a part of themselves. An imaginative stroke during or at the end of the war would have paid dividends. Such investment is rarely spontaneous and rather requires inventiveness and commitment; and that was the moment, when the nation was amenable to major change, when it was enjoying some sense of its own togetherness and, importantly, because cricket is regarded as a game of some solemnity, when it was undergoing an exceptional round of attachment to serious matters and self-improvement.

The war, as wars do, spawned bright ideas. Some of them were orientated towards the military, such as the spectacular developments in aircraft. Some of them were more indirectly concerned with warfare, like the introduction of pay as you earn from 1943 or the switch over the war years in agriculture, from 12 million acres arable and 18 million acres grassland to the exact reverse. In music, in broadcasting, in dancing, in a variety of fields, innovations occurred regularly. Cricket religiously withstood the temptation and emerged from the war unsullied by novelty.

Victory exhausted Britain. It was a classic sacrifice, a national analogue of its own heroes – Wolfe at Quebec, Nelson at Trafalgar – dying at the moment of triumph. The prosaic facts were desperate enough. Two-thirds of the country's export trade had vanished; the merchant fleet was a third smaller than in 1939; a tenth of the nation's wealth had been destroyed; the country's debts stood at £46 billion; and, in 1946, we spent £300 million more abroad than we earned. The catastrophe was, ironically, worsened by the fast end to the Japanese war. Lease Lend stopped abruptly on VJ day while, of course, stricken continental Europe made immediate demands on international aid. There was no slow demobilization or easy economic run down, and, by some accounts, the outmoded methods, complacent management and turgid labour relations that were to create problems in decades to come were already covertly present.

Alongside the economic collapse went the self-delusion of political grandeur, a smug sense of occupying an important place on the world stage. Britain, dreaming of its hegemony during the Victorian epoch, rightfully proud of its contribution to the defeat of fascism, could not realize its day was over. From the entry of America and Russia into the war, Britain's hour was done, and she was committed to second-class statehood. There is nothing at all wrong with that status, provided those possessing it are happy to come to terms with it, and not indulge in the folly of a Suez or the absurdity of a Falklands. Otherwise, and especially for a broken-backed nation, it is a taxing and tiresome business.

It was in this context that cricket turned to the extremely moist summer of 1946, determined to sustain what Rowland Bowen called 'the holy game' which was no more than just a game. As Bowen argued, the MCC 'refused to study any remedy', and the rot set in. It epitomized the national dilemma. Some had fought for a return to the old days and ways, which included that dimension of world authority, with, an illustration, the MCC lording it over the other cricketing nations. Others had fought for a distinct improvement, for a great change from the ancient régime and, by and large, sought domestic security and the comfort and good cheer of a homely life, without too much worry about involvement elsewhere. That is a simplification, for there were all manner of cross-strands and complications. None the less, Macaulay's lines spring to mind, from his description of how Horatius kept the bridge.

> Was none who would be foremost
> To lead such dire attack;
> But those behind cried 'Forward!'
> And those before cried 'Back!'

The cricket establishment fell wholly into the second category, and there was no serious breach of tradition. Judgement on cricket's war depends on one's stance. Students of the American constitution claim that is open to a 'loose' and to a 'tight' interpretation and wartime cricket, including the planning for its own future, is likewise open to opposite assessments. A charitable view would be that cricket had a good war, performing miracles of ingenuity, providing sparkling entertainment and raising lots of money. All this seemed like an achievement, meritorious and inspired. A harsher view would examine wartime cricket by the criteria of the possibilities open to it then and in the aftermath of war and by comparison with other similar cultural forms. By those severer standards, cricket had not too good a war.

About 11.30 on Saturday 4 May 1946, H. Griffith of Cambridge University, S. Banerjee of India, A. W. H. Mallett for the MCC and D. H. Macindoe of Oxford University bowled to, respectively, C. Washbrook of Lancashire, A. P. Singleton of Worcestershire, R. J. Gregory of Surrey and C. J. Barnett of Gloucestershire. A full-scale first class programme had begun. On Wednesday 8 May, 1946, J. Sperry, very properly at Lord's, opened the bowling for Leicestershire against J. D. Robertson of Middlesex. It was the first ball bowled in the county championship since that damp Friday, at Hove six and a half years earlier, when, in Hedley Verity's last first-class match, Yorkshire had routed Sussex.

Father Time, the symbol of Lord's perpetuity, had been dislodged by a barrage balloon cable after a gale in the November of 1940. It had been kept in the committee room. Now it was returned to its traditional place on the Grand Stand, a token of cricket's changeless character.

Index